TRANSACTIONS 3

Intercomprehension AND Plurilingualism

ASSETS FOR ITALIAN LANGUAGE IN THE USA

EDITORS
Roberto Dolci AND Anthony Julian Tamburri

JOHN D. CALANDRA ITALIAN AMERICAN INSTITUTE
QUEENS COLLEGE, CITY UNIVERSITY OF NEW YORK

The Calandra Institute TRANSACTIONS series documents studies and analyses of demographics, language, sociological activities, and emerging issues that impact Italian-American culture.

The editors wish to thank, first and foremost, Italy's Ministry for Foreign Affairs for its financial support from: Capitolo 2619/3 della DGSP – Ufficio III del Ministero degli Affari Esteri relativa a "Contributi ad enti ed Associazioni, per corsi di formazione ed aggiornamento per docenti di lingua italiana," esercizio finanziario 2013.

The editors also thank the staff of the John D. Calandra Italian American Institute, especially Rosaria Musco, Lucia Grillo, and Carmine Pizzirusso.

TRANSACTIONS
VOLUME 3

©2015 by the authors
All rights reserved
Printed in the United States of America

John D. Calandra Italian American Institute
Queens College, CUNY
25 West 43rd Street, 17th floor
New York, NY 10036

ISBN 978-1-939323-03-3
Library of Congress Control Number: 2014958251

CONTENTS

vii   Preface
        ANTHONY JULIAN TAMBURRI

ix   Foreword
        CARLO DAVOLI

xiii   Introduction
        ROBERTO DOLCI

1   On America's Foreign Language Education Policy and the Foreign Language Deficit
        ROBERTO DOLCI

29   Intercomprehension Studies in Europe: History, Current Methodology, and Future Developments
        ELISABETTA BONVINO

61   The Ties That Bind: Italian for Spanish Speakers in Intercomprehension
        CLORINDA DONATO and CEDRIC JOSEPH OLIVA

79   We Can Learn Through Languages Because We Are Defined by Languages
        PIERRE ESCUDÉ

101   Integrating Plurilingualism into Curriculum Design: Toward a Plurilingual Shift
        BARBARA SPINELLI

145   The Florida State University Experience: Design, Development, and Implementation of Italian for Spanish Speakers Courses
        FABRIZIO FORNARA and IRENE ZANINI-CORDI

171   The French/Italian for Spanish Speakers Project:
      From Idea to Permanent Program
      MARKUS MULLER

191   Mona Lisa in the Classroom: An Educational Proposal
      for Integrated Training in Intercomprehension
      DIEGO CORTÉS VELÁSQUEZ

217   French and Italian for Spanish Speakers: San Pedro High School—
      A Practical Study of the Logistics of Teaching Another Romance
      Language to Spanish Speakers
      IDA LANZA and DIANE HARTUNIAN

241   Contributors

245   Index of Names

Preface

Anthony Julian Tamburri
The John D. Calandra Italian American Institute

This book is the result of our first workshop on "intercomprehension," a new method of teaching Italian, this time specifically to speakers of another Romance language. Organized by Roberto Dolci and myself, the workshop took place in September 2013 and included seven speakers, while in this book two more joined the others.

"'Intercomprehension' & Multilingualism: Teaching Italian to Romance Languages Speakers" is part of a series of workshops and symposia sponsored by the Italian Language Resource Laboratory (ILRL) of the John D. Calandra Italian American Institute. The goal of the ILRL is to contribute to a greater understanding and improvement of both the teaching and the learning of Italian.

The goal of our 2013 workshop was to introduce both the high-school and college teacher of Italian to new methodologies in teaching the target language to students who are native speakers or have an excellent knowledge of another Romance language. The basic goal was to demonstrate how the student's knowledge of that Romance language could facilitate his/her learning of Italian. Through teaching strategies specific to this multilingual student, his/her knowledge of Italian can be more readily acquired and absorbed as s/he moves forward in studying Italian.

In providing the teacher of Italian with those methodologies and strategies that will create the ideal classroom for this specific student profile, we eventually create a body of students who will move forward in their study of Italian with greater facility and, equally important, at a faster pace. As a result, both the teaching and the learning of Italian should prove more efficient, and the potential for a greater number of students at the advanced levels increases.

In dealing with the various challenges of such a new methodology, there were other issues to take into consideration, one being geography. The workshop leaders also focused on geographical variances. Hence, some spoke to the teaching of Italian to those whose native Spanish originated from Central and South America as well as from the Caribbean. One leader, in turn, dealt with ways of employing the web for successful implementation of "intercomprehension." Yet another discussed the causation of a paradigmatic shift in foreign language teaching. Namely, from the curricular perspective, what are the development, changes, and potential improvements that, for instance, a French/Italian for Spanish Speakers program might have on a language department.

Our six workshop leaders first lectured and subsequently engaged in a question-and-answer session and eventual discussion about the advantages of intercomprehension with the approximately 50 participants who spanned the K-16 teaching levels. The significance of such a range of levels is important also to a greater degree of collaboration and a coincidental coordination of teaching Italian at and across the K-12 and college levels. Such coordination can only lead to a smoother transition for the student as s/he passes from high school to college.

Another very much desired result is that those students who already speak a Romance language will surely advance further in high school and thus enter into more upper-level courses in Italian at the college level. A greater population of students in advanced Italian courses in our colleges and universities will also allow these institutions to pursue the following: (1) to offer more courses *in lingua* on literature, culture, and cinema; (2) to assist in sustaining major programs in Italian, and, (3) potentially to provide for a larger population of students at the graduate level whose language competency will be greater than what we now find at this juncture.

As we moved more than 60 years ago to the so-called audio-visual methods of records, placards, and short films, we now not only adapt today's more advanced technologies of those earlier inventions, but we seek out new frontiers, so to speak. The binomial "intercomprehension and multilingualism" constitutes one of the new frontiers in language teaching for us to explore and, once there, where we shall ultimately develop greater and more efficient language teaching and learning methodologies for the wider expansion of a multilingual society.

Foreword

Carlo Davoli
Education Office Director
Consulate General of Italy

Carissimi,

Porgo innanzitutto il saluto del nostro Console Generale, Ministro Natalia Quintavalle, che ha comunque manifestato notevole interesse per questo incontro e per gli sviluppi che da questo possono discendere.

Io non entro nel merito degli aspetti tecnici che saranno molto meglio di me trattati dai relatori. Vorrei invece soffermarmi, senza tema di esagerazione, su quella che ritengo possa essere definita una giornata "storica," perché per la prima volta, sulla medesima tematica, e contemporaneamente, viene investita l'intera nazione, segno evidente dell'importanza che il nostro Ministero, la nostra Ambasciata e tutta la rete consolare italiana negli Stati Uniti annettono alla formazione cui oggi prenderemo parte.

É una nuova frontiera, che inizia a prendere forma anche nell'East Coast, dopo le pioneristiche esperienze californiane. E questo grazie all'intuizione, anzi direi la constatazione, di illuminati studiosi, alcuni dei quali qui presenti, che hanno compreso che la didattica delle lingue straniere offriva ancora spazi inesplorati, e che possedeva in nuce una ulteriore branca, invisibile ai più in quanto trasversale. Conoscevamo le cellule, ma non anche la loro interconnessione.

Adesso, per mettere a sistema quanto fin qui acquisito, bisognerà procedere su più binari:

- da una parte andrà predisposto un percorso scientificamente tarato e validato, un "prodotto" (tra virgolette) che sia qualitativamente, commercialmente ed editorialmente proponibile:
- dall'altra parte una proposta che sia "politicamente" (sempre tra virgolette) presentabile.

Occorrerà definire i prossimi passaggi, individuare i giusti interlocutori, declinare compiti, tempi, e strategie.

Occorrerà individuare e coinvolgere le persone giuste all'interno delle rappresentanze dei paesi di lingua neolatina; chi, come noi, possa innamorarsi dell'idea-forza, credere nel progetto, ed avere la capacità di intravederne l'enorme potenzialità e gli sviluppi concreti.

Io sono estremamente fiducioso, e sono convintissimo che gli sviluppi di questa avventura contribuiranno ad allargare la base della piramide, innalzandone la vetta, conducendo anche ad un incremento del numero degli esami AP Italian, tanto cari alla nostra Ambasciata, ed in particolare al Ministro Maggipinto, che approfitto per ringraziare per aver creduto lui per primo nel nuovo approccio metodologico.

Sono convinto che le comuni matrici culturali dei popoli latini, ancor prima delle assonanze linguistiche, a fronte di una seria offerta formativa alternativa all'attuale curricolo, prenderanno per mano migliaia di giovani americani, e li condurranno con più facilità allo studio dell'Italiano.

Da responsabile dell'Ufficio Scolastico del Consolato di New York sono compiaciuto per il fatto che in California l'esperienza dell'Intercomprensione abbia toccato non soltanto le università, ma che abbia trovato disseminazione anche nelle scuole superiori, e mi riferisco in particolare alla San Pedro High School, trasformata in un vero e proprio laboratorio didattico-metodologico.

Sono inoltre orgoglioso di poter annunciare che un corso basato sul metodo dell'intercomprensione verrà attivato dall'ente gestore America Italy Society a Filadelfia.

Assieme al Console Generale d'Italia (a Filadelfia) abbiamo incontrato il locale Console Generale del Messico, cosa che faremo anche qui a New York, assieme ai nostri diplomatici e all'Ente Gestore IACE, guidato dal suo instancabile Presidente Berardo Paradiso. Una volta stabilite le giuste alleanze, con il "prodotto" in mano, unitamente alle forti associazioni italo-americane, guidati dalla nostra Ambasciata, potremo sottoporlo all'attenzione delle autorità politico-scolastiche americane. La partita è appena iniziata, e ce la dovremo giocare bene.

Consentitemi in ultimo, a nome del Consolato Generale d'Italia a New York, di ringraziare i relatori, studiosi di fama tra i più qualificati al mondo in materia di intercomprensione.

Ringrazio anche i docenti partecipanti, veri ed insostituibili messaggeri della nostra lingua, ma soprattutto il Preside Tamburri ed il prof. Roberto Dolci, lungimiranti visionari e ospitali padroni di casa, che dimostrano oggi di aver chiaro in mente quanto lontano possa portare questo progetto, la cui capacità di pervasione potrà regalare interessantissimi risultati nell'azione di promozione della nostra lingua.

Introduction

The Plurilingual Approach:
Assets To Promote Italian Language

Roberto Dolci

In recent years among scholars, a new perspective on bilingualism / multilingualism has emerged. First of all, the very definition of *bilingual* has changed, from a person who is ambilingual (an individual with native competency in two languages) to a person who possesses a certain degree of competence in more than one language (Bloomfield, 1933; McNamara, 1967; Titone, 1972; Valdes, 2005, among others).

Moreover, the advantage of being multilingual and how this can facilitate not only one's cognitive abilities in a broader sense (Farrell, 2011; Byalistock, 2007), but specifically, in the learning of other languages has been pointed out—and scientifically proven (Cenoz and Gorter, 2011; Kramsch, 2012, among others).

Starting from these assumptions, many approaches and methods have been developed that take advantage of the students' previous knowledge of other languages and of the presence of many languages in the classroom. They are commonly defined as "plurilingual approaches," and they are spreading in colleges and K–12 schools in the United States.

In the United States the bilingual/multilingual approaches have been adopted mainly in those schools where a large number of recent immigrants asked for an instruction with languages (normally one) other than English. Even though a great part of the research, grants, and experimentation have been concentrated on the bilingual education of Spanish/English, nonetheless other languages of immigration are involved (Potowsky, 2010). These programs have been the source of considerable controversy and debate in the education community (Amselle, 1995). In recent years, the underlying theory, the aims, and the public have completely changed. The goal of bilingual/multilingual education is not to help disadvantaged students, but to give them an opportunity to enhance their foreign language capabilities in a faster and better way. It is also the opportunity to teach and learn less-taught foreign (and other) languages and to preserve them. It might also help the diffusion of Italian language in the United States.

We don't have data on how many Americans speak (some) Italian. We have only partial data. The American Community Service (ACS) survey reports that from 1980 to 2010 the number of Americans who speak Italian at home decreased by 55 percent; the worst result among the 20 languages most spoken.[1] Italian as a heritage language is in danger. But if we examine the data about ancestry, we find that the U.S. population who self-identifies as being of Italian ancestry rose of 44 percent from 1980 to 2010.[2] Does this mean that fewer people speak Italian as a heritage language, but more people are proud of their Italian identity? If so, this could be good news for the Italian language, and the data should be better analyzed in order to make more attractive the possibility of learning and knowing Italian as part of their cultural identity.

Around 80,000 students take Italian language and culture courses at the college level (Furman, Goldberg and Lusin, 2009), 4.78 percent of the students enrolled in foreign language courses. At K–12 level only around 78,000 students are enrolled in Italian language courses (0.8 percent of the students enrolled in foreign language courses) (ACTFL, 2008). Now the first question is: Why such a difference between K–12 and college and university students? Perhaps a contribution to the answer comes from the results of a specific question about which foreign language high-school students are more interested in studying: 36 percent of them says Italian (ACTFL, 2008).

While we know that there is a great interest in studying Italian, at both the college and high-school levels, there are not as many opportunities for students to take Italian language and culture courses as we might suspect; even fewer at the K–12 level than at college. This interest is part of the growing "proud to be Italian" sense of identity in the Italian-American population. It is necessary to advocate for more courses and consequently more

---

[1] American Community Survey Report. Language Use in the United States: 2011. United Census Bureau. The raw data are: from 1,618,344 in 1980 to 725,223 in 2010.

[2] United Census Bureau (1980) and American Community Survey 1-year estimates (2010). In raw data from 12,183,692 to 17,235,941

teachers, but it is also important to find new ways to offer the Italian language, based also on new curricula and syllabi.

In the recent years, some schools and universities adopted a plurilingual approach in order to offer students new opportunities to learn Italian. In this volume, we will present different experiences in various educational environments: California, Florida, and New York schools and colleges. The methods adopted by the researchers can be defined as a hybrid between the method of intercomprehension and the integrated approaches, as defined by Candelier (2012). All are designed for students of Italian, or French, who already have a competence in other Romance languages—as a mother tongue or because they have studied them previously. Also, differently from the classical intercomprehension methods, all the student's learning skills and competences are involved, not just reading.

It seems to be particularly promising to develop methods that are specifically addressed to students of Latin American descent and who haveproficiency in Spanish and/or Portuguese. The combination of Spanish/English/Italian or Spanish/English/French is definitely prevalent.

In 2011, in the United States 24 percent of students at the K–12 level were Hispanic, with peaks of 40 percent in the West. The Hispanic population in the country is expected to reach a majority , 30 percent, in 2023.[3]

In 2014, approximately 15 percent of undergraduate college students were of Hispanic ethnicity. A survey carried out by the John D. Calandra Institute in 2010 reported that 16.6 percent of high-school students studying Italian were Hispanic. To this data we must add how many non-Hispanic students studied or are studying another Romance language (Spanish, French, Italian, and Portuguese) and who therefore might be facilitated in learning another Romance language.

At the K–12 level in 2008, 72.87 percent studied Spanish as a foreign language, while 15 percent studied French (ACTFL, 2010). Some of them might be interested in learning Italian because of its ease; or to learn Italian and Spanish or French at the same time. In college, students enrolled in Spanish courses make up more than 52 percent of the students who take for-

---

[3] National Center for Education Statistics. http://nces.ed.gov/programs/coe/indicator_cge.asp.

eign language courses, while French is studied by 12 percent of the students.[4]

One datum is particularly worrying: The difference in number between those who follow the introductory courses and students taking advanced courses is very high. This is confirmed by the fact that the difference in the number of students enrolled in Italian courses at the undergraduate and graduate level is very high: Only one in 10 follows graduate-level courses.

Once again, Italian language seems to be very popular, but it is difficult to "retain" for the students; it seems they are not offered the opportunity to continue. Another significant problem for Italian is that with such a low percentage of students in graduate courses, it is very difficult to properly train a sufficient number of teachers and specialists with good language competence.[5]

Therefore, proposing courses of Italian language for Spanish speakers or students with different levels of proficiency in another Romance language is definitely a way to proceed in the future if we want Italian to grow faster.

Many foreign language teachers often combine a certification in Italian with one in Spanish, or French and vice versa. We should train them to take

---

[4] Enrollments in Languages Other Than English in United States Institutions of Higher Education, Fall 2009, MLA, 2010

[5] While this book was in printing, the results of the survey of MLA, referring to 2013, were made public. It was not possible to make an accurate analysis of these data, but at a first glance shows that there is a general decline of students enrolled in language (-6.7%) with the most common languages, such as Spanish, French, and German with declines of around 10%. The Italian slightly exceeds this threshold, with a decrease of 11.3% compared to 2009. The positions remain the same with the Italian language as fifth among the most studied, with 71,285 students. Also the figures on the percentage of students that pass from introductory courses to advanced worsen for Italian: only 8,5% of the students attended courses in higher level. In 2009 they were 10%. French, German, and Italian are the three languages that showed a steady decline in the transition from early to advanced courses, from 2006 to 2013, but still Italian has the worst result. In general, we can say that the picture is worrying though not dramatic. In fact, if the decline of the foreign language learners is general, this is also accompanied by a decrease in the number of students enrolled in Higher Education: -709,472 from 2011 to 2013 (NCES, 2014 as reported in MLA 2015). Anyway, for Italian the decline is worrying and even more the decline of students enrolled in the advanced courses. These data does not change the general analysis and the conclusions made in these papers. On the contrary, it becomes even more necessary to rethink the educational offer in terms of objectives and content to meet the needs of students and become more attractive. Again, the use of a multilingual and multicultural approach can be a valuable asset to reverse the trend.

advantage of their Romance language competence.

This could be important for school administrators whose schools may offer more interesting ways of learning foreign languages—and for students and parents as well who would see their efforts in learning foreign languages optimized.

From the point of view of research, this field is very promising, and the challenge for scholars involved in theory application, and in policy making, is interesting. In this volume experts from colleges and high schools present methods and activities that show how to put this approach into practice. The results are encouraging.

In the first essay, Roberto Dolci analyzes some aspects of U.S. language policy and how its objectives are linked to strategic and economic interests. During the past 70 years, strategic plans to improve Americans' language skills have been promoted, but not always successfully. Scholars and institutions currently affirm and demonstrate that the development of multilingual approaches in schools and universities can be much more effective in preparing America and American citizens for the challenges that await them.

Elisabetta Bonvino, in turn, traces the history of intercomprehension and describes its theoretical basis and the development of its methodology and application. Intercomprehension became the focus of much research, and applied projects financed by the European Union are considered strategic assets for the European Union's language policy. This led to the construction of various methods that are presented by the author within their theoretical framework and context.

Clorinda Donato and Cedric Joseph Oliva in their essay —also referring back to the debate on multilingualism developed in the United States in recent years—present an adaptation of the method of Intercomprehension in an American context and, in particular, in California in which they operate, characterized by a strong presence of speakers of Spanish. The program developed at the California State University at Long Beach can be considered the first developed in the United States, adopting and reinterpreting the principles of intercomprehension until then mainly used in Europe. Through examples and data the scholars show its validity and effectiveness.

Pierre Escudé stresses the value of multilingualism and how this can be considered an advantage in a country such as the United States. He points out that, in teaching foreign languages, instructors should have a goal of facilitating the awareness of what languages have in common, stressing how important it is not to focus on differences but on the similarities between languages. These principles are the basis of a method, Euromania, dedicated mainly to younger learners, developed by the scholar, and presented here.

Barbara Spinelli introduces the term *multiliteracy* and states that one of the objectives for language learning in the global world is to develop multiliteracy and pluriligualism. Her essay presents a classroom project aimed at developing these competences via an intensive elementary Italian language course for Romance language speakers at a university in New York. The intensive course is a hybrid that includes the use of the authoring tool "Wiki" to build a multilingual electronic space. Her essay describes the challenges encountered when integrating such an instructional approach into a more "traditional" classroom. Qualitative data are examined in order to analyze students' responses to such a method, and further practical applications for language teaching are suggested.

Fabrizio Fornara and Irene Zanini-Cordi show yet another context where the intercomprehension method proves a valuable aid for teaching and learning Italian, given the strong presence of speakers of Spanish. In the chapter's first part, the researchers present the university context in which they work, the impact and the solutions adopted in the language program and curriculum, while the second half of the essay describes the teaching strategies used, with particular reference to the use of technology and social media.

Markus Muller presents an administrator's perspective and describes the impact that the adoption of a method like intercomprehension and plurilingualism between Romance languages has on the program of a language department at college level. A correct application of these methods necessarily affects the curriculum of more than one language and requiresa remodel aiming at a strong integration between them on at least the three most common languages, Spanish, Italian, and French and necessitating a rethinking of the entire program.

Diego Cortés Velazquéz presents the practical application of what can be considered the method most updated and disseminated: EuRom5, through the description of the activities proposed and implemented in a course of Italian to Spanish speakers.

Ida Lanza and Diane Hartunian demonstrate how the method of intercomprehension can be effectively applied also at the high-school level in a context where there is a strong presence of Spanish speakers. Even high-school students are strongly stimulated by a method that develops their multilingual awareness and reinforces their sense of belonging and identity. The two teachers apply intercomprehension also to AP Italian classes. Data show that it works very well, and students learn more quickly and more efficiently, suggesting that applying the principles of plurilingualism and intercomprehension to AP-level courses in high school would be a great asset for AP Italian language and culture courses and exams.

BIBLIOGRAPHY

ACTFL, (2008), *Students Survey Report*, http://www.actfl.org /news/reports/ 2008-actfl-student-survey-report. Retrieved 20 January 2012

ACTFL, (2010) *Foreign Language Enrollments in K–12 Public Schools. Are Students Prepared for a Global Society?*, (2010), ACTFL. Retrieved 20 January 2012

Amselle, J. (ed.) (1995) The Failure of Bilingual Education, Washington D.C.: Center for Equal Opportunity.

Bloomfield, L. (1933) Language. New York: Holt, Rhinehart and Winston

Bialystok, E. (2007), Cognitive Effects of Bilingualism: How Linguistic Experience Leads to Cognitive Change, International Journal of Bilingual Education and Bilingualism, 10, 3.

Candelier, M. (coord.) (2012), FREPA: A Framework of Reference for Pluralistic Approaches to Languages and Cultures, Strasbourg: Council of Europe Publishing.

Cenoz, J., Gorter, G. (2011), A Holistic Approach to Multilingual Education: Introduction, *The Modern Language Journal*, 95, iii, pp. 339-343

Farrell, M. (2011), Bilingual competence and students' achievement in Physics and Mathematics, International Journal of Bilingual Education and Bilingualism, 14, 3.

Furman, N., Goldberg, D. and Lusin, N., (2009) "Enrollments in Languages Other Than English in United States Institutions of Higher Education, Fall 2009", Modern Languages Association of America, http://www.mla.org/pdf/2009_en roll ment_survey.pdf, retrieved July 6, 2014.

Goldberg, D., Furman, N., and Lusin, N., (2015) ""Enrollments in Languages Other Than English in United States Institutions of Higher Education, Fall 2013", *Modern Languages Association of America*, http://www.mla.org/pdf/2013_enroll ment_survey.pdf, retrieved February 27, 2015.

Kramsch, C. (2012), Authenticity and Legitimacy in Multilingual SLA, *Critical*

Multilingualism Studies, 1:1, pp 107-128

Macnamara, J. (1967) "The Bilingual's Linguistic Performance. A Psychological Overview," Journal of Social Issue, 23,58-77.

Potowski, K. (ed.) (2010) *Language Diversity in the USA*, Cambridge: Cambridge University Press.

Titone, R. (1972) *Bilinguismo precoce ed educazione bilingue*. Roma: Armando Editore.

Valdes, G. (2005) "Bilingualism, Heritage Language Learners, and SLA Research: Opportunities Lost or Seized?" *The Modern Language Journal* 89.3.

On America's Foreign Language Education Policy
and the "Foreign Language Deficit"

Roberto Dolci

1. America's Language Education Policy

In his speech at the American Council on the Teaching of Foreign Languages summit in 2005, the sociolinguist Bernard Spolsky stated that the United States does not have a real language policy.[1] This statement might seem strong, but many scholars agree that in the United States language is a matter related to the sphere of human rights or a reaction to external events, more than to a long-term strategy (Spolsky 2004; Shohamy 2006; Wright 2004; Morris 2003).

For example, there is no reference to language per se in the Constitution, although it is written in English; and there is no specific law regulating the use of languages in the United States. According to Spolsky and all the participants at the summit (politicians, experts and representatives of associations and government agencies), the current era urges the United States to adopt a language policy in order to meet the challenges caused by internal migration, to remain competitive in the global market, and to guarantee the nation's safety.

Historically, in the United States, foreign language (FL) policy went through several phases of contraction and expansion depending on the political and economic situation. In specific historical periods of high-stress international relations, the United States insisted that only a strong investment in education could provide an answer to these challenges determined by their strategic role. These initiatives—at the federal or national level—mainly focused on the development of sciences and foreign languages.

The ASTP (Army Specialized Training Program) is a good example of

---

[1] ACTFL US Language Policy plan of Action http://www.actfl.org/us-language-policy-plan-action?pageid=3725 , 2005, accessed July 2014.

these education initiatives. The program started during World War II in order to quickly and adequately train soldiers who would then go to fight in Europe and Asia. The program included also the teaching of as many as 37 foreign languages, among them Italian (Santosuosso, 1954).

The impact of the ASTP has also been substantial for the theoretical and methodological development in language pedagogy, bringing a revolution in content, methods, and techniques that have become the basis of the communicative approach in language teaching.

Another critical moment for the United States occurred in 1957 when the Soviet Union launched the satellite Sputnik, temporarily gaining supremacy in the space race. As the historian Daniel Boorstin remembered later: "Never before had so small and so harmless an object created such consternation" (Borstin 1974). The response of President Eisenhower was the introduction of the National Defense Education Act (NDEA).

This program was designed to encourage the training of teachers and students in order to address particularly acute national manpower shortages in teaching, specifically in the fields of science, mathematics, engineering, and modern foreign languages (Flattau, 2006, II-5). Within a few years, the number of Americans who had access to higher education had more than doubled. However, while some sectors such as education and science increased significantly, students of foreign languages, a field that had increased until 1970, then began a downturn (Flattau, 2006, II-8).

At the end of the twentieth century, America faced another challenge that it did not feel ready to confront: the globalization of the century that was to come. Data showed that education imparted in schools and universities was not adequate and could undermine the primacy of the United States in various fields. Once again, the answer was a federal law: the Bush Administration initiative named "American 2000" continued under the Clinton presidency's initiative "Goals 2000: Educate America Act," signed in 1994. The law was primarily intended to improve American students' skills to better face global competition through a reform of the curricula and the promotion of a national system of standards and certifications. Additionally, "Goals 2000" stated that it was crucial to "Provide an international education exchange program" (*Goals 2000*, Title VI).

Like the ASTP program mentioned above, the impact of this law was particularly important for FL teaching in the United States. The launch of the

ACFTL Standards for Foreign Language Learning was a consequence of these two initiatives, which had an evident impact in U.S. K-12 schools since their publication in 1999.[2]

The debate on how to encourage the study of foreign languages continued in the following years and focused on two main topics: promoting internationalization, and fostering plurilingualism.

2. The Debate on the Foreign Language Deficit

In the nineties, theories on FL teaching and learning focused on the idea that FL knowledge needed to be linked to a solid cross-cultural competence. Communicative competence in a foreign language includes not only linguistic but also cultural and pragmatic components. Therefore, a learner needs to understand others in a broader sense, developing an intercultural competence. Learners need to interpret the world from plural perspectives, to respect the different value systems, and avoid stereotypes. In this process learners can appreciate without bias the system of values of their own culture. It was for this reason that stakeholders stressed the importance of merging students into the target culture, for instance through study-abroad programs.

Therefore, the need of defining a policy aimed at emphasizing the internationalization of U.S. education became a pivotal issue at different levels including the institutional, scientific, and associative. This need combines with the two traits that have always driven the educational and language policy of the United States: economic development and security. The main impetus for this interest was globalization and the challenges it entails, accompanied by the 9/11 attacks, which were far more tragic than the launch of Sputnik in 1957.

While in 1957 effort was focused particularly on extending students' access to higher education, after 2001, the policy's main goal was increasing students' foreign language competence through different strategies: international exchanges, access to foreign students in American universities, and encouraging American students to study abroad.

In the last 10 years many associations and research centers such as the IIE (Institute of International Education), ACTFL, JNCL-NCLIS (Joint Nation-

---

[2] In Europe, a similar debate started some years earlier. It then led to the creation of the *Common European Framework of Reference for Languages*, *CEFR*, published in 2001.

al Committee for Languages-National Council for Languages and International Studies), CFR (Council on Foreign Relations), ACE (American Council on Education), LRC (Language Resource Centers), and NAFSA (Association of International Educators) promoted numerous initiatives and projects.

For instance, in 2000 the Department of Education's Office of Postsecondary Education stated that "It should not take another Sputnik launch and a Cold War to galvanize our nation into action on international education. The launch of the Internet and global competition should be enough."[3] Also, President Clinton, in 2000, and President Bush, in 2001, stressed the importance of international education.

And so it was that, in 2005, at the ACTFL summit in Baltimore, many experts and politicians discussed the need for a plan of action for increasing opportunities for American students to study abroad and to study foreign languages. The main goal of this plan was to raise "the American public's awareness of the need and value of learning languages and understanding cultures."[4]

In 2006, President Bush promoted the National Security Language Initiative, which allocates millions of dollars for the dissemination of foreign languages in schools and the training of new teachers in order to ensure the competitiveness in international languages with the goal of promoting greater cultural understanding and as a result to strengthen national security.

In 2008 the Department of Education opened a special office for the International and Foreign Language Education, which aimed at "encouraging and promoting the study of foreign languages and cultures of other countries at the elementary, secondary, and postsecondary levels in the United States."[5]

In 2010 Secretary Arne Duncan, at the Foreign Language Summit held at the University of Maryland, quoting President Obama's words, pointed out that the "Sputnik moment" for the current generation is "now" and added: "The Soviet satellite was a wake-up call that launched a wave of innovation and reform in American schools, particularly in math, science, and language

---

[3] US Department of Education, "Learning Without Limits. An Agenda for the Office of Postsecundary Education", 2000, http://www2.ed.gov/offices/OPE/AgenProj/report/index.html, accessed July 2014.
[4] ACTFL, US Language Policy plan of Action http://www.actfl.org/us-language-policy-plan-action?pageid=3725 accessed July 2014.
[5] http://www2.ed.gov/about/offices/list/ope/index.html.

instruction. Today's call to action is an economic one. We need to build a strong foundation for growth and prosperity."[6] At the same summit, Leon Panetta, as director of the Central Intelligence Agency, also stressed the importance of developing FL language competences to guarantee U.S. national security and competitiveness.[7]

The final report (2005), called "Securing America's Future: Global Education for a Global Age," conceived by the Strategic Task Force on Education Abroad established by NAFSA, became the reference for future actions at the federal level. An example of these actions was the creation of the Study Abroad Foundation in 2009 on Senator Paul Simon's initiative.

NAFSA involved many stakeholders (e.g., senators, presidents of universities, directors, and scholars) in order to improve future generations of Americans' foreign language knowledge and intercultural competence.[8] In fact, the report stated that while in the world students learn at least two foreign languages, including English, foreign language teaching in the United States is still too little encouraged.

The Task Force suggested that only a period abroad can allow American students to develop language skills and multiple ways of interpreting different actions and behaviors of target cultures. In order to emphasize the importance of living abroad, the document quotes a passage of the speech that President Bush (Bush, 2001, quoted in NAFSA 2003) gave after 9/11:

---

[6] US Department of Education, "Education and the Language Gap" http://www.ed.gov/news/speeches/education-and-language-gap-secretary-arne-duncans-remarks-foreign-language-summit, accessed July 2014.

[7] He stated: "For the United States to get to where it needs to be will require a national commitment to strengthening America's foreign language proficiency. A significant cultural change needs to occur. (…) Language skills are vital to success in an interconnected world, and they are fundamental to US competitiveness and security.(…) Language is the window through which we come to know other peoples and cultures, (…) Mastery of a second language allows you to capture the nuances that are essential to true understanding. (…) This is not about learning something that is helpful or simply nice to have. It is crucial to CIA's mission C.I.A., "CIA Director Calls for a National Commitment to Language Proficiency at Foreign Language Summit," https://www.cia.gov/news-information/press-releases-statements/press-release-2010/foreign-language-summit.html accessed July 2014.

[8] According to the report, it's precisely because of this that the U.S. is unprepared to address the challenge of globalization and security against new worldwide emergencies. "We are now in another Sputnik moment. We can remain as ignorant of the outside world as we were on September 11, or do the work necessary to overcome this handicap" (NAFSA 2003, 3).

By studying foreign cultures and languages and living abroad, we gain a better understanding of the many similarities that we share and learn to respect our differences. The relationships that are formed between individuals from different countries as part of international education programs and exchanges can also foster goodwill that develops into vibrant, mutually beneficial partnerships among nations. (5)

The document also provided examples of good practices, among which we find the Erasmus program promoted by the European Union. Since 1987 this project allowed more than 2 million European students to spend a period abroad to study in the target academic context. This mobility in Europe generated what is called the "Erasmus generation" and is the prototype of the future European citizens.

Consequently, the Task Force established the "Abraham Lincoln Study Abroad Fellowship Program," which later became the "Paul Simon Study Abroad Foundation Act," in honor of the senator, who died in 2003. The Foundation aims at reaching 1 million American students going to study abroad programs in the next ten years and at encouraging universities to develop international programs. The act had the endorsement of dozens of organizations. Were the foundation to be finally approved, it would represent the most remarkable change in the internationalization of education policy in the United States.

THE OUTCOMES OF THE INTERNATIONALIZATION POLICIES

What was the impact of all these internationalization initiatives on schools, universities, and particularly on students' educational formation?

In U.S. higher education, internationalization programs have a long history. Since the early twentieth century the prestigious foundation Rhodes funded scholarships for studying at Oxford, while after World War II the Fulbright Foundation helped to improve mobility of thousands of students and professors between the United States and foreign countries.

Most American universities and colleges have programs for internationalization and study abroad, as do many high schools. The number of students who attend study abroad programs has grown tremendously in recent years. Although we are far from the 1 million expected by the Simon Foundation, the number of students has more than tripled, approximately from 80,000 in 1990 to 270,000 in 2010. However, this number represents less than 1 percent of students enrolled in college (Institute of International Education [IIE], 2013).

According to the IIE survey, the study areas mostly covered in these programs are the Social Sciences (22.4 percent), Business and Management (20.5 percent), Humanities (10.8 percent), Physical/Life Sciences (8.6 percent), and Fine or Applied Arts (7.8 percent). Foreign Language students represent only 5.3 percent, with a decrease of 3.0 percent over the past year (IIE, 2013).

Among the geographical areas, Europe is chosen by half of the American students, Latin America by 15 percent, and Asia by 12 percent. The most popular destination is the United Kingdom with 34,660 students, accounting for 12.2 percent. Italy stands in second place, with 29,645 students representing 10.5 percent of the total, but with a decrease of 2.4 percent over the past year, followed by Spain, France, China, Australia, and Germany.

The number of foreign students who come to study in the United States is very different. In 2012/2013 there were 819.644, an increase of 33 percent compared to 2000. The countries most represented are China, with 235,597 students (an increase of 21 percent over the previous year), followed by India, South Korea, Canada, Taiwan, Saudi Arabia, Japan, Mexico, Turkey, and Nepal, among others. In the first 25 positions there are only four European countries: Germany (12th), UK (13th), France (17th), and Spain (25th).

FOREIGN LANGUAGES AT SCHOOLS AND COLLEGES

As far as foreign language education is concerned, in 2007-2008 only 18.5 percent of K-12 students were enrolled in foreign language courses in American public schools. These outcomes are considered unsatisfactory by the ACTFL, which underlines the need of studying a foreign language at an early ages in order to create a multilingual population. In fact, the ACTFL (2010) states that the U.S. "economic, military, and humanitarian needs require a multilingual population that begins with foreign language education throughout grades K-12."[9]

However, if we take into account only grades 9-12, data are much better.

---

[9] http://www.actfl.org/enrollment-survey.

According to the National Center of Educational Statistics (NCES) the percentage of students enrolled in foreign language programs increased from 20.9 percent in 1948 to 42.3 percent in 2000 (NCES, 2011). Nonetheless, about half of high-school students do not attend language courses. The most-studied languages at the K-12 levels are Spanish, followed by French, German, Latin, Japanese, and Italian (ACTFL, 2010).

Skorton and Altschuler (2012, 1) identified one of the main reasons why the offering of foreign language instruction tremendously decreased in private and elementary schools (from 31 to 25 percent from 1997 to 2008) and in middle schools (from 75 to 58 percent) as being budget cuts. According to this study, these cuts also affected the quality of foreign language teaching offered within these educational contexts.

In higher education, the situation is not much better. If there was a sharp increase in numbers of students attending language courses especially since 1995, in 2009 only 8.6 percent of all undergraduate and graduate students were enrolled in language courses (MLA, 2009). The languages most studied are Spanish, French, German, American Sign Language (ASL), Italian, Japanese, and Chinese. Learners of Spanish at all levels of instruction exceed the sum of all other foreign language students.

The relevant position of Spanish compared to the other foreign languages demonstrates that Spanish can no longer be considered a "foreign language" in traditional terms, but rather a second language, given its spread, albeit uneven, in the United States. In fact, in 2009 the number of U.S. residents who spoke Spanish at home was 35 million, 12 percent of U.S. residents.[10]

Interestingly, the highest number of foreign language students in college was reached in 1965 (16.5 percent). From that moment, there was a slow but evident decrease in enrollments, and it was only starting in 1995 that there was a change. This probably means that the National Defense Education Act (NDEA) was successful in increasing enrollment at college but not for foreign language courses. According to Furman, Goldberg, and Lusin (2010) this decline may be due to the decline in language requirements.

The data related to foreign language knowledge at the different levels of education mirror the general situation of languages spoken by the population

---

[10] US Census Bureau, http://www.census.gov/newsroom/releases/archives /facts_for_features _special_ editions/cb11-ff18.html, accessed July 2014.

in the United States. Secretary of Education Arne Duncan (2010) comparing the United States with Europe stated that "just 18 percent of Americans report speaking a language other than English, while in Europe 53 percent of citizens speak more than one language."[11]

3. THE UNITED STATES: A MULTILINGUAL COUNTRY AND SOCIETY

The efforts of the United States in promoting foreign language knowledge are not limited to improving the internationalization of students and universities. Success in promoting FL knowledge among American citizens also depends on a cultural and educational change, using the resources that already exist. If monolingualism is interpreted as a negative aspect, it is also true that the United States have never been a monolingual country.[12] This is true elsewhere as well. Contrary to popular belief, bilingualism and not monolingualism seems to be the common practice in the world.

Francois Grosjean (2010), one of the most important scholars on bilingualism, affirms that:

> Whenever I give a talk on bilingualism, I surprise my audience with the following estimate: More than half of the world's population uses two or more languages (or dialects) in everyday life. Bilingualism is present on all continents, in all classes of society, in all age groups.[13]

It is nonetheless necessary to make a distinction between multilingual countries and multilingual populations. For instance, the United States has always been a multilingual country because of the diverse languages of immigrants, which added to hundreds of languages spoken by Native Americans.

The U.S. Census Bureau, collecting language data in its decennial censuses until 2000, listed 381 languages spoken in the nation. The American Community Survey (ACS), which collects language data after 2000, lists over 300 languages spoken at home. If we look closer at everyday contexts in which languages are used, we discover that: Voting ballots are in 28 lan-

---

[11] Actually, the data on Americans are underestimated. See below.
[12] Actually, monolingualism has a negative connotation mainly for linguistics and educators. For politicians and the conservative part of the population, it is bilingualism that was (and is) that is seen as a problem.
[13] http://www.psychologytoday.com/blog/life-bilingual/201011/bilingualisms-best-kept-secret.

guages; the Social Security website is written in 19 different languages; the drivers license exams are in 23 languages; and the Census 2000 instruction guide was written in 50 different languages.[14]

In 2011, 60.5 million people (21 percent) out of the 291.5 million people aged 5 and over, spoke a language other than English at home. These languages range from a few thousands (or hundreds) of speakers of some Native-American languages that are at risk of extinction, to millions of speakers of Spanish. These data clearly show that the United States is a multilingual nation. However, that is not sufficient to affirm that bilingualism or multilingualism is a normal condition in the country. In fact, how many American citizens can be considered at least bilingual? How many of the 21 percent who speak another language at home speak English as well? In order to answer this question, first of all we need to determine what being bilingual or multilingual means.

Bilingualism and multilingualism are areas of interest for many different scientific fields: psychology, linguistics, educational linguistics, sociology, politics, and pedagogy. In fact bilingualism/multilingualism is a multidimensional phenomenon that involves cognitive, social, cultural, and emotional aspects along with people's age, language needs, and competence. In this sense, the definition of bilingualism/multilingualism depends on the researcher's perspective (Naharro, 1998; Paradis, 1987; Fabbro, 1996; Hamers & Blanc, 2000).

From the linguistics (theoretical, applied, and educational) point of view the question of how to define bilingualism or multilingualism is obviously not a new one, and many scholars have given interpretations that differ considerably (Grosjean, 2010; Cenoz and Gorter, 2011; Hamers and Blanc 2000; Baker, 2006). Baetens-Beardsmore's (1982, p.1) definition is widely cited and interprets bilingualism as a term that "has open-ended semantics." However, scholars agree that there are two main interpretations. A narrow definition considers being bilingual as being "two times monolingual." For instance, Bloomfield (1933, p.36) asserted that bilingualism is the "native-like control of two languages." McNamara (1967), instead, suggests that one can be bilingual even with only a basic competence in one of the four language skills (speaking, writing, reading, and listening) in a language different

---

[14] Source: http://us-english.org/view/307.

from his/her mother tongue. A similar, but more precise, definition is given by Titone (1972):

> ... il bilinguismo consiste nella capacità di un individuo di esprimersi nella seconda lingua aderendo fedelmente ai concetti e alle strutture che a tale lingua sono propri, anziché parafrasando la lingua nativa.[15]

In recent years, most scholars tend to accept a definition that is closer to Mcnamara's and Titone's definition. Valdes (2005) explains this with the equation: "multilingualism=more than one."

According to Valdes (2005) we can define a bilingual/multilingual person as *ambilingual* (having native competency in two languages), but bilingual/multilingual is also a person who possesses different levels of proficiency in two or more languages and distinctively among all the productive and the receptive skills. According to this perspective one can define many different types of bilingual/multilingual competence and classify them along a continuum. Figure 1 shows the L1/L2 User Continuum (adapted form Valdes, 2005):

Monolingual   Monolingual

A A_b A_b A_b A_b A_b AB aB aB B_a B_a B_a B_a B_a B

Figure 1 The L1/L2 User Continuum (adapted form Valdes, 2005)

In Figure 1, different size fonts indicate different language strengths in language A and language B for different L1/L2 users. A recently arrived immigrant, for instance, might be represented as Ab ("A" dominant in the immigrant language and in the beginning stages "b" of learning English). Similarly, a fourth-generation L1/L2 user could be represented as Ba ("B" having acquired English as a L1, dominant in English, and still retaining some profi-

---

[15] Bilingualism is the ability of an individual to express him/herselves in a second language adhering to the concepts and structures that are peculiar to that language, rather than paraphrasing the native language (my translation).

ciency "a" in the immigrant language).

In minority language communities all over the world, such different types of L1/L2 users live together and interact with one another and with monolinguals on a daily basis, using one or the other of their two languages. L1/L2 users will fluctuate in their preferences or perceived strengths in each language, depending on the nature of the interaction, the topic of discussion, the domain of activity, and the formality or the informality of the situation (Valdes, 2005, p. 414).

All types of bilingual speakers are included within this continuum. For instance, individuals who have learned one or more languages at school—either as child or as adult—or have spent a period of time abroad can be considered bilingual. The description of the continuum may be much more complex and multidimensional if we add the knowledge of other languages. As mentioned above, according to this definition, a person can be bilingual/multilingual if he/she has some degree of proficiency in producing, comprehending, and interacting in more than one language, even at different levels of performance in each skill. In this chapter we accept and use this definition, even though it may have some limits.[16]

By taking into consideration this definition of bilingual/multilingual we can interpret the ACS data differently. As mentioned above, these data showed that in 2011 60 million people, 21 percent of the total, declared that they spoke a language different from English at home. However, the survey asked people to self-evaluate their own speaking ability in English. Of the respondents, 58.2 percent declared "very well," and 19.4 percent said "well." Only 7 percent did not speak English at all.

Therefore, if we interpret these data according to our definition, we can affirm that 77 percent of this population is at least bilingual—that is 47 million of people, around 17 percent of the total population.

However, if we want to know how many bilinguals or multilinguals live in the United States, these data are not enough. We do not have enough information about the languages spoken outside the home by the 230 million

---

[16] One problem could be, for instance, what degree of language proficiency we can consider as threshold level for bilingualism/multilingualism. In fact, this level may depend on many variables (e.g. the domain of use, social orientation, and the speaker's needs). For example, Grosejean (2010), stating that "bilingualism is the use of two or more languages in one's everyday life," takes into consideration the two aspects of context and needs.

people who said they speak only English at home. Do they speak at least one foreign language at a certain level of proficiency? Unfortunately, the Census does not provide any information about these factors. However, in many states, we can easily conclude that many English-speaking Americans speak a language other than English outside their homes. For instance, in states like Florida, Texas, and California, the great majority of the respective populations interacts in Spanish at some point during the day.

As Michael Herard points out in his article published in the *New York Times*, the Census should ask the same question that the European Commission used in its surveys to investigate languages spoken in Europe, that is, what are the languages that you speak well enough in order to be able to have a conversation?[17]

Taking this into account, the data presented by Secretary of Education Duncan in 2010 are strongly underestimated[18]—and we can probably assume that Americans are more multilingual (or less monolingual) than is commonly believed. But there is no room for complacency. All experts, politicians, commentators, and stakeholders agree that this is not enough in order to take on the challenges that the globalized world poses to the United States.

4. A Shift in SLA and FL Methodology

A possible answer to these difficulties is to consider bilingualism and multilingualism as a resource to be exploited from kindergarten age. Research should focus on the development of theories, approaches, methods, and programs that promote multilingualism and take into consideration students' different linguistic background in multilingual classroom.

During the 1990s, theoretical research on Second Language Acquisition (SLA) underwent an important shift due to what was called the "multilingual turn in SLA" (Cook, 1992, 1995; Kramsch 2009, 2012, May 2014) as a reaction to "monolingual bias" (Firth & Wagner, 1997; Cook, 1997; Ortega, 2008; Cenoz and Gorter, 2011). This turn called for an important change in approaches and methods in language education.

---

[17] Are we really Monolingual? By Michael Erard. Published on January 14, 2012. In EU in 2012 54% of the population declared to be able to have a conversation in at least one foreign language, while 25 % declared that can have a conversation in at least two foreign languages.
[18] See above. "http://www.ed.gov/news/speeches/education-and-language-gap-secretary-arne-duncans-remarks-foreign-language-summit.

The main idea was to question the traditional assumption that the goal in learning a language is to reach the competence of a homogeneous and ideal "native speaker." In other words, the concept of monolingualism was abandoned in favor of multilingualism, which provided language learning with a more pragmatic and realistic social dimension and emphasized the notion of a learner's multilingual competence (Cook, 1991, 2012). In their seminal paper Firth and Wagner (1997)[19] wrote:

> In essence, we call for work within SLA that endeavors to adopt what we have referred to as a holistic approach to and outlook on language and language acquisition, an approach that problematizes and explores the conventional binary distinction between "social" and "individual" (or cognitive) approaches to language use and language learning, that attends to the dynamics as well as the summation of language acquisition, that is more emically and interactionally attuned, and that is critically sensitive towards the theoretical status of fundamental concepts (particularly "learner," "native," "nonnative," and "interlanguage"). (296)

In a subsequent paper written in 1998, in response to Long (1997) and Kasper (1997), Firth and Wagner (1998) reaffirm:

> It is surely time to take seriously the possibility of deconstructing such dichotomies as use versus acquisition, sociolinguistics versus psycholinguistics, and language use versus communicative act." (93)

This position radically modifies the definition of the language learner. Kramsch summarizes it by saying that a learner is not a *language learner* but rather a *language user*, "not a *deficient non-native speaker*, but a *savvy navigator* of communicative obstacles" (Kramsch, 2011, 108). The multilingual perspective on SLA places in doubt many of the traditional assets of foreign language teaching, such as the standardization of the norm against the use of different languages according to students' communicative needs and the author-

---

[19] Firth, A., & Wagner, J. (1997). "On discourse, communication, and (some) fundamental concepts in SLA research." *Modern Language Journal* 81: 285–300.

ity of the institution in deciding what has to be learned (Kramsch, 2011; Cenoz and Gorter, 2010).

This point of view appears to be the most appropriate response to the needs of people and to the demands of globalization, and language policy makers were aware of that. During the 1990s, either in Europe or in the United States, stakeholders asked for a change in language education policy. As a result, two important documents that changed language education came out: the *Common European Framework for Languages (CEFR)* in Europe (2001) and the *Standards for Foreign Language Learning* in the USA (1996).

Since the 1960s the Language Policy Division of the Council of Europe (CoE) adopted a plurilingual approach, convinced that the rich heritage of languages and cultures in Europe was a valuable resource to be protected and promoted. Therefore, only a plurilingual and pluricultural approach could convert that diversity "from a barrier to communication into a source of mutual enrichment and understanding" (*CEFR*, 2001, 2).

Starting in the early 1990s, the CoE asked a group composed of experts in theoretical and applied linguistics, sociolinguistics, educational linguistics, as well as teachers and administrators to prepare a framework that could help one to become a "European democratic citizen." In 2001, the last version of the *CEFR* was launched. The *CEFR* is the most important language education policy document in Europe, and it has worldwide influence. The *CEFR* (2001) is based on the fundamental assumption of the promotion of plurilingualism and pluriculturalism as stated below:

> The plurilingual approach emphasizes the fact that as an individual person's experience of language in its cultural contexts expands, from the language of the home to that of society at large and then to the languages of other peoples (whether learnt at school or college, or by direct experience), he or she does not keep these languages and cultures in strictly separated mental compartments, but rather builds up a communicative competence to which all knowledge and experience of language contributes and in which languages interrelate and interact.[20] (4)

---

[20] The *CEFR* makes a distinction between multilingualism and plurilingualism. It defines multilingualism as "the knowledge of a number of languages or the co-existence of different languages in a given society." (4). In this sense, multilingualism can be considered only as a

This perspective completely transforms the approach to language education by asking for a change at each level, from curriculum planning to classroom activities, as the CEFR points out in the following:

> From this perspective, the aim of language education is profoundly modified. It is no longer seen as simply to achieve "mastery" of one or two, or even three languages, each taken in isolation, with the 'ideal native speaker' as the ultimate model. Instead, the aim is to develop a linguistic repertoire, in which all linguistic abilities have a place. This implies, of course, that the languages offered in educational institutions should be diversified and students given the opportunity to develop a plurilingual competence. (5)

It is easy to understand how this perspective acquires a fundamental value for the European Union, where 24 different official languages coexist. The European Union values all the languages spoken in Europe at the same level: Language and cultural diversity are a asset, not a problem.

In the same period in the United States a debate began on what the most appropriate educational policies for the challenges of the new millennium might be.[21]

First published in 1996, the *Standards for Foreign Language Learning. Preparing for the 21st Century*, by ACTFL, represents a document that changed the way to teach foreign languages in the United States from the K-12 levels.

This document also seeks to provide an educational response to the new challenges that the United States will face in the near future: those externally represented by globalization and those internally characterized by an increasingly pluralistic society.

Even if the context is completely different, the *Standards* shares with the *CEFR* the same theoretical background. The *Standards* wants to educate students to communicate successfully in both a pluralistic American society as

---

description of a reality, while plurilingualism is an attitude and a competence. Nowadays the two terms seem interchangeable with a preference for multilingualism that is widely spread in the literature also with the meaning given to plurilingualism.

[21] As we said before, promoted and financed by the Bush Administration with the *America 2000 Education Initiative* continued under *Goals 2000* in the Clinton Administration

well as abroad, developing and maintaining proficiency in English and at least one foreign language and giving opportunities to children from non-English backgrounds to develop bilingual/multilingual competences. The document (ACTFL, 1996) stresses that:

> The United States must educate students who are linguistically and culturally equipped to communicate successfully in a pluralistic American society and abroad. ALL students will develop and maintain proficiency in English and at least one other language, modern or classical. People from non-English backgrounds should also have opportunities to develop further proficiencies in their first language. (1)

Even though there is no explicit mention of a multilingual approach, it is clear that these standards also consider the student as a *language user* who learns how to navigate and to communicate through different cultures and languages by comparing them, making connections with other kinds of knowledge, and participating in diverse multilingual communities. This goal is successfully summarized by the Five Cs: *Communication, Cultures, Connections, Comparisons, and Communities.*[22]

In 2007, a team of experts from the MLA prepared another important document on language education policy for the United States. The title perfectly explains the rationale: *Foreign Languages and Higher Education: New Structures for a Changed World*. While it does not offer any specific standards, the ad hoc committee of experts does recognize that college FL programs are inadequate, and they thus ask for a change in FL academic programs in order to fill "the nation's language deficit" and to comprehend better the globalized world. Their mission is to "pave the way toward a multilingual future for students in the higher education system in the United States" (2007, 9). The goal is to develop translingual and transcultural competence through a reform

---

[22] By 2012, 46 States adopted the Common Core State Standards for K-12 students. There are not specific Foreign Language Standards described in the CCSS; only for English Language and Arts and other areas. In any case, the discussion about the application of the CCSS also involves a discussion about bilingualism and multilingualism in the USA classroom. For an interesting analysis about the CCSS and bilingualism, see Garcia & Flores (2014).

of the curriculum.[23]

The language education policies and standards and the new theories of SLA outline a different model for accomplishing the multilingual requirement. It is up to the more theoretically applicative disciplines—applied linguistics and educational linguistics, first of all—to translate these principles into approaches and methods that are consistent with the theory in order to adapt them to the needs of the society.

None of the documents mentioned thus far suggests or describes a method, but they define the key principles according to which the approaches and methods must be respected.

As the CoE (Language Policy Division of CoE, 2005) states, a plurilingual person has:

- a repertoire of languages and languages varieties;
- competence of different kinds and levels within the repertoire.

In turn, plurilingual education promotes:

- an awareness of why and how one learns the language one has chosen;
- an awareness of and the ability to use transferable skills in language learning;
- a respect for the plurilingualism of others and the values of languages and varieties irrespective of their perceived status in the society;
- a respect for the cultures embodied in languages and the cultural identities of others;
- an ability to perceive and mediate the relationship which exist among languages and cultures;
- a global integrated approach to language education in the curriculum. (5)

However, what are the implications for education, linguistics, researchers, administrators, teachers, and students in adopting a plurilingual approach?

---

[23] See Spinelli in this volume for a deeper discussion about this document.

Kramsch (2012), among others, states that "it is also necessary to take advantage of the increasingly multilingual composition of language classes and to draw on the students' multilingual competences, even if they are learning a single language" (107).

She suggests some plurilingual practices as follow:

1. Treat L1, L2, and L3 as available semiotic repertoires, not as structural rules and self-enclosed systems;
2. Explicitly teach the relation between multiple modalities, registers, and genres;
3. Engage with texts on multiple levels of indexicality (…);[24]
4. Bring back translation, full or partial, into our L2 literary practices;
5. Mainly discuss with colleagues in FL departments: For whom are we teaching foreign languages? (…). (123)

In 2011, *The Modern Language Journal* dedicated a special issue to multilingual practices in school, where numerous authors presented many different methods.[25] Cenoz and Gorter, the editors, called the approach "Focus on Multilingualism." Cenoz and Gorter (2011, 341) reaffirm that the goal of the ideal of native-speaker competence is a mistaken one. That goal creates a feeling of failure and incompleteness in students. They consider multilinguals and learners in the process of becoming multilingual as "possessing unique forms of competence, or competencies, in their own right." In traditional classrooms there is a separation between the language taught and other languages. In traditional methods and classroom-language practices, phenomena like codemixing, codeswitching, and translanguaging are not allowed by the teachers. On the contrary, the proposed multilingual and holistic approach looks at these phenomena as characteristics of the multilingual practice. Their approach valorizes the other languages present in the classroom as a result of the different experiences and identities of the students. Cenoz and Gortez also point out that a holistic multilingual approach can be realized only if there

---

[24] This includes any sign that helps to identify a community or a group (Ochs, 1990).
[25] "Toward a Multilingual Approach in the Study of Multilingualism in School Contexts," Special Issue. *The Modern Language Journal*, 95, iii (2011).

is a strong coordination among teachers and the school in proposing an integrative language curriculum that takes advantage of the presence of different languages in the school and the classroom focusing on the relationships between them (341).

Candelier (2012) defines pluralistic approaches as those that "use teaching/learning activities involving several (i.e., more than one) varieties of languages and cultures."

He identifies four main pluralistic approaches:[26]

- The intercultural approach, which encourages reflection over different cultural areas and focuses on teaching how to avoid possible intercultural conflicts;
- The integrated didactic approach, which helps students to establish links between a limited number of languages, those taught in the curriculum;
- The intercomprehension between related languages approach, where a student works on two or more languages of the same family, one of them being his/her mother tongue;
- The awakening to language (*éveil aux langues*) approach. Candelier defines this one as the most extreme one since students work with several languages. It is not limited to the languages in the curriculum but "integrates all sort of other linguistic varieties—from their homes, from the environment, and from all over the world." (7)

Each approach has its characteristics. The choice, or the integration between them, is up to the school and the teacher, and it depends on the different contexts and goals of language education. Candelier (2012) proposes a Framework of Reference for Pluralistic Approaches (FREPA) in order to cre-

---

[26] It is impossible here to accurately present each approach. The intercomprehension approach will be deeply explained thorough this volume. For the other approaches see Candelier (2012).

ate synergy among them. The set of descriptors allows schools and teachers to co-ordinate their use in a harmonized curriculum.[27]

In conclusion, the challenge is to consider bilingualism and multilingualism as a resource to be exploited, starting from K-12 and at the university level, and to develop methods and programs that take advantage of the linguistic diversity present in the society. In this way, the presence in the classroom of students with different language skills becomes an advantage. Even though biligualism/multilingualism is widespread in the United States, it must be nurtured and cultivated. It cannot be considered an obstacle, but rather must serve as a resource that needs to be properly utilized.

---

[27] Candelier and his colleagues developed many teaching activities, research papers, and other useful materials free to download from the ECML (European Centre for Modern Languages) website. See http://carap.ecml.at/CARAP/tabid/2332/language/en-GB/Default.aspx.

BIBLIOGRAPHY

National Standards in Foreign Language Education Project. (1996), *Standards for foreign language learning: Preparing for the 21st century.* Lawrence, KS: Allen Press.

ACTFL, (2008) *Students Survey Report,* http://www.actfl.org /news/reports/ 2008-actfl-student-survey-report. Retrieved 20 January 2012

ACTFL, (2010) *Foreign Language Enrollments in K-12 Public Schools. Are Students Prepared for a Global Society? (2010).* ACTFL, 2010

Amselle, J. (ed.) (1995) The Failure of Bilingual Education, Washington D.C.: Center for Equal Opportunity.

Baetens Beardsmore, H. (1982) *Bilingualism: Basic Principles.* Clevedon: Multilingual Matters.

Baker, C. (2006) *Foundations of Bilingual Education and Bilingualism.* (4th edition). Clevedon: Multilingual Matters.

Baucom, L., (2005) "U.S. Language Policy Plan of Action," ACTFL, http://www.actfl.org/us-language-policy-plan-action?pageid=3725, accessed July 3 2014.

Bloomfield, L. (1933) Language. New York: Holt, Rhinehart and Winston.

Bolen, C. M. (ed.) *A Guide to Outcomes Assessment in Education Abroad*, Forum on Education Abroad, 2007

Boorstin D.J. (1974) *The Americans: the democratic experience*, Vintage book.

Bush, George W., (2001) "International Education Week 2001 Message, (November 13, 2001)," Global Education, http://globaled.us/now/fullstatementbush.html, accessed July 20, 2014.

Bialystok, E. (2007) Cognitive Effects of Bilingualism: How Linguistic Experience Leads to Cognitive Change, International Journal of Bilingual Education and Bilingualism, 10, 3.

Candelier, M. (coordinator) (2012) FREPA: A Framework of Reference for Pluralistic Approaches to Languages and Cultures, Strasbourg: Council of Europe Publishing.

Cenoz, J., Gorter, G. (2011) "A Holistic Approach to Multilingual Education: Introduction," *The Modern Language Journal*, 95, iii: 339-343.

Clinton W. J. (2000) "Memorandum for the Heads of Executive Departments and Agencies", The White House, http://www.nafsa.org/uploadedFiles/NAFSA_Home/Resource_Library_Assets/Public_Policy/president_clinton_issues_1.pdf?n=173, accessed July 20 2014.

Cook, V. (1992) 'Evidence for multi-competence', *Language Learning*, 42, 4, 557-591.

Cook, V. (1997) 'Monolingual bias in second language acquisition research', *Revista Canaria de Estudios Ingleses*, 34: 35-50.

Cook, V. (2012) *Multicompetence*, http://homepage.ntlworld.com/vivian.c/Writings/Papers/MCentry.htm.

Council of Europe (2005) Plurilingual Education in Europe, Strasbourg: Council of Europe Language Policy Division.

Dolci, R. "Study in Italy" (2013) in Anthony Julian Tamburri & R. Dolci (eds.) *Why Study Italian*, New York: John D. Calandra Italian American Institute.

Dolci, R., (2006) "Il *Quadro* e gli Standards for Foreign Language Learning", in Mezzadri M. (ed.), *Integrazione linguistica in Europa: Il Quadro comune di riferimento per le lingue*, Torino: Utet Libreria, 60-84

Dolci, R., Tamburri, Anthony Julian (2013) (eds.) *Why Study Italian,* New York: John D. Calandra Italian American Institute.

Doyle, D. (2009) "Holistic Assessment and the Study Abroad Experience" *Frontiers*, Vol. XVIII: 143-156.

Duperron, L., Overstreet, M.H., (2009) "Preparedness for Study Abroad: Comparing the Linguistic Outcomes of a Short-Term Spanish Program by Third, Fourth and Sixth Semester L2 Learners," *Frontiers*, Vol. XVII: 157-179.

Fabbro, F. (1996) *Il cervello Bilingue*, Roma: Astrolabio.

Farrell, M. (2011) Bilingual competence and students' achievement in Physics and Mathematics, International Journal of Bilingual Education and Bilingualism, 14, 3.

Firth, A., & Wagner, J. (1997). "On discourse, communication, and (some) fundamental concepts in SLA research," *Modern Language Journal*, 81: 285-300.

Firth, A., Wagner, J. (1998) "SLA Property: No Trespassing!" *The Modern Language Journal* Volume 82, Issue 1: 91-94.

Flattau, P. E. et al. (2006) *"The National Defense Education Act of 1958: Selected Outcomes"* Science and Technology Policy Institute, Washington, DC, Institute for Defense Analyses, https://www.ida.org/upload/stpi/pdfs/ida-d-3306.pdf, retrieved 20 July 2014.

Furman, N., Goldberg, D. and Lusin, N., (2009) "Enrollments in Languages Other Than English in United States Institutions of Higher Education, Fall 2009", Modern Languages Association of America, http://www.mla.org/pdf/2009_enrollment_survey.pdf, retrieved July 6, 2014.

Garcia, O., Flores, N. (2014) "Multilingualism and Common Core State Standards in the United States", in May, S. (ed.), *The multilingual turn*, New York: Routledge.

Grosjean, F. (1989) 'Neurolinguists, beware! The bilingual is not two monolinguals in one person', *Brain and Language,* 36: 3-15.

Grosjean, François (2010). *Bilingual: Life and Reality.* Cambridge, Mass: Harvard University Press.

Hamers, J. F. & Blanc M. H. A. (2000) Bilinguality and bilingualism, Cambridge: Cambridge University Press, 2nd Edition.

Hayward, F. M., Siaya L. M., (2003) "Mapping Internationalization in US campuses," American Council on Education, http://www.acenet.edu/bookstore/pdf/mapping.pdf retrieved July 6 2014.

Hayward, F. M., Siaya L. M. (2001) "Report on Two National Surveys about International Education", American Council on Education, http://www.acenet.edu/bookstore/pdf/2001-intl-report.pdf, retrieved July 15 2014.

NCES (National Center of Educational Statistics) (2011) "Digest of Education Statistics 2011," US Department of Education, http://nces.ed.gov/pubsearch/pubsinfo.asp?pubid=2012001, retrieved 12 July 2014.

IIE (Institute of International Education) (2013) "Open doors. Report on International Educational Exchange 2013" http://www.iie.org/en/Research-and-Publications/Open-Doors retrieved July 3, 2014.

Jimenez-Jimenez, A., (2010) "A Comparative Study on Second Language Vocabulary Development: Study Abroad vs. Classroom Settings," *Frontiers* 19: 105-124.

Kasper, G. (1997) "A" Stands for Acquisition: A Response to Firth and Wagner," *The Modern Language Journal* 81:3: 307–312.

Kramsch, C. (2010) *The Multilingual Subject*. Oxford: Oxford University Press.

Kramsch, C. (2012) "Autenticity and Legitimacy in Multilingual SLA," *Critical Multilingualism Studies* 1:1: 107-128

Long, M. (1997) "Construct validity in SLA research: A response to Firth and Wagner," *Modern Language Journal* 81: 318-323.

Macnamara, J. (1967) "The Bilingual's Linguistic Performance. A Psychological Overview," Journal of Social Issue, 23,58-77.

Maurais, J. and Morris, M.A., (eds.) (2003) *Languages in a Globalising World*. Cambridge: Cambridge University Press.

May, S. (ed.), (2014) *The Multilingual Turn*, New York: Routledge.

Mohajeri Norris, E., Steinberg, M., (2008) "Does Language Matter? The Impact of Language of Instruction on Study Abroad Outcomes," *Frontiers* 17: 107-131.

NAFSA, (2003) "Securing America's Future: Global Education for a Global Age," http://www.nafsa.org/uploadedFiles/NAFSA_Home/Resource_Library_Assets/Public_Policy/securing_america_s_future.pdf?n=3894, retrieved July 13, 2014.

Naharro, M. (1998) "Note sul bilinguismo e problemi con esso correlate," *Atti del XVII Convegno dell'Associazione Ispanisti Italiani: Milano 24-25-26 ottobre 1996*. Vol. 2. 11-22.

Nichols, P. C. and Coleon, M. (2000) "Spanish Literacy and the Academic Success of Latino High School Students: Codeswitching as a Classroom Resource," *Foreign Language Annals* 33(5).

Norris, E. and Gillespie, J. (2009) "How Study Abroad Shapes Global Careers Evidence From the United States," *Journal of Studies in International Education* 13.3: 382-397.

Ochs, E. (1990) "Indexicality and socialization" in *Cultural psychology: The Chicago Symposia*. J. Stigler, G. Herdt, & R. Shweder, eds. Cambridge: Cambridge University Press.

Orahood, T., Kruze, L., Easley Pearson, D. (2004) "The Impact of Study Abroad on Business Students' Career Goals," *Frontiers* 10: 117-130.

Ortega, L. (2008) *Understanding Second Language Acquisition*. New York: Routledge.

Paradis, M. (1987) *The Assessment of Bilingual Aphasia*. Hillsdale, NJ: Lawrence Erlbaum.

Pennycook, A., (2010) *Language as a Local Practice*, London: Routledge.

Potowski, K. (ed.) (2010) *Language Diversity in the USA*, Cambridge: Cambridge University Press.

Robinson, J. P., Rivers, W.P., Brecht, R.D. (2006) "Speaking Foreign Languages in the United States: Correlates, Trends, and Possible Consequences", *The Modern Language Journal* 90.4: 457-472.

Rundstrom Williams, T., (2009) "The Reflective Model of Intercultural Competency: A Multidimensional, Qualitative Approach to Study Abroad Assessment," *Frontiers* 18: 289-306.

Santosuosso J. J. (1954) "ASTP Characteristics in 55 colleges: 1941-1951", *Italica* 31.2: 99-105.

Shohamy, E., (2006) *Language Policy*. New York: Routledge.

Skorton, D. Altschuler, G. (2012) "America's Foreign Language Deficit," *Forbes*, August, 27.

Spolsky, B., (2004) *Language Policy*, Cambridge: Cambridge University Press.

Sutton, R. C., Rubin, D. L., (2010) "Documenting the Academic impact of Study Abroad–Final Report," Presentation held at the NAFSA Annual Conference. June 2010, http://glossari.uga.edu/?page_id=42&did=24, retrieved July 20 2014.

Thompson, J. W., (2003) "An Exploration of the Demand for Study Overseas from American students and Employers", NAFSA, http://www.nafsa.org/_/File/_/study_by_iie_daad_bc.pdf, retrieved July 13, 2014.

Tillman, M., (2005) "Impact of Education abroad on Career Development, Vol. I", AIFS, http://www.aifsabroad.com/advisors/pdf/Impact_of_Education_AbroadI.pdf, retrieved July 3, 2014.

Titone, R. (1972) *Bilinguismo precoce ed educazione bilingue*. Roma: Armando Editore.

Trooboff, S., Van De Berg, M., Ryman J., (2008) "Employer Attitudes toward Study Abroad," *Frontiers* 15: 17-34

US Census Bureau, "Total Ancestry Reported," 2011, http://factfinder2.census.gov/faces/tableservices/jsf/pages/productview.xhtml?pid=ACS_11_1YR_B04003&prodType=table, accessed July 15, 2012

US Department of Education (2000) "Goals 2000 Educate America Act", H.R. 1804, 103 Congress of the USA, http://www2.ed.gov/legislation/GOALS2000/TheAct/index.html, retrieved 20 July 2014.

US Department of Education "International and Foreign Language Education," Office of Postsecondary Education, http://www2.ed.gov/about/offices/list/ope/iegps/index.html, Accessed July 4 2014.

US Department of Education (2006) "Teaching Language for National Security and American Competitiveness", US Department of Education, http://www2.ed.gov/teachers/how/academic/foreign-language/teaching-language.pdf, retrieved July 25, 2014.

US Department of Education, (2000) "Learning Without Limits. An Agenda for the Office of Postsecondary Education", http://www2.ed.gov/offices/OPE/AgenProj/report/index.html, retrieved July 16, 2014.

Valdes, G. (2005) "Bilingualism, Heritage Language Learners, and SLA Research: Opportunities Lost or Seized?" *The Modern Language Journal* 89.3.

Wright, S., (2004) *Language Policy and Language Planning*, New York: Palgrave MacMillan.

Intercomprehension Studies in Europe: History, Current Methodology, and Future Developments

Elisabetta Bonvino

1. Intercomprehension

The prototypical representation of linguistic interaction is based on speakers sharing a single code: in order to interact, speakers produce and understand utterances belonging to the same language.

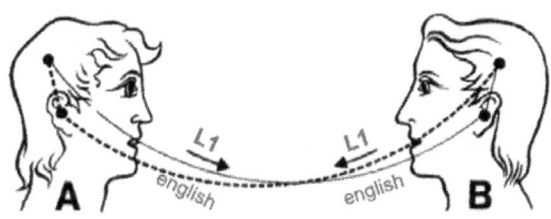

Figure 1. Communication between L1 speakers

It should however be emphasized that even in cases of total monolingualism the sharing of the code is only ever partial, not only at a lexical level (we do not know a word or we do not give it the same meaning) but also at other levels: pragmatic, syntactic, morphological, and even phonological.

In a communication model as shown in Figure 1, the speakers may have different competence levels when using a single code for interaction that may not coincide with their mother tongue (see Figures 2 and 3).

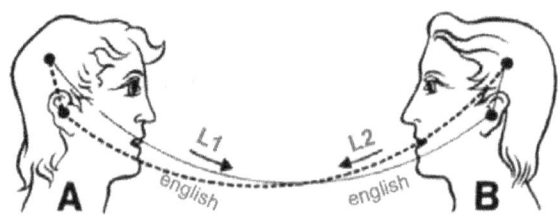

Figure 2. Communication between L1 speaker and L2 speaker

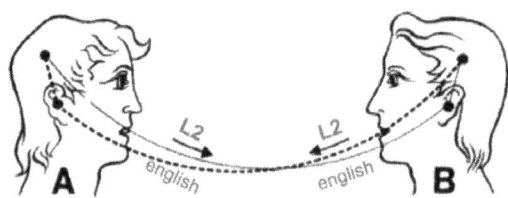

Figure 3. Communication between L2 speakers

A communicative situation seemingly different from the one given in Figures 1 and 2 is that in which those participating in the interaction only partially share the code; that is to say they are able to "understand languages without speaking them" (Blanche-Benveniste and Valli, 1997) (see Figure 4). A form of plurilingual communication may arise from this "partial" competence (understanding and not speaking)[1]—with two distinct codes being used—in which those who take part in the communicative event understand the language of the others and express themselves in the language or languages they know.

---

[1] On partial competence, see 3.2.

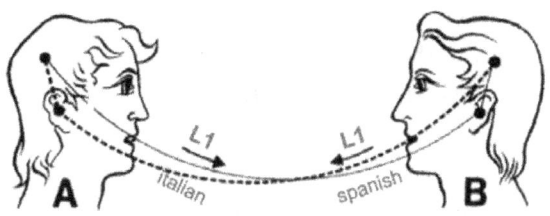

Figure 4. Communication between speakers using their different L1

This phenomenon—called intercomprehension (from now on referred to as IC)—is a widespread practice for millions of speakers who regularly come into contact with speakers of other languages, especially similar or related ones and therefore have the chance to exchange linguistic elements. Communication in IC exploits the same linguistic, inferential, and cognitive strategies that make communication in the same language possible and is favoured both by the characteristics of the languages and their pragmatic nature and by the variable competency levels of individuals.

Studies on IC deal with the spontaneous phenomenon[2] and attempt to make a detailed description of the comprehension processes, with the aim of proposing operational models in order to carry out teaching programs that will increase not only comprehension skills but also the ability to interact in IC.

IC studies is a wide field of research that has common objectives with other related studies like mutual intelligibility, semi-communication, and receptive multilingualism, on one side, and, on the other, with second-language acquisition, studies on multilingualism and plurilingualism, studies on bilingualism and heritage language learners. Research on IC provides a privileged point of view and highlights some of the phenomena being studied from the fields mentioned above. In particular, IC is able to offer significant data and reflections on:

- Linguistic (but not only) comprehension processes.
- Input processing on interlanguage development.
- Social representation of:

---

[2] By *spontaneous* we mean a phenomenon that does not happen as a result of explicit teaching.

- language learning,
- languages and linguistic varieties,
- monolingualism vs. bilingualism vs. plurilingualism and multilingualism.

Furthermore, as we will show in this article, a learning program based on IC is interesting for the following reasons:

- IC proposes rapid access to groups of languages and promotes plurilingualism and preserves multilingualism.[3] It is an approach that is particularly suitable for multilingual contexts in which there are targeted language policies aimed at promoting the languages used locally, including minority languages that are not often studied. It is therefore an approach in line with the language policies hoped for in Europe.
- IC can be useful for language learning in multilingual contexts linked to immigration, e.g., in the case of heritage language learners (see Donato in this volume).[4]
- IC highlights the importance of the mother tongue in the learning/teaching of languages.
- IC develops learners' cognitive and metacognitive skills.
- IC develops the prior knowledge of individuals, and, from a constructivist point of view, it favors the development of competences in other languages (that is, other than those already acquired by learners) by exploiting the knowledge learners already have.

---

[3] "Multilingualism' refers to the presence in a geographical area, large or small, of more than one 'variety of language' i.e. the mode of speaking of a social group whether it is formally recognized as a language or not; in such an area individuals may be monolingual, speaking only their own variety. 'Plurilingualism' refers to the repertoire of varieties of language which many individuals use, and is therefore the opposite of monolingualism; it includes the language variety referred to as 'mother tongue' or 'first language' and any number of other languages or varieties. Thus in some multilingual areas some individuals are monolingual and some are plurilingual". CEFR, (p. 5) http://www.coe.int/t/dg4/linguistic/Division_en.asp

[4] By Heritage Learner we mean an individual who is raised in a home where a language is spoken that is different from that of the context in which he/she lives. The learner may speak or merely understand the heritage language and be, to some degree, bilingual in the language of the context in which he/she lives (e.g. English) and in the heritage language (adapted from Valdés 2000, 1).

- IC blends with other existing approaches, such as Content and Language Integrated Learning (CLIL), and can offer valid tools for professions in which the use of more than one language is important.
- Last but not least, it improves comprehension skills, develops metacognitive competences, and favors interaction, but it can also be the first phase of a program for the global learning of languages (Ollivier, 2011).

2. Evolution of The Concept: a Short Overview

In the past twenty years, IC has been the focus of several European cooperation projects ranging from financing for the production of teaching materials (see § 4) to the establishment of a pool of universities and organizations involved in IC (REDINTER, www.redinter.eu) and the creation of training courses on IC (Euroforma, Formica, Intermar).

The first research projects were started up in France, Germany, and Denmark between the 1970s and 1980s. In the French field, a conference titled "La Latinité aujuord'hui" (1983) gave rise to the idea of developing a dialogue on Latin intercommunicability.

According to the participants, this intercommunicability could easily be achieved as long as there was the political will to do so and teaching practices were developed that were able to develop the transparencies emerging from the contact of the Romance languages (Caddéo & Jamet, 2013). These ideas, expressed in an issue of *Français dans le monde*, by André Reboullet (1983), echoed two articles published in the 1970s. The first one was by Francis Debyser (1970) and encouraged the exploitation of the similarities among the Romance languages for the purposes of written comprehension by passing from one language to another. Another article, titled "L'enseignement de l'espagnol aux francophones: pour une didactique des langues voisines," written by Louise Dabène (1975), later the coordinator of the Galatea Project, reached the conclusion that the processes of learning vary according to the learner's perception of the gap with the L2. According to Dabène, this is due not only to the formal similarity of the languages but also to the learner's attitude and "organizational" activity. These processes, which today we will refer to as cognitive operations are, for example, generalizations, the perception of analogies and differences, becoming aware of systems, and so on.

In the same period, Claire Blanche-Benveniste, a French linguist who grew up in a multilingual environment (Russian, Yiddish, Greek, Spanish Judean, Turkish, Portuguese, and French) began to consider the possibility of a simultaneous approach to the teaching of Romance languages.

In the 1990s some European teams began to work more or less independently and in parallel on projects now considered to be IC milestones: the team coordinated by Claire Blanche-Benveniste for the EuRom4[5] project; the team coordinated by Louise Dabène for the Galatea[6] project; Franz Joseph Meissner, Horst Klein, and Tilbert Stegmann for the German Eurocomrom project; and finally the Danish project launched by Jørgen Schmitt Jensen, which concluded with the publication of some comparative grammars developed in order to facilitate IC (see Bach, Brunet, and Mastrelli, 2008).

The increase in the number of projects with European financing and the interest of the European Commission in IC have ensured a certain continuity in the research and supported the development of teaching tools (see paragraph 5).

Over the years, we have witnessed a conceptual evolution of the notion of IC, directly related to the communicative aims of the processes to be developed, to developments in technology and to the availability of teaching materials (Capucho, 2012).

The first projects (EuRom4, Eurocomrom, and so on), following in the wake of the above-mentioned studies, concentrated on developing written comprehension abilities. There are some more recent and promising research on oral IC that concentrates mostly on pure reception[7] and oral dimension is present in some tools created for IC training, although the development of this skill is rarely the primary objective (Jamet, 2011, p. 252). In IC tools the oral is often used as a support, as in the case of EuRom4 and 5 and other educational practices (Blanche-Benveniste, 2009; Bonvino & Caddéo, 2008; Escudé and Janin, 2010). The Fontdelcat approach to orality stands out, the premises of which favor the aspects of face-to-face communication by means of comprehending audiovisual materials (Martin, 2008, 2012). As we will see, attention to the development of comprehension and in particular to writ-

---

[5] Universitè d'Aix en Provence (FR); Università degli Studi di Roma Tre (IT); Universidad de Salamanca (ES); Universidade de Lisboa (PT)
[6] They then merged into Galanet, Galapro and now MIRIADI. See below.
[7] see Blanche –Benveniste 2009; Cortés 2012; Jamet 2007, 2009, 2011.

ten comprehension have contributed to the creation of the epistemological basis of IC. All of these initiatives hold great promise for developing written and oral skills and will make an important contribution to L2 comprehension.

The development of new technologies such as chat and discussion forums has made it possible to go beyond basic reception. Some projects, especially Galanet and now Miriadi, have gone from comprehension of written materials to mainly, but not only, written interaction.

The educational experiences (Euroforma, Formica, and Intermar) have also created contexts and developed teaching practices for oral interaction (Bonvino, Escudé and Caddéo, 2011).

In 2011 one of the most important projects realized in IC came to an end. It was the European Intercomprehension Network—Redinter (Lifelong Learning Program, www.redinter.eu), coordinated by Filomena Capucho, who gathered together most of the university institutions involved in this field of research, thus favouring and increasing contacts among researchers from various countries. The main aims of this network included the surveying and assessment of IC's good practices, the creation of a bibliographical corpus, and a census of educational interventions through IC.

3. TEACHING INTERCOMPREHENSION: PRINCIPLES

We have seen that IC, understood as a phenomenon, follows communication processes and that, although there has been an evolution, most current IC projects develop above all the reading comprehension. It is therefore proper to ask what the projects labeled as IC have in common and what distinguishes them from L2 reading or listening courses. The principles that typify IC's approach to teaching may be summarized as follows:

- plurilingual approach
- partial competences
- attention to comprehension
- learning transversality
- reflection on languages and role of L1

3.1 *Plurilingual approach in IC means more than one language in one course.*

One of the most interesting characteristics shared by most of the approaches is the idea that IC ability can be developed in more than one language at the same time or at least in the context of a single teaching program. Learning a language means learning something of other languages or at least paving the way for learning other ones (Simone, 1997, p. 32).

IC is therefore part of the framework of the plural approaches defined by CARAP (2007, p. 3) as those teaching approaches that set up activities include more linguistic and cultural varieties. According to this theoretical framework, plural approaches follow four directions that are not necessarily in contrast with one another: IC, Language Awareness (*Éveil aux langues*), Intercultural Approach, and the Integrated Didactic Approach.

As we saw above,[8] according to the Common European Framework of Reference (from now on referred to as CEF), a plurilingual person has a repertoire of languages, language varieties, and competences of different kinds and levels within that repertoire. The term *repertoire* implies a concept of competence that can be broken down into diversified sub-competences, in which diversified competences of different linguistic varieties are found, each of which occupies "a sector, a particular position, and has a different range of use and different functions" (Berruto, 2004, p. 125). Another fundamental idea for language education, closely linked to the conception of plurilingualism, is that languages are not to be considered as watertight compartments to be tackled and learned separately.

> [...] the aim of language education has been profoundly modified. It is no longer seen as simply to achieve "mastery" of one or two, or even three languages, each taken in isolation, with the "ideal native speaker" as the ultimate model. Instead, the aim is to develop a linguistic repertoire, in which all linguistic abilities have a place (CEF, 2001, p. 5)

The IC teaching methodology has given particular strength to plurilingualism by directly or indirectly challenging traditional conceptions of languages and the learning of languages being in watertight compartments (Coste, 2010, p. 194). As Jean-Claude Béacco (Escudé and Janin, 2010) argues, IC presents itself as being one of the possible resources for diversifica-

---

[8] see footnote 4.

tion in language teaching since it distances itself from the classic division "one course = one language."

Finally, it should be underlined that work carried out on several languages simultaneously is extremely useful from a learning point of view as it promotes linguistic comparisons.

3.2 Partial competence is a very important concept in IC epistemology.

According to the CEF, "plurilingualism" does not necessarily mean a complete mastering of all the abilities, but rather the integration of various repertoires. Plurilingualism, therefore, starting from the integration of various repertoires, becomes a multiple competence, which is functional to a specific and limited objective (CEF, 2001, p. 8). The competences in an individual's linguistic repertoire may, of course, also be partial. The concept of partial competence is today a pillar of language education and is also the starting point for research on the assessment of competences. This idea of partial competence implies the possibility of separating various linguistic abilities by isolating, for example, the written and oral comprehension skills. An example of partial plurilingual competence in this context is that which allows a Spaniard to possess a productive competence in Castilian but a purely receptive competence in Catalan.

Although it is not always easy to isolate the different elements of linguistic competence, which are closely interdependent, it is clearly possible to have different degrees of competence in the various linguistic abilities; for example, it is well known that there is a gap between receptive and productive abilities, with the former being of a higher level, and learners acquire comprehension skills much more rapidly than production skills.

Every linguistic repertoire is composed of different linguistic varieties, partial or otherwise, and has above all the great advantage of diverging from monolingualism and taking steps toward plurilingualism. Possessing receptive skills in more than one language can answer the needs of some groups of learners (for example, journalists who need to gather information from various and authentic sources), and it can be achieved in a short period of time, if the learning process involves more than one language and concentrates on receptive skills.

3.3 Attention to the processes and strategies for comprehension leads toward learner autonomy.

There is agreement about the fact that input is essential for the process of second-language acquisition (cf., among others, Gass, 1997; Krashen, 1985), and many studies on second language acquisition have dealt with how input is processed during the second-language learning process and how it is incorporated into the learner's interlanguage system, as well as the quantity of input needed for learning and the characteristics that input must have in order to facilitate learning. Most studies agree that the need for input that is at least partially comprehensible for learning and comprehension is therefore a crucial element.

In spite of this, most of the practices and tools for L2 learning/teaching are heavily oriented toward the development of written and oral production. Even the assessment of comprehension abilities is mainly carried out through production, for the obvious reason that the results of production are more tangible. The processes of written or oral perception and comprehension are very often neglected in teaching practice: Learners are not taught how to understand and put useful cognitive and metacognitive strategies into practice for the purposes of comprehension.

Research in the field of L2 reading and listening has led to the emergence of many works that have made it possible to identify and classify those cognitive and metacognitive strategies that allow access to texts. They also underline the importance of a teaching intervention that does not neglect reading and listening techniques and that centers on the product (testing understanding) and also on the process, understood as the set of strategies and actions used during reading or listening activities in order to be able to understand (see Bouvet and Bréelle, 2004 for reading and Vandergrift, 2007, for listening).

A first general definition of a strategy may be that it is a "line of organized, targeted, and controlled action that an individual chooses in order to carry out a task" (CEF, 2001, p. 12). In the field of language learning, a "strategy" may be considered as an attitude or a set of actions aimed at favoring learning in general or at completing a particular linguistic task, which in the case of reading or listening might be understanding a text in ways appropriate to the type of text and to the objectives of the reader or listener. Learning strategies are often classified according to the typology of O'Malley et al. (1985, p. 582–584), as metacognitive, cognitive, and socio-affective.

As indicated above, the approach to IC ascribes great importance to the understanding process. Within this approach the various methodologies aim at developing cognitive and metacognitive strategies through different practices but that contribute to learners becoming aware of how to use such strategies and of their importance. Some examples are given below.

In the case of EuRom5, a methodology that proposes the reading and comprehension of texts in five Romance languages, worthy of note is the technique of the "transposition" of meaning into L1, where learners are required to put the flow of their thoughts on record during a silent reading and make a sort of "translation" at the same time, however approximate it may be, of the text in the target language in front of the class. This technique recalls the think-aloud protocol (or verbal report) and prioritizes careful observation and class sharing in the strategies used by the reader while reading, with the objective of highlighting the cognitive process being employed. This technique is usually used in experimental contexts. The operations forming the basis of think-aloud are quite complex, and their scientific credibility has often been criticized.[9] However, the EuRom5 experience leads to a consideration of the benefits of the application, even if partial, of the technique of recording everything for teaching purposes, especially regarding learners becoming aware of the cognitive and metacognitive strategies for reading.

One further example of how strategies for comprehension are implicit in IC training is the description of the EuroCom project. One of the basic concepts of the EuroCom method is the definition and classification of different types of transfer. The five types of transfer described by the EuroCom researchers are i) intralingual in the source language, ii) intralingual in the bridge language, iii) intralingual in the target language, iv) interlingual, and v) transfer of learning. Special emphasis is put on the transfer of learning, which is defined as instrumental knowledge that affects the acquisition of linguistic structures and that is basically a transfer characterized by metacognition (Meissner and Klein, 2004). This type of transfer, according to Meissner, is an operation that contributes to the creation of a "monitor" that keeps

---

[9] For a debate on the usefulness of the *Think-aloud* protocol in L2, see the recent review by Bowles (2010).

the behavior of learning under surveillance through the management of the comprehension strategies required to perform other types of transfer.

Still another example comes from those projects that involve written interaction in IC on an online platform. Various teams associated with the Galanet program have completed observations on the interactions on the platform. These exchanges provide a rich corpus of communication exchanges among various Romance languages, which makes it possible to understand how interlocutors negotiate production and comprehension and what the implications of plurilingual interaction are. During these events it is possible to observe significant metalinguistic activity carried out in the same language or in different languages, where one interlocutor communicates with another. The interlocutors therefore face each other with various strategies for overcoming difficulties such as, for example, reframing words in their own language to check their comprehension, using the other person's language, adjusting their production if necessary to the other's receptive competences, and asking for help from and being helped by others according to the reciprocal principle of tandem learning (Degache, 2004, p. 38). Thus they also become aware of aspects such as place, together with the importance and influence of the cultural dimensions of interactions.

3.4 *Transversality and linguistic features allow comprehension between closely related languages.*[10]

As is well known, the Romance languages share a common origin: Their variations are located along a continuous space that makes possible a mutual comprehension in neighboring areas (apart from the discretionary limits introduced by modern state borders). From a typological point of view, too, these languages are very similar, with the partial exception of French, which differs from the other Romance languages because of some well-known characteristics, such as the stricter word order and the overt expression of the subject, which makes it more similar to a Germanic language. The similarity between Romance languages covers all aspects of the organization of the lan-

---

[10] Intercomprehension is obviously easier for languages belonging to the same family, such as the Romance languages which come from Latin, even though affinities between languages can be found and exploited in unrelated languages too.

guage (among which especially the lexicon) and facilitates mutual understanding.[11]

The CEFR highlights more than once the fact that an individual's linguistic repertoire, like the rest of his/her network of knowledge, is not divided into watertight compartments. Instead there is a transferability of knowledge: Whatever is learned in one sector of experience can be transferred to other sectors. This transferability is also found in the learning of languages: What is known in general about language by those who speak a language, together with specific knowledge of their L1 and other knowledge that may also be partial, all guide and facilitate the comprehension of linguistic input from other L2s (see Bettoni, 2001, p. 25; Klein, 1986, p. 64).

In order to understand a text in a language, learners belonging to the same linguistic group can use various elements (lexical, phonological, morphological, and syntactic) that make things easier thanks to the similarities among the languages. One of the main objectives when teaching IC is precisely teaching learners to exploit the affinities and similarities among languages in order to increase comprehension skills. These affinities are traditionally neglected in language teaching because they tend to be seen as a danger rather than a resource. This legacy of contrastive analysis leads to the discussion of "false friends" while "real friends" are ignored, that is to say all the cases in which there is clear transparency among languages (see Bonvino, Fiorenza, Pippa, 2011).

---

[11] For a wider treatment of the aspects of affinities among languages and the exploitation of lexical transparency see Bonvino (2010).

In the case of the Romance languages the similarity is obvious at all languages levels, starting from the lexicon (Table 1):

Table 1
Lexical similarities between Romance languages

Portuguese	Spanish	Catalan	Italian	French
infantil	infantil	infantil	infantile	infantile
diretor	director	director	direttore	directeur
enervação	inervación	innervació	innervazione	innervation

3.5 IC promotes reflection on languages and exploits the role of L1.

In the last few decades the debate on grammar and metalinguistic competence has been focused on the possibility of transforming explicit knowledge of a language into procedural knowledge, in order to improve the executive competences of a language. However, recently it has been emphasized that metalinguistic reflection, besides facilitating and accelerating the process of language learning, should have a central value in educational linguistics. Indeed, it makes it possible to activate cognitive competences, which are useful for improving general learning competences.

As has been pointed out, the simultaneous learning of more than one language and attention to receptive skills make it possible to go into more detail and therefore to become more aware of some very important aspects of communication, such as how to express oneself in order to be understood, how to adapt to others (i.e., the close relationship between comprehension and production), the various ways in which languages function, language levels (standard/non standard, formal/informal), and textual typologies.

By exploiting positive transfer, the plurilingual approach makes the best use of L1. The use of L1 during the learning process has three effects: It reassures learners, it facilitates access to other languages, and above all it provides space for reflection. Thanks to the discovery of how other languages function, learners also discover their L1 (Bonvino, 2012; Caddéo and Jamet, 2013). In the Chainstories project and in the production tasks in L1 that may be part of a reading activity with EuRom5 (cf. Cortés, in this volume), the objective is to write a story in L1 in a collaborative way starting from what learners have understood in an L2. The positive effects on L1 and on learners' ability to reflect on languages are very clear.

4. Teaching Intercomprehension: Materials

The teaching tools used in the IC approach are aimed at specific audiences and are very efficient and have been able to successfully exploit the principles of transferability of knowledge, the partiality of competences, and plurilingualism.

The Redinter project was a chance to make a census of some good practices and some training courses dedicated to IC. Benucci and Cortés (2012) infer that the Galanet, Galatea, Galapro, EurocomRom, Itinéraires Romans, Euromania, EU&I and EuRom4/5 projects are present in several educational fields, and this widespread presence bears witness to their recognized value and makes evident their quality values, such as the reproducibility, efficiency, coherence, and accessibility of these teaching tools.

In order to give an idea about the typology and variety of the existing tools, the following list groups together some practices based on the following characteristics:

1. Reading and understanding other languages
2. Written interaction on platforms
3. IC through a bridge language
4. IC beyond the Romance languages family
5. IC beyond language families
6. Oral IC through audiovisuals
7. IC for children and adolescents
8. IC for specific audiences

4.1 *Reading and understanding other languages*

Reading and understanding other languages is the main goal of the Galatea and EuRom4[12] (see Interlat, Interrom, Eurom.Com.Text, ICE, IGLO) projects. These first IC projects, exclusively aimed at the family of Romance languages, concentrated on written reception as it is more accessible compared to oral reception and made the most of the characteristics of the reading process and the transparency among the languages. Subsequently, other projects were born in the wake of EuRom4, each of which introduced new ideas.

4.2 *Written interaction on platform*

Written interaction on platforms as Galanet (see Table 2), Galapro, and Babelweb (see Table 3) give speakers of the various Romance languages (but not exclusively) the chance of plurilingual training, especially in French, Italian, Portuguese, and Spanish, through the practice of IC in written interaction. The objective of working on the Galanet and Galapro platforms is respectively the development of collaborative projects between groups of students from different Romance language countries and between teachers doing IC training (De Carlo, 2011).

---

[12] EuRom4 is the project from which EuRom5 stemmed, see Cortés in this volume.

Table 2
Main features of Galanet project

Name:	Galanet–Plateforme de formation à l'intercompréhension en langues romanes
Years:	2001–now
Intended for:	Adults, adolescents, and university students
Languages involved:	French, Italian, Spanish, and Portuguese
Support:	Online platform for plurilingual communication
Description and methodology	
This a hybrid methodology halfway between training oriented toward action and a teaching project that exploits the potentialities of the TIC. Some groups of students from different Romance language countries interact on a web platform, each one using their own language. This communicative interaction is motivated by the construction of a common project that develops over various work sessions. During each work session the participants meet in the virtual room, which contains various resources: a forum space, a meeting room, a chat room, a group notice board, and a personal notice board. The forum is where discussion takes place and where each person has to communicate with the others to decide the discussion topic to be worked on by the group.	

Table 3

Main features of Babelweb project

Name:	Babelweb – action-oriented approach and on-line learning of Spanish, French, and Italian
Years:	2008–now
Intended for:	Adults, adolescents, and university students
Languages involved:	Spanish, French, Italian, Portuguese, Catalan, and Romanian
Support:	Web platform
Description and methodology	
Babelweb is a site for IC teaching based on the exchange of texts, aimed at speakers of at least one Romance language (L1 or L2). The project centers on an innovative teaching concept: an interactive methodology based on IC that proposes real-life tasks, which are thought of more as social interactions than language lessons. The site has various resources such as blogs, forums, and wikis that help students carry out the tasks in the Romance languages: describing a film, talking about a holiday, reviewing a film, writing poems or recipes, and so on. The work on this site provides a chance not only to learn the Romance languages but also to use them in an interactive situation in which all the users take part in the spaces for publication. With the aim of guaranteeing the interactions, the site has been created following the principle of invisible teaching, a concept developed during the project that is one of its main characteristics thanks to the use of web 2.0.	

4.3 *IC through a bridge language*

IC through a bridge language is possible for Meissner, a researcher from EuroCom project (see Table 4), who defines IC as "la capacité de comprendre une langue étrangère sur la base d'une autre langue sans l'avoir apprise" (2003, p. 31). In this case the emphasis is on "another language," which does not necessarily have to be one's mother tongue, given that the work group is aimed at German-speaking students who know French and can therefore access all the other Romance languages.

Table 4
Main features of EuroCom project

Name:	EuroCom
Years:	1995–2003
Intended for:	German students
Languages involved	Romance languages, Germanic languages, and Slavic languages
Support	Handbook and website

> **Description and methodology**
>
> The Eurocom method follows the teaching of plurilingualism and aims to contribute to the development of reading comprehension skills in more than one language simultaneously. It is intended for German speakers who use a Romance language as a bridge language.
>
> The linguistic section of EuroCom, called "Seven sieves," aims to filter the linguistic material from Romance languages in order to separate the transfer elements of form and function from the nontransferable elements. According to this methodology, learners can apply some filters to understand a text, the above-mentioned seven sieves, which will make possible the passage from one language to another. The seven sieves for Romance languages are:
>
> 1. An international lexicon
> 2. The lexicon shared by the same language family: the "pan-Romance" lexicon
> 3. The phonological similarities that concern a certain number of interlinguistic regularities
> 4. Spelling and pronunciation
> 5. The pan-Romance syntax, which makes it possible to identify the position of articles, nouns, adjectives, verbs, and conjugations
> 6. The morphosyntactic elements, which make it possible to recognize the basic elements of the words and syntax of the Romance languages
> 7. The prefixes and suffixes that make it possible to recognize many words

4.4 IC beyond the Romance languages family

IC can go beyond the Romance languages family. Although most of the teaching practices have been developed in the field of Romance languages, some projects such as IGLO, ICE, EuroComSlav, and EuroComGerm (part of EuroCom project, see above) propose the exploitation of linguistic similarities in other language families. In particular, the EuroCom researchers have added a module for Slavic languages (EuroComSlav) and one for the Germanic languages (EuroComGerm) to the Romance languages module. The IGLO and ICE projects are particularly aimed at the latter addition.

4.5 IC beyond language families

The possibility of extending the IC concept beyond the languages of the same family has been considered by some scholars (Capucho 2005, Doyé 2005 and Ollivier 2011). Peter Doyé (2005, p.13) believes that even though the first work on IC concentrated on language families, this does not mean that the family frontiers are insurmountable. The basic principle of this widened IC approach is that of raising awareness of languages.[13] In fact, in 2003 the EU&I (European Awareness and Intercomprehension, see Tab. 5) research began, which widened the field of research to plurilingual research between languages of different families. The Intercom, Intermar, e CINCO projects are working in the same direction.

Table 5
Main features of EU&I project

Name:	EU&I
Years:	2003–2007
Intended for:	The general public. People working in the social field with migrants, students, and adults in mobility programs (Erasmus and so on.) as well as students and instructors for instructors involved in the dissemination and use of the teaching materials produced.
Languages involved:	Bulgarian, German, French, Greek, Italian, Portuguese, Spanish, Swedish, and Turkish.
Support	CD-Rom and website

---

[13] « il y a éveil aux langues lorsqu'une part des activités porte sur des langues que l'école n'a pas l'ambition d'enseigner » (CARAP, 2007)

Description and methodology
The aim of the project is to contribute to the improvement of language awareness in Europe through the development of a method for teaching IC skills. This is to be done through both the creation of learning materials and the dissemination of the notion of IC and its concrete applicability to the daily life of common citizens. EU&I groups together a series of play and pragmatic activities, such as booking a hotel room in Portugal, understanding a weather forecast in Dutch, or listening to a short story in Swedish, which allow users to face comprehension tasks in various languages and develop an awareness of strategies with which they can access unknown languages.

4.6 Oral IC through audiovisuals

Oral IC has been experienced through videos for researchers on the FontdelCat project, centred on the development of understanding of Catalan, that propose an interesting and little-explored line of research and teaching application: the use of audiovisual materials. Meaning is conveyed by the images and by the voices of the actors who take part in scenes of student life on a university campus.

4.7 IC for children and adolescents

IC has been proposed also for children and adolescents through Euromania, Chainstories, Itinéraires Romans, and Limbo, all of which are very different both in objectives and methodology. However, what they all have in common is an interest in children and adolescents, which differentiates them from most teaching practices that are aimed at university students. The most structured work, which is full of pedagogical implications, is EuRomania,[14] which has the great merit of combining content and language integrated learning and IC, a combination to be hoped for in tools for adults too.

4.8 IC for specific audiences

---

[14] See Escudé in this volume.

Some specific audiences have been the target of Intermar (see Tab. 6) and CINCO, which are among the most recent projects. The former is a Life Long Learning project that aims to promote plurilingualism and the learning of languages through IC in a maritime context by means of courses offered by the military and merchant Naval Academies. The material prepared for the course, accessible on the Moodle platform, is organized according to a task-based approach, and the courses have been tested in eight academies. The aim of the CINCO project is to make IC a part of the professional training in order to provide tools for cooperation among Romance language speakers.

Table 6
Main features of Intermar project

Name:	Intermar
Years:	2011–2013
Intended for:	Adults; workers in naval occupations
Languages involved:	English, Dutch, German, Swedish, Russian, Latvian, Lithuanian, Portuguese, Spanish, French, Italian, and Romanian
Support	Online learning platform for intercomprehension and maritime English courses

> Description and methodology
>
> Work at sea involves frequent contact with people speaking different languages and coming from diverse cultures, either onboard or ashore. Communication is ensured by the use of both general and specialized English. Yet double synergies may be developed between the learning of Maritime English and the construction of IC competences, paving the way for other languages through specific IC activities and tasks.
>
> The EU project Intermar is creating a European community of maritime and naval institutions that share an IC approach to foreign languages. Starting from existing materials, it will build adapted products to create an effective course toolbox, available online on a learning platform. On this platform, teachers and learners will find custom-designed modules for IC and Maritime English, containing learning materials, concrete scripts for collaborative tasks, and assessment tools.
>
> Intermar will thus promote innovative practices in foreign language acquisition for maritime professionals in Europe in the context of the initial or in-service training activities offered to navy personnel and seafarers.

5. Directions for Future Research

In the past few years IC has proved to be a very productive field both in terms of research and teaching. However there are still many aspects to be examined in detail, in particular those in the list given below.

1) The first aspect that needs to be studied in more detail is the assessment of IC. Only with an assessment system can IC truly aspire to being part of curricula. In spite of some interesting thoughts on this point, there are still no shared theories or practices on which competences to assess (IC syllabi) or on how to assess the development of competences acquired during an IC course, by using valid, effective, and reliable assessment tests.

2) Research on oral IC is only at the beginning, and, although it has been integrated into many teaching practices, it has not created many teaching tools, which would be very useful.
3) A highly promising field for IC is the one linked to specific audiences who are interested, for example, in the management of plurilingual information and in teaching subjects using languages.
4) It would also be useful to gather further experimental data on the development of comprehension between related languages, especially on input processing and integration into the learner's interlinguistic system.
5) The data on the development of comprehension in IC could also be useful from the point of view of capitalizing on what has been learned in one IC program in a subsequent course that includes interproduction or also production.

Table 7
Main features of more disseminated IC projects

Project name	Target languages	Target audience	Website
Babelweb	ROA: cat, fra, ita, por, ron, spa	Adults	www.babel-web.eu
Chainstories	ROA: cat, fra, glg, ita, oci, por, ron, spa	Kids	www.chainstories.eu
CINCO	ROA: fra, ita, por, ron, spa	Adults	www.projetocinco.eu
EU&I	GEM: deu, swe ROA: ita, fra, por, spa SLA: bul Other: tur, ell	Adults	www.eu-intercomprehension.eu

EuroCom	ROA GEM SLA	Adults	www.eurocomprehension.eu
EuRom5	ROA: cat, fra, ita, por, spa	Adults	www.eurom5.com
Euromania	ROA: cat, fra, ita, oci, por, ron, spa	Kids	www.euro-mania.eu
FontdelCat	ROA: cat, fra, ita, por, ron, spa	Adults	ice.uab.cat/fontdelcat
Galanet	ROA: fra, ita, por, spa.	Adults	www.galanet.eu
ICE	ROA: fra, ita, por, ron, spa GEM: deu, eng, nld	Adults	http://logatome.eu/ice.htm
IGLO	GEM: deu, nld, eng, nob, dan, swe, isl	Adults	http://www.hum.uit.no/a/svenonius/lingua/
Intercom	GEM: eng, deu. ROA: fra, por SLA: bul Other: ell	Adults	www.intercomprehension.eu
Intermar	GEM: eng, nld, deu, swe, SLA: rus BAT: lav, lit ROA: ita, ron, por, spa, fra	Adults	www.intermar.com.ax

Itinéraires Romans	ROA: fra, ita, por, ron, spa.	Kids	http://www.unilat.org/DPEL/Intercomprehension/Itineraires_romans/
Minerva	ROA: cat, fra, ita, por, ron, spa,	Adults	
Miriadi	ROA: ast, cat, fra, ita, mfe, oci, por, ron, spa. GEM: deu, eng	Adults	www.miriadi.net

In Table 8 is presented a classification of target languages by linguistic families of the projects in Table 7 and their codes according to ISO 639-3.[15] From both tables it is possible to see the massive presence of Romance language in this domain.

Table 8

Target languages of IC projects classified in linguistic families

Romance Languages (ROA)	Germanic Languages (GEM)	Slavic Languages (SLA)	Other
Asturian: ast Catalan: cat French: fra Galician: glg Italian: ita Occitan: oci Portuguese: por Romanian: ron Spanish: spa Mauritian creole: mfe	Danish: dan Dutch (Nederlands): ndl English: eng German: deu Icelandic: isl Norwegian Bokmål: nob Swedish: swe	Bulgarian: bul Russian: rus Balto-slavic (BAT): Latvian: lav Lithuanian: lit	Greek: ell Turkish: tur

---

[15] Language code used by Ethnologue and Summer Institute of Linguistics.

BIBLIOGRAPHY

Bach, S., Brunet, J. & Mastrelli, A. (2008). *Quadrivio romanzo. Dall'italiano al francese, allo spagnolo, al portoghese.* Firenze: Accademia della Crusca.

Benucci, A. & Cortés Velásquez, D. (2012). Le pratiche dell'IC: una visione d'insieme. In Degache, C. & Garbarino, S. (Eds.) *Intercompréhension: compétences plurielles, corpus, intégration.* Université Stendhal Grenoble 3 (France). http://ic2012.u-grenoble3.fr/OpenConf/papers/24.pdf

Bettoni, C. (2001). *Imparare un'altra lingua.* Bari: Laterza.

Berruto, G. (2004). *Prima lezione di sociolinguistica.* Bari: Laterza.

Blanche-Benveniste, C. (2009). Suggestions de recherches à mener pour entraîner la perception orale d'une langue romane à d'autres. In Jamet, M.C. (Ed.) *Orale e intercomprensione tra lingue romanze. Ricerche e implicazioni didattiche* (pp. 19-32). Venezia: Cafoscarina editrice.

Blanche-Benveniste, C. & Valli, A. (1997). L'Intercompréhension: le cas des langues romanes. *Le français dans le monde, Recherches et applications.* [Numéro spécial]. Janvier, 1997

Bonvino, E. (2010). Intercomprensione. Percorsi di apprendimento/ insegnamento simultaneo di portoghese, spagnolo, catalano, italiano e francese. In Mezzadri, M. (Ed.) *Le lingue dell'educazione in un mondo senza frontiere* (pp. 211-222). Perugia: Guerra Edizioni.

Bonvino, E. (2012). Lo sviluppo delle abilità di lettura nell'ottica dell'intercomprensione. In Bonvino, E., Luzi, E. & Tamponi, A. (Eds.) *(Far) apprendere, usare e certificare una lingua straniera* (pp. 139-152). Formello (RM): Bonacci editore.

Bonvino, E., Caddéo S. & Escudé P. (2011). Euro-Forma: de la formation à la pratique orale en intercomptéhension. In Capucho, F., Degache, Ch.; Meißner, F.J. & Tost, M. (Eds.) *Intercomprehension. Learning, teaching, research* (pp. 386-401). Tübingen: Narr.

Bonvino, E. & Caddéo, S. (2008). Intercompréhension à l'oral : où en est la recherche ? In Capucho, F., Martins, A., Degache, C. & Tost, M. (Eds.), *Dialogos em intercompreensão* (pp. 386-394). Lisbona: Universitade Católica Editora.

Bonvino, E., Fiorenza, E. & Pippa S. (2011). EuRom5, una metodologia per l'intercomprensione: strategie, aspetti linguistici e applicazioni pratiche. In De Carlo, M. (Ed.) *Intercomprensione e educazione al plurilinguismo* (pp. 162-18). Porto Sant'Elpidio: Wizarts Editore.

Bouvet, E. & Bréelle, D. (2004). Pistage informatisé des stratégies de lecture: une étude de cas en contexte pédagogique. *Apprentissage des langues et systèmes d'information et de communication. ALSIC*, VII (1), 85-106.

Bowles, M. A. (2010). *The Think-Aloud Controversy in Second Language Research.* New York/London: Routledge Taylor & Francis Group.

Caddéo, S. & Jamet, M.C. (2013). *L'intercompréhension: une autre approche dans l'enseignement des langues.* Paris: Hachette.

Candelier, M., Camilieri-Grima, A., Castellotti, V., De Pietro, J. F., Lörenz, I., Meissner, F.-J., & Schröder-Sura, A. (2007). *CARAP—Cadre de référence pour les approches plurielles des langues et des cultures.* Graz: Conseil de l'Europe.

Capucho, F. (2012). L'Intercompréhension–un nouvel atout dans le monde professionnel. In Degache, C. & Garbarino, S. (Eds.) *Intercompréhension : compétences plurielles, corpus, intégration.* Université Stendhal Grenoble 3 (France), http://ic2012.u-grenoble3.fr/OpenConf/papers/67.pdf

Capucho, F. (2005). EU&I: On the notion of intercomprehension. In Martins, A. (Ed.) *EU&I. European Awareness in intercomprehension* (pp.11-18). Viseu: Universidade Catolica Portuguesa.

Cortés Velásquez, D. (2011). Aspetti metacognitivi e processuali della comprensione di un testo audiovisivo in spagnolo da parte di italofoni. *Redinter Intercompreensão*, II, 203-226.

Cortés Velásquez, D. (2012). Dalla comprensione scritta alla comprensione orale con EuRom5: una sperimentazione in Colombia. *Redinter Intercompreensão*, [Attraverso le lingue. L'intercomprensione in ricordo di Claire Blanche-Benveniste], III, 269-291.

Cortés Velásquez, D. (2013). *Intercomprensione orale e metacognizione.* Tesi di dottorato in Linguistica e Didattica della lingua italiana a stranieri, XXV ciclo, Università per Stranieri di Siena. Unpublished.

Coste, D. (2010). L'intercompréhension à la croisée des chemins? *Synergies* Europe, 5, 193–199.

Council of Europe (2001). *Common European Framework of Reference for Languages: learning, teaching, assessment.* Cambridge: Cambridge University Press.

Dabène, L. (1975). L'enseignement de l'espagnol aux francophones : pour une didactique des langues voisines. *Langages*, 39: 51-64.

De Carlo, M. (Ed.) (2011). *Intercomprensione e educazione al plurilinguismo.* Porto Sant'Elpidio: Wizarts Editore.

Debyser F. (1970). La linguistique contrastive et les interférences. *Langue française.* 8, 31-61.

Degache, Ch. (2004). Interactions asynchrones et appropriations dans un environnement d'apprentissage collaboratif des langues (Galanet). *Repères & Applications*, IV, 33-48.

Degache, Ch. & Garbarino, S. (Eds.) (2012). *Actes du colloque IC 2012. Intercompréhension : compétences plurielles, corpus, intégration.* Université Stendhal Grenoble 3 (France) http://ic2012.u-grenoble3.fr /index.php? pg=10&lg=fr

Doyé, P. (2005). Towards a methodology for the promotion of intercomprehension. In Capucho, F. & Oliveira, A. (Eds.) *Building bridges: European awareness & intercomprehension*, (pp. 23–26). Viseu: Universidade Católica Editora,

Escudé, P. & Janin, P. (2010). *Le point sur l'intercompréhension, clé du plurilinguisme.* Paris: Clé International.

Gass, S. M. (1997). *Input, Interaction, and the Second Language Learner.* Mahwah, NJ: Lawrence Erlbaum Associates Publishers.

Jamet, M.C. (2011). Parliamo di orale! Il suo posto nella didattica dell'intercomprensione oggi e domani. In De Carlo, M. (Ed.) *Intercomprensione e educazione al plurilinguismo*, (pp. 252-263), Porto Sant'Elpidio: Wizarts Editore.

Jamet, M.C. (2009). *Orale e intercomprensione tra lingue romanze, Ricerche e implicazioni didattiche.* Venezia: Cafoscarina editrice.

Jamet, M.C. (2007). *À l'écoute du français. La compréhension de l'oral dans le cadre de l'intercompréhension des langues romanes.* Tübingen: Gunter Narr Verlag.

Klein, W. (1986). *Second Language Acquisition.* Cambridge: Cambridge University Press.

Krashen, S.D. (1985). *The Input Hypothesis: Issues and Implications.* New York: Longman.

Martin, K. E. (2012). Les tests d'intercompréhension orale : portée et limites d'une modalité quantitative. In Degache, C. & Garbarino, S. (Eds.). *Intercompréhension : compétences plurielles, corpus, intégration.* Université Stendhal Grenoble 3 (France). http://ic2012.u-grenoble3.fr /OpenConf /papers/64.pdf

Meissner, F.-J., Klein, H. G., & Stegmann, T. D. (2004). *EuroComRom—Les sept tamis: lire les langues romanes dès le départ.* Shaker: Aachen.

Ollivier, Ch. (2011). Représentations de l'intercompréhension chez les spécialistes du champ. *Redinter- Intercompreensão*, 1, 29-51.

O'Malley, J. M., Chamot, A. U., Stewner-Manzanares, G., Russo, R., Kupper, L. (1985). Learning strategy applications with students of English as a second language. *TESOL Quarterly*, 19, 285-296.

Reboullet, A. (1983). La latinité : une idée à reconstruire. *Le Français dans le monde*, 179, 19-20.

Simone, R. (1997). Langues romanes de toute l'Europe, unissez vous! *Le français dans le monde, Recherches et applications,* [Numéro spécial], 25-33.

Valdés, G. (2000). *"Introduction" Spanish for Native Speakers*. New York: Harcourt College.

Vandergrift, L. (2007). Recent developments in second and foreign language listening comprehension research. *Cambridge Journal: Language Teaching*, 40, 191–210.

THE TIES THAT BIND:
ITALIAN FOR SPANISH SPEAKERS IN INTERCOMPREHENSION

CLORINDA DONATO AND CEDRIC JOSEPH OLIVA

1. INTRODUCTION

The philosophy of second language acquisition in the United States is quietly undergoing a potentially radical transition from belief in monolingual, mono-directional acquisition patterns to multilingual, multidirectional learning models that correspond far more closely to the language realities of transnational subjects whose blended identities are lived and/or expressed in more than one language. To quote Stephen May from *The Multilingual Turn*, "Multilingualism, it seems, is the topic du jour—at least in critical applied linguistics. Driven by globalization…critical applied linguists have increasingly turned their attention to the dynamic, hybrid, and transnational linguistic repertoires of multilingual (often migrant) speakers in rapidly diversifying urban conurbations worldwide." (May, 2013 p. 1) In response to both the need to operate in increasingly multilingual contexts as well as the reality of bilingual, trilingual, and often multilingual language learners populating language classes, multilingual pedagogies are needed. Our approach has been informed by the ongoing need for the acquisition of a target language; at the same time, however, it proposes strategies for conducting this acquisition within a multilingual context, making ours a multilingual, multicultural strategy.

Growing numbers of students in North American high schools, colleges, and universities possess a working knowledge of Spanish, which they acquired as heritage speakers or through formal study at school.[1] Statistics on

---

[1] At the post-secondary level in the United States, 862,688 students studied Spanish in 2009. By comparison, 215,954 students studied French, 80,672 learned Italian, and 11,371 studied Portuguese. See Nelly Furmin, David Goldberg, and Natalia Lusin, *Enrollments in Languages Other Than English in United States Institutions of Higher Education*. Modern Language Association. Web Publication. Modern Language Association, Autumn 2009. http://www.mla.org/

the growing population of Spanish speakers in the United States can be found in media outlets everywhere, and institutions of higher learning are beginning to ask themselves how they can better respond to Latino students.[2] To mention only a few of these statistics: 1) The United States is the fifth-largest Spanish-speaking country in the world at 38.3 million; and 2) Spanish is the most widely spoken world language among non-Hispanics in America.[3] This background in Spanish creates automatic linguistic and cultural ties with the entire family of the Romance languages. These ties, i.e., the bridges that allow students to "cross" from one language to another within the same language family, bind learners to accelerated language acquisition through the method of intercomprehension, which teaches them strategies for expanding their learning capacity. Our contribution will cover the ways in which Euro-

---

cgi-shl/docstudio/docs.pl?flsurvey_results. Retrieved on September, 29, 2014. See Also Dolci (this Volume)

[2] On January 21, 2014 Pearson advertised the following Webinar via e-mail to university professors: "The Time is Now--Success Strategies for Latino Students." The Webinar was held on Wednesday January 29, 2014, with the following description: "The number of Latino college students has been on a steady climb since the mid–2000s with enrollments spiking by nearly 25% between 2009 and 2010, according to the U.S. Census Bureau. This growing population faces a unique set of educational challenges, many of which will require individualized diagnosis and intervention to guide each student down the path to scholastic success." No mention is made of language study. Though the link is no longer active, here is a copy of the e-mail:

> Don't miss this enlightening presentation during which Deborah Santiago, Chief Operating Officer and Director of Research of Excelencia in Education, and Graciela Vasquez, Director of Adult Education and Diversity Programs at Cerritos College, will discuss Latino student success in higher education and their experiences implementing effective practices to achieve this goal.
> Speakers:
> Graciela Vasquez, Director of Adult Education and Diversity Programs, Cerritos College
> Deborah Santiago, Chief Operating Officer and Director of Research, Excelencia in Education
> David Pluviose, Executive Editor, Diverse: Issues In Higher Education
> Jonell Sanchez, Vice President for College & Career Readiness, Pearson

[3] See A. Gonzalez Barrera, and M. H. Lopez, "Spanish is the most spoken non-English language in U.S. homes, even among non-Hispanics," Pew Research Center, August 13, 2013, http://www.pewresearch.org/fact-tank/2013/08/13/spanish-is-the-most-spoken-non-english-language-in-u-s-homes-even-among-non-hispanics/ (cite checked on February 2, 2014).

pean-based intercomprehension has served as a model for what we can call "American intercomprehension," in which Spanish as well as English are dominant resources in the language acquisition process. While the variety of Spanish recognized by European intercomprehension is that of Spain, American intercomprehension differs in that all varieties of Spanish are viable, coexisting within the same classroom together with English. These include Caribbean, Latin American, and Mesoamerican Spanish, including the Spanish of Los Angeles, Miami, New York, etc., not to mention Spanglish.

This discussion will include the heritage learner and intercomprehension, as well as the methods we are developing for integrating intercomprehension into the Italian language classroom. Three specific examples (lexical, grammatical, and advanced reading) will be provided that serve both to outline the direction that language module creation is taking on our campus and to provide replicable examples for the writing of such modules by instructors for their own classrooms. Closing reflections will touch briefly upon the multiple contact zones that the Hispanic and Italian languages and cultures share. Though a sidebar in this particular article, these multiple contact zones constitute a topic worthy of further attention as we build polyphonic teaching and learning programs.[4]

2. History

This article reports on the series of Italian course offerings known as "Italian for Spanish Speakers" at California State University, Long Beach, that have been taught since 2009. These courses integrate intercomprehension into the communicative language classroom. Intercomprehension is a form of plurilingual communication across languages of the same family that began in Europe in the 1970s and has evolved in a variety of directions, yielding collaborations, projects, and pedagogical materials (See Bonvino, this volume and Escudé, this volume). Our foray into intercomprehension began in 2007, when funds from the French Government brought intercomprehension experts Pierre Escudé and Pierre Janin to our campus for a series of presentations and workshops (Escudé and Janin, 2010). In the course of these workshops, we became aware of the many intercomprehension projects currently

---

[4] See Clorinda Donato, "Italians and the Hispanic World in the United States: Latinos in Trans-historical Perspective."

under way in Europe that offer inspiration and salient points of reference for work in this field of second-language acquisition in America.[5] In the case of Italian, our work has been enriched as well through consultation and collaborative workshops with Elisabetta Bonvino, co-author of *EuRom5*, a textbook for teaching those who possess knowledge of one Romance language to learn to read in four more, the five Romance languages being Portuguese, Catalan, Spanish, French, and Italian, following the order of proximity related to their geographical provenance (See also Muller, this volume).

In 2006, the Department of Romance, German, Russian Languages and Literatures at California State University, Long Beach, began a collaboration with the University of Toulouse II on an iteration of intercomprehension that integrates it into a program of language production in French or Italian for selected cohorts of Spanish-speaking students. In 2009, we began the program to teach Italian to similarly selected cohorts of Spanish-speaking students. The CSULB program is among the first in the United States to implement specialized pedagogies in French and Italian language acquisition for Spanish speakers. It should be noted that there is some degree of overlap with the many programs that teach Portuguese to Spanish speakers, as well as some degree of distance from European intercomprehension. Like our colleagues in Portuguese for Spanish speakers, our goal is that of teaching a particular group of students a particular language, in all four skills (reading, writing, speaking, and listening), while European intercomprehension has heretofore focused almost exclusively on acquisition of reading knowledge, though some European scholars have begun to experiment with, and advocate for, the development of all four skill levels in intercomprehension as well (Caddéo and Jamet, 2013). The project responds to the realization among professionals in the language sciences that the growing numbers of students with competency in Spanish need a language acquisition curriculum that takes advantage of their preexisting skills. It includes theoretical reflection as well as practical application for the Italian language classroom.

3. ITALIAN FOR SPANISH SPEAKERS: LESSONS FROM THE HERITAGE SPANISH SPEAKERS LEARNING COMMUNITY

---

[5] See "Les Méthodes et les Ressources en Circulation, Fiches Pratiques," in Caddéo and Jamet, *L'Intercompréhension: une autre approche pour l'enseignement des langue*, 141–174.

Both our French and Italian for Spanish speakers programs began with acceleration in language acquisition as the primary goal of instruction. We had no particular theoretical basis from which to draw, with the exception of intercomprehension, whose immediate goals of teaching reading comprehension of several Romance languages simultaneously offered an intriguing beacon for our rethinking of language instruction to Spanish-speaking students. Indeed, intercomprehension proffered immediately applicable strategies for reading and most importantly for incorporating into our classes reading materials that are far more advanced than the readings provided by textbooks. However, we also realized that teaching to our Spanish-speaking students, the vast majority of whom are heritage speakers, also required a far better understanding of who they were as Spanish speakers and the variety of levels of Spanish they might individually possess as they entered our classrooms. The role of language in their lives and their relationship with language acquisition had to be understood.

As instructors, it behooves us to acknowledge the far more fluid boundaries of language acquisition and usage in our students' lives, not to mention the fact that language acquisition is driven by need, not culture, in migratory populations, while for non-migratory populations, language acquisition is driven by culture, not need. Our students' relationship with English and Spanish often draws from these two realities. Another important relationship linking our approach to Romance language acquisition and heritage language research is the growing emphasis on practice, i.e., what people actually *do* with language as opposed to what people *can* do with language, the latter of which is the goal of the ACTFL proficiency guidelines. This is not to say that ACTFL guidelines are unimportant or irrelevant—on the contrary, they may be applied in ways that emphasize the greater oral narrative capacity (especially in the use of past tenses) of Spanish speakers acquiring Romance languages.[6] However, language practice, in particular what the heritage language community refers to as "translanguaging" with its corollary, "transculturing," offers American intercomprehension an important touchstone for understanding how students relate to, learn, and use what they are learning in the

---

[6] Chantal Thompson referred to the greater capacity for narrating in the past in "Assessing and Teaching for Proficiency at the Advanced and Superior Levels," an ACTFL workshop that took place in Orlando, FL, on November 21, 2013, during the annual convention.

Italian for Spanish speakers classroom. More specifically, translanguaging and transculturing become vital tools for the development of pedagogical approaches such as ours that propose to augment our students' multilingual propensities and capacities through the distinct awareness that we are indeed teaching languages to a multilingual subject whose ability to "represent the world in different linguistic codes" should engender "[a] multilingual perspective on foreign language education...different from the traditional monolingual perspective taken up to now" (Kramsch 2009, p. 188).

The term *translanguaging* originally referred to the deliberate alternating of languages throughout the four competencies of speaking, writing, reading, and listening (Baker, 2001, 2003). It has been expanded upon to encompass the global dimension of the ways in which people communicate in globalized societies in which linguistic resources are multiple and mobile (Hornberger & Link, 2012). In these contexts, language acquires a transnational, flexible dimension in which use, meaning, and referents may spill across every kind of border, including neighborhoods, families, friends, cities, nations, and of course classrooms. Just as transnational literacies concern literacy practices that link the local to the global, translanguaging in intercomprehension connects local language, knowledge, and cultural practices to global ones. Translanguaging also offers language learners, instructors, and linguists a far more nuanced perspective of code-switching, as well as code-meshing, which comes from the discipline of world Englishes. We believe that code-meshing, "a strategy for merging local varieties with Standard Written English in a move toward gradually pluralizing academic writing and developing multilingual competence for transnational relationships," (Canagarajah, 2009, p. 1625) is proving to be a useful tool for intercomprehension as well, especially with heritage speakers of Spanish who often possess multiple varieties of Spanish. Thus the implications of code-meshing for intercomprehension and the practices we are pursuing in our classes are many, particularly in light of Canagarajah's talk at the 2014 MLA meeting, where he referred to the multilingual speech among women from Zimbabwe who were living in London and conversing in a variety of languages as "polyglot dialogue," a term that is also in use, along with "receptive multilingualism," to mean intercomprehension. Intercomprehension, however, is the preferred term for referring to understanding across the Romance languages (Beerkens, 2010).

While the positive, enriching, and high-level competencies are engaged in by the code-switching speaker, writer, reader, or listener and the description of how code-switching can be a marker of a dual-language sophistication (Nichols and Colón, 2000), the focus tends to rest on languages as systems, i.e., language interference or the way linguistic borrowing occurs. Instead, translanguaging addresses the *practice* of language and all forms of communication (García, 2009), while providing a way to activate all levels of a student's bilingual and growing multilingual competencies along the continua. What can be done with bilingual scaffolding (Saxena, 2010) and flexible bilingual pedagogies (Blackledge and Creese, 2010) is being done in our French and Italian for Spanish speakers classes as supportive *multilingual* scaffolding and flexible *multilingual* pedagogies. These classes "offer possibilities for teachers and learners to access academic content through the linguistic resources and communicative repertoires they bring to the classroom while simultaneously acquiring new ones" (Hornberger and Link, 2012, p. 268). Indeed, the term *translanguaging*, with everything it incorporates as discussed above, accurately captures and characterizes the environment in our multilingual French and Italian for Spanish speakers classrooms. By accessing contemporaneously the dual linguistic and communicative resources and repertoires of English and Spanish, no matter where they are on the continua of competency in these two languages, we are able to employ multilingual strategies and teach them multilingual tools that network their knowledge to new knowledge that immediately belongs to them. Instead of working within the vacuum of the Krashen-based comprehensible input that rigorously dictates the order of lexical, grammatical, and syntactical acquisition, devoid of the encouragement to connect that input to any other previously acquired knowledge, American intercomprehension works in a flexible, networked, multi-pathed road that engenders self *and* group direction through language acquisition.

Translanguaging is reflected in multiple classroom practices that would be anathema in the communicative language classroom, such as exercises that foster code-switching, or code-meshing, or more importantly, exercises that utilize multilingual presentation models of course content as shall be seen in the modules presented here. Among the many strategies that come from the heritage, or bilingual teaching field, we also have found affinities with the Portuguese for Spanish speakers courses that exist throughout the United

States. Indeed, the motivations driving Portuguese for Spanish Speakers courses in the United States cohere closely to those driving our Italian for Spanish speakers courses, including the opportunity to capitalize on the similarities between Spanish and Italian, the expansion of students' language competencies, and in most cases the ability to move students from being bilingual to multilingual subjects with the inherent set of cultural understandings that translingual and transcultural education entails (Carvalho, Freire, and da Silva, 2010).

Carvalho, Freire, and da Silva cite the lexical similarities that reach 85 percent between Spanish and Portuguese, thus facilitating reading. They stress the need for the creation of materials geared specifically toward the Spanish bilingual who engages in acquiring Portuguese. We fully agree with this position, as well as the importance of showing Spanish speakers the grammatical structures of Italian, Spanish, and English through comparative or contrastive analysis to point out the "bridges" linking one Romance language to the others.

We also agree to a large extent with Carvalho's opinion that "the communicative approach (…) is useless for Spanish speakers" (Carvalho [Interview], 2013 p. 3). She cites the boredom factor for students who understand with full transparency the majority of grammatical and lexical content that is taught in the typical communicative classroom. She discusses the ability of monolingual Spanish speakers and monolingual Portuguese speakers to understand each other, corroborating the approach of intercomprehension. She also remarks upon the inappropriateness of "made-up, oversimplified language" to a population that understands written Portuguese from day one. Instead, she opts for readings "written by and for L1 Portuguese speakers" (Ibid). The role of reading is similarly important in our Italian for Spanish speakers program. Through experimentation, we realized that it was possible to offer students authentic reading materials, enabling them to read with interest about the most important topics of the day at a level that engages them as adults and elicits their opinions. We have observed their spontaneous desire for and interest in exchanging information with both teacher and fellow student alike.

4. THE ITALIAN FOR SPANISH SPEAKERS PROGRAM AT CALIFORNIA STATE UNIVERSITY, LONG BEACH

The Italian for Spanish speakers program at California State University, Long Beach, is and has been a multilingual program taking place in a multilingual classroom environment since its inception. The sheer ability to set up an administrative structure allowing for multilingual learning on a semester by semester basis has been a feat unto itself, one that over the years will offer our team the ideal setting for conducting much of the research that is so sorely needed in this field and whose need is alluded to in numerous publications (Creese and Martin, 2003). Many of the multilingual projects that were the object of study in Creese and Martin addressed language and identity in an effort to support language maintenance or restore a language of cultural identity where the identity remained intact but the language had been lost and was being restored. This is the case of Corsican and French, where children and even adults identify as Corsican but may have little linguistic competency in the language, despite the fact that the Corsican language use carries a high value in Corsican society (Jaffe, 2003). The kind of data that we will collect in our multilingual language courses reflects a unique situation for the study of multilingual language acquisition, one in which questions of language and identity reverberate among three reference languages and identities—English, Spanish, and French or Italian.

5. TEACHING MODULES

In intercomprehension, the use of several Romance languages is a crucial element to one's teaching strategy. The Italian for Spanish speakers' class in our program integrates principles of intercomprehension that are applied to the teaching of Italian as a foreign language. In this environment, the languages are categorized as target, reference, and auxiliary languages.

English and Spanish have both been used as "reference languages." The "auxiliary languages" include the periodic exploration of short examples in other Romance languages, including Portuguese, Catalan, French, Italian, Corsican, and Romanian. There is a specific emphasis on French in the Italian class as an auxiliary language, while the emphasis is on Italian in the French class, due in large part to the fact that we teach French and Italian for Spanish speakers, and we try to encourage connections among those classes. In the Italian for Spanish speakers class, Italian does remain the "target language," and the exercises are designed to be experienced in Italian for the purpose of learning Italian. Like the teachers of high-school language classes, we, too, have an obligation to comply with standard course outlines and meet benchmarks. However, we are going about that teaching differently, as described in this chapter. Through the multilingual examples offered here, learners are given an opportunity to explore, deduce, and hypothesize about the concordances and divergences between target, reference, and auxiliary languages while essentially performing exercises in the target language. They are invited to pay attention to practice and to form as they begin to understand the rules they are learning in the target language.

These intercomprehensive tools include work on valuable lexical (Oliva, forthcoming[7]), grammatical, and cultural proximities, while students learn how to become independent, self-reliant, and advanced readers. The exercise featured in figure 1 shows an example using English, French, Italian, and Spanish, which can be performed in the target language. After filling in the blanks in the target language bubble with the verbs provided on the labels (*mi chiamo, sono, ho, abito*), students are encouraged to associate the same labels (*il nome, la nazionalità, l'età, la residenza, l'occupazione*) with the sentences in the reference and the auxiliary languages from which an exercise of knowledge transfer has been derived. Students are then asked to transfer information in these bubbles into the targeted language as if the students were helping an Italian speaker understand the information provided in the other languages. This is empowering for our students who perform the task of providing information they understand in the reference language in the language they are learning. Additionally, questions such as "*Come si chiama il personaggio messicano?*" or "*Quanti anni ha Anthony?*" are encouraged.[8]

---

[7] Cedric Joseph Oliva is currently discussing this material in "Lexical Transparency: From Legitimacy to Predictability" to appear in a forthcoming publication.

[8] The recently published e-book, *Juntos: Italian for Speakers of English and Spanish* offers several examples of this kind of transfer.

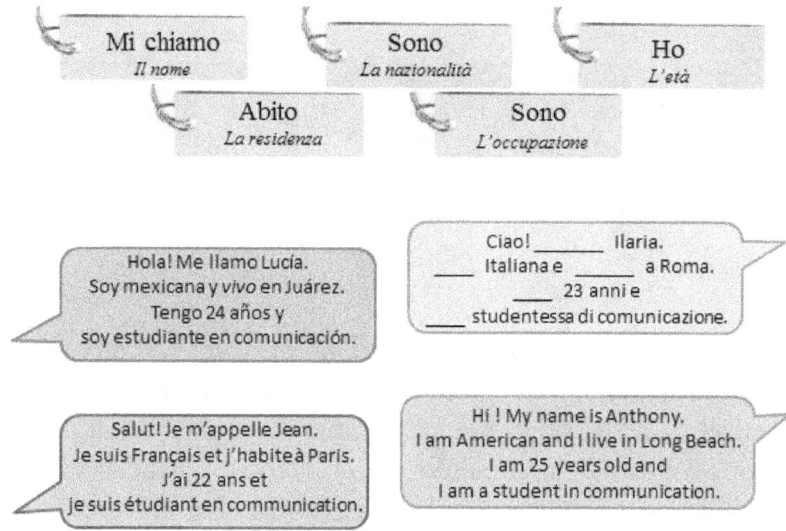

Figure1: I-100: Italian for Spanish Speakers

In this module, the intercomprehensive work on lexical proximities occurs at two levels, which we have described in accordance with the intercomprehensive terminology in usage (Castagne, 2007), i.e., *relaying* (figure 2.a) and *bridging* (figure 2.b).

An example of lexical relaying in this module can be found in the way students experience the understanding of the Italian verb *abitare* (to live). Transparent verbs exist in both Spanish *habitar* and English *to inhabit*. Their meaning is closely related to *abitare* (to live) in Italian and certainly transparent enough to provide the desired "relay" to meaning. A "landscape" example from the world of cinema provides an opportunity to contemplate an authentic usage that could be easily seen on a marquee, i.e., the case of the 2011 Almodóvar film titled *La piel que habito* (*lit:* the skin which I inhabit), which was otherwise translated as *The skin I live in* for commercial purposes. Thus learners are invited to understand *abito a Roma* (I live in Rome) by looking at either *habitar* or *inhabit* as relaying words in their reference languages and to understand *abitare* as *vivir* (to live) in Spanish or *to live* in English.

IT : abitare → **habitar** → vivir : SP
IT : abitar → in**habit** → to live : EN

Figure 2a: Relaying

The relaying is made possible by checking through the corpus of related words, i.e., adjectives, other nouns, etc., for the existence of connections that will most likely yield a bridge, though at times they might result in the identifying and rejecting of "false-friends" a process that our students already apply within the framework of their bilingual (English–Spanish) logic, albeit often unconsciously. These types of exercises guide them in recognizing and applying these same processes to learning the target language. The other type of lexical work relies on intercomprehension bridges. This second example shows how one may speculate on lexical proximities between Italian and English–Spanish:

Spagnolo	Francese	Italiano	Inglese
Educa**ción**	Éduca**tion**	Educa**zione**	Educa**tion**
Comunica**ción**	Communica**tion**	Comunica**zione**	Communica**tion**

Figure 2b: Bridging

In English, the words ending in –tion, which can be considered in "common usage,"[9] represent a pool of 899 words. When students encounter a lexical intercomprehensive bridge, they learn how to maximize it through a broad input of words they can recognize via the use of the bridge; this in turn leaves room for work on specific words that happen to be different, whether

---

[9] For the purpose of this example, we will consider words in "common usage" as words that have an occurrence superior to one in one million.

they are opaque or false-friends and need separate learning. Preliminary studies on 100 of the most common words ending in *–zione* show that, to an Anglo-Spanish speaker learning Italian, up to 92 percent (Oliva, forthcoming) of these words can be perceived as transparent with the help of intercomprehension.

Finally, figure 3 shows an example of work on grammatical proximity such as the Romance concordance in expressions that are often identified as the "idiomatic use of *tener* (to have)" in Spanish teaching. The example includes: *tener* in Spanish, *avoir* in French, and *avere* in Italian.

Spagnolo	Francese	Italiano	Inglese
(Yo) **tengo** 24 años	J'**ai** 22 ans	(Io) **ho** 23 anni	I **am** 25 (years old)
(Ella) **tiene** __ años	Elle **a** __ ans	(Lei) **ha** __ anni	She **is** __ (years old)

Figure 3: Grammatical proximity

Using the texts provided in figure 1, learners fill in a chart that addresses the age of the characters as shown in figure 3. As students do so, they are offered an opportunity to compare the verbal structures and assess their similarities leading to the discovery that, unlike English, which requires a "to be" formulation, i.e., "I am xx years old," the Romance languages all concur in their use of a structure that uses "to have"—which would, for example, literally translate, "I have xx years." The next step is for students to apply their realizations to other expressions that they already know in English and Spanish, and for which they would use "*to be*" in English but "*tener*" in Spanish, which also applies to Italian: "*ho xx anni*" (I am *xx* years old), "*ho fame* (I am hungry), *ho sete* (I am thirsty), *ho paura* (I am scared), *ho ragione* (I am right), and so on.

> **LO SVILUPPO DEL linguaggio**
>
> [...] La tendenza è di fare un sacco di domande non tanto per soddisfare un'autentica curiosità quanto per obbligare l'adulto (la mamma, il papà o altri) a rispondere e quindi ad animare una conversazione. In questo periodo, soprattutto intorno ai 4 anni, il bambino è felice di inventare parole buffe che fanno ridere i grandi, e di usare spesso anche parole un po' sconvenienti, prevalentemente riferite alle sue funzioni fisiologiche. [Quando il bambino ha] 5 anni il linguaggio può considerarsi sostanzialmente completo.
>
> Nella conversazione con un bambino è molto importante dedicargli una vera attenzione, così come è importante quando si parla con lui introdurre sempre nuove parole che, se non vengono subito capite, devono essere spiegate, così come lo si deve fare quando si legge e si incontrano parole che il bambino non comprende. Utile è ripetere storie e fiabe: piace al bambino e lo aiuta a ricordare le parole nuove. [...]

Figure 4: Advanced text "Quanti anni hanno i bambini?"[10]

The next step is for students to apply the learned formulas to an advanced text that picks them up, as is the case in figure 4, for the text entitled *Quanti anni hanno i bambini?*, which uses age statements and words ending in *–zione* with their plural forms as well as *avere/tener/to be* structures.

Students are encouraged to work on making such contrasts and connections among the languages as they apply their bilingual logic and perspectives to the learning of another language. Once the linguistic perspective and metacognitive process are ignited by these guided explanations, students are more likely to be successful at, and engage in, textual exploration. They are prepared to move beyond their comfort zones and to take apart more complex texts, because these students can read advanced texts, create and hypothesize about unknown rules, and develop their own sets of rules to understand the text.

6. Points of Convergence with the Heritage Language Reality of Spanish in Italy

While France has been a country of immigration and migration in the modern period due in large part to its colonial past, the same has not been true for Italy until the last 25 years, when low birth rates and a relatively sta-

---

[10] GSK. "Lo sviluppo del linguaggio." *Tu e il tuo bambino, 14-16*. http://www.leggerepercrescere.it/attach/Content/Menu_footer_b/1521/o/tueiltuobambinoda1a5.pdf

ble Italian economy in the 1980s and 1990s brought to Italy "cittadini extraeuropei" i.e., people coming from countries that lie outside of the European Union, including Eastern Europe, North Africa, Africa, the Philippines, and increasingly, Latin America and Mesoamerica. While the current state of the Italian economy would not appear to be capable of supporting further immigration, the prevailing economic and political conditions in the countries from which peoples regularly migrate to Italy has continued to erode, with increasing numbers of migrants seeking not only work, but political asylum. As Italy begins to address cultural and linguistic integration, the particular case of Spanish speakers in Italy has become an ongoing topic of research, with programs being designed that promote language maintenance while fostering multilingualism. Thus new audiences of Spanish speakers as a recognized group within Europe have begun to change the landscape for Spanish within the E.U. The initiatives currently being undertaken to recognize this group of "cittadini extraeuropei" respond to a set of conditions that is very similar to those of the heritage language Spanish speakers in the United States. Studies on "Italiano L2" for Spanish speakers have begun to call our attention to the evolving cultural, linguistic, and social conditions in Italy that will warrant increased attention in the years to come (Oliviero, Potowski and San Felice, 2013).

7. State of the Field and A Look toward the Future

The field of Romance language study for Spanish speakers in the United States can unequivocally be called rich and promising. Our work over the past seven years has moved from the obvious, anecdotal observation of what could be done with learners who shared Spanish language competencies, whether those learners be L1, L2, or Heritage speakers of Spanish. Once again, we encounter a great deal of similarity between our experiences teaching Italian to Spanish speakers and those described in the published work of professors and researchers of Portuguese for Spanish speakers. In the interview with Ana Carvalho cited previously, she discusses the trajectory of Portuguese for Spanish speakers research in the United States, with comparative error analysis between speakers of English and Spanish who are learning Portuguese. She also calls for more rigorous research methods that will provide us with a far more nuanced picture of our Spanish-speaking students and, most importantly, how to welcome Spanish into the American language classroom.

It is not surprising that intercomprehension has had difficulty gaining traction in the United States, where second-language acquisition focused on the acquisition of English by speakers of an infinite variety of languages. With little reason to contemplate how similarities across language families might maximize learning, many useful tools lay dormant. Today, with an increasing presence of Spanish in the spaces in which we teach, live, learn, and work, the practice of languages in synergy in the Americas forges a new brand of American intercomprehension that now bridges and binds our lives through shared linguistic and cultural experiences we are now free to explore.

BIBLIOGRAPHY

Baker, C. (2001). *Foundation of bilingual education and bilingualism.* Clevedon, UK: Multilingual Matters.

Baker, C. (2003). Biliteracy and Transliteracy in Wales: Language planning and the Welsh national curriculum. In N.H. Hornberger, (ed.) *Continua of biliteracy: An ecological framework for educational policy, research, and practice in multilingual settings,* (pp.71-90). Clevedon, UK: Multilingual Matters.

Beerkens, R. (2010). *Receptive Multilingualism as a Language Mode in the Dutch German Border Area.* Münster: Waxmann Verlag.

Blackledge, A., and Creese, A. (2010). *Multilingualism: A Critical Perspective.* London, UK: Continuum.

Caddéo, S., and Jamet, M. C. (2013). *L'Intercompréhension: une autre approche pour l'enseignement des langues.* Paris: Hachette.

Canagarajah, A. S. (2009). The Place of World Englishes in Composition: Pluralization Continued, in S. Miller (ed.), *The Norton book of Composition Studies,* (pp.) 1617-42. New York: Norton

Carvalho, A. M. (2013). The Field of Portuguese for Spanish Speakers in the U.S. An Interview conducted by Lyris Wiedemann, Fernanda Consoni, and Michael Ferreira http://www.ensinoportugues.org/wp-content/uploads/2013/10/Carvalho _Interview_10-1-13-FINAL.pdf retrieved September, 26, 2014

Carvalho, A.M., Freire J. L., and da Silva A. J. B. (2010). "Teaching Portuguese to Spanish Speakers: A Case for Trilingualism." In *Hispania,* 93, (1), 70-75.

Castagne, E. (2007). "Transparence Lexicales Entre Langes Voisines. In E. Castagne (ed.) *Les enjeux de l'intercompréhension,* (pp 155-166). Coll. ICE 2, Reims: Epure

Creese, A., and Martin, P. (eds.). (2003). *Multilingual Classroom Ecologies: Interrelationships, Interactions and Ideologies.* Clevedon, UK: Multilingual Matters.

Donato, C. (2013). Italians and the Hispanic World in the United States: Latinos in Trans-historical Perspective, in , R. Dolci & A. J. Tamburri, (eds.) *Why Study Italian? Diverse Perspectives on a Theme,* (9-17). New York: Calandra Institute Transactions 2.

Donato, C., Oliva, C. J., Romero, M. and D. Zappador-Guerra. (2014). *Juntos: Italian for Speakers of English and Spanish*, 1st Ed., The George L. Graziadio Center for Italian Studies, Long Beach, available through Red Shelf, The California State University.

Escudé, P., and Janin., P. (2010). *Le Point sur l'Intercompréhension, Clé du Plurilinguisme.* Paris: Clé.

García, O. (2009). *Bilingual education in the 21st century: A global perspective.* Malden, MA: Wiley-Blackwell.

Hornberger, N.H., and Link H. (2012). Translanguaging and transnational literacies in multilingual classrooms: a biliteracy lens, *International Journal of Bilingual Education and Bilingualism*, 15 (3), 261-278.

Jaffe, A. (2003). Talk Around Text: Literacy Practices, Cultural Identity and Authority in a Corsican Bilingual Classroom. In Creese, A. and Martin, P. (eds.) *Multilingual Classroom Ecologies: Inter-relationships, Interactions and Ideologies*, (pp. 61-76). London: Multilingual Matters.

Kramsch, C. (2009). *The multilingual subject: What foreign language learners say about their experience and why it matters.* Oxford: Oxford University Press.

May, S. (2013). *The Multilingual Turn. Implications for SLA, TESOL and Bilingual Education.* New York: Routledge.

Nichols, P. C., and Coleon, M. (2000) "Spanish Literacy and the Academic Success of Latino High School Students: Codeswitching as a Classroom Resource." *Foreign Language Annals,* 33(5*).*

Oliviero, C., Potowski, K., and San Felice, L. (2013). La enseñanza del español como lengua de herencia' en Génova. In D. Carpani and P.-L. Crovetto (eds.) *Migrazioni, Lingue, Indentità*, (pp. 65-98). Genova: ECIG.

Simões, A. R. M. (1992). *Com licença.* Austin: University of Texas Press.

Simões, A, R. M. (2009). *Pois Não: A Brazilian Portuguese Course for Spanish Speakers with Basic Reference Grammar.* Austin: University of Texas Press.

Simões, A. R. M., Ana Maria Carvalho, and Wiedemann, L. (2004). *Português para falantes de espanhol. Portuguese for Spanish Speakers.* Campinas: Pontes Editores.

We Can Learn Through Languages Because We Are Defined by Languages

Pierre Escudé

1. America is a Multilingual Country

The United States is a relatively new country, a land of hope and mass immigration. It has always been a multilingual country, where European languages especially have coexisted from the start. Because of that reality, the American identity is not defined by a single, original, historical language. Being American means subscribing to a common set of values while remaining what one is. Therefore, being able to master the English language as a common language from the perspective of one's own native language, or to enter a real multilingualism from the perspective of one's own native English represents a major challenge.

Circulation between languages is more than a mere technique. It is a dynamic virtue that helps one to develop what one is while developing the will and the ability to be American. For here in the United States, you can't deny the reality of the diversity of the coexisting languages, contrary to what has often been done in Europe. One of the great challenges of the United States, therefore, is in the didactic treatment of this coexistence.

Obviously, the natural and social place for that is school, from early childhood to university. How to master the English language while mastering other languages that are a crucial asset in a multilingual nation and a multilingual world? That is where intercomprehension can contribute to the debate.

1.1 *A historical and dynamic reality*

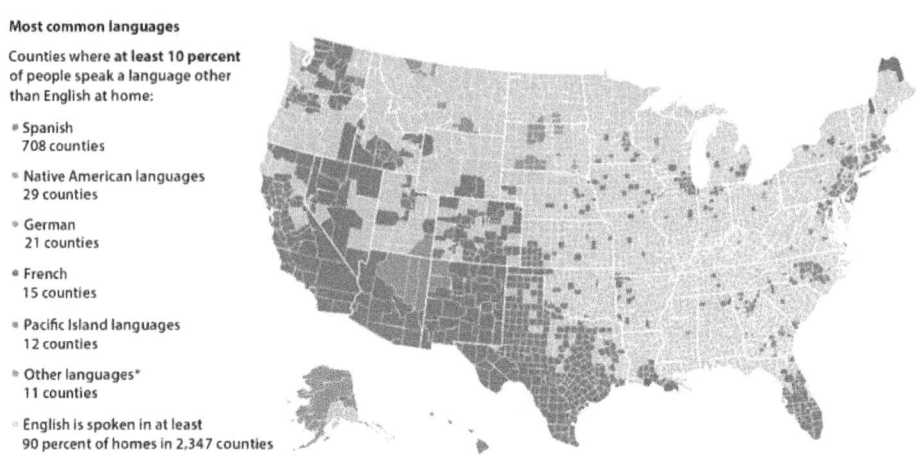

Figure 1

This 2011 map[1] shows the counties where at least 10 percent of the population speaks another language than English at home. This suggests four things. One: English is spoken by an overwhelming 90 percent in 2,347 counties—75 percent of the territory. Two: Spanish is spoken in 708 counties (22.4 percent of the territory) geographically distributed between the Southwest and the larger urban centers. Spanish represents 62 percent of the non-English languages spoken in the United States. It is by far the second American language. Three: Two European languages—French and German—are also historically inscribed in the geography of 36 counties. Four: The native American languages remain present on some geographical spots of 23 counties, reminding us that America, originally a multilingual nation, still hosts many native languages.[2]

The map shows specific linguistic presences that bear witness to the demographic pressure of large neighboring centers (the southern border for Spanish) and to the weight of history (as in Louisiana and the Quebec border for French). Other than English, three important European languages that came over with the first migrations are French, Spanish, and German.

---

[1] http://www.washingtonpost.com/wp-srv/special/national/us-language-map/
[2] Between 100 and 150 distinct languages in the USA and in Canada, spoken by more than half a million people.

1.2 Are the current diversities problems or assets?

Government statistics make it possible to observe the evolution of the languages spoken in the United States over a period of 30 years (1980–2010). They make it very clear that the reality of bilingualism has increased tremendously. Indeed, while the global population has increased by 37.6 percent over 30 years, the share of Americans speaking another language besides English at home has increased by 158.2 percent.[3] Is that a problem or an asset? Although this phenomenon only concerns a minority as nearly 80 percent of all Americans speak only English at home, it does require some explanation.

The strongest progression of non-English languages most spoken at home reflects the most recent immigration waves: Vietnamese (+599.2 percent), Russian (+393.5 percent); Chinese (+345.3 percent); Korean (+327.1 percent); Persian (+256.5 percent); Spanish (+232.8 percent) or Tagalog (+231.9 percent). However, the languages belonging to more ancient immigration waves tend to disappear from family usage: Italian (-55.2 percent); Yiddish (-51 percent); German (-32,9 percent) or Polish (-25,9 percent). The (growing in-)ability to speak the language of one's original community may be an indicator of social integration or inclusion in the new society in particular through intermarriage or dwindling new arrivals.

Beyond the figures, it is worth trying to qualify the action of speaking a language other than English in the family and private circle. Language inclusion—as in the ability to speak several languages at home: one's mother-tongue and English—is all the more frequent as the population is socially favored. The 2011 survey questioned Americans on their own estimation of the quality of their spoken English[4]: 25.9 percent of the nearly 38 million Spanish speakers said they do not speak English well, of whom 9 percent said they do not speak English at all. The Chinese figures are very similar: 29.6 percent (of whom 9.7 percent are non-English speakers). The French-speaking community, on the other hand, has very few monolingual individuals (0.6 percent) while the "French Creole" speaking population has about 4.3 percent.

---

[3] Cf. U.S. Census Bureau, 1980 and 1990 Census. Census 2000, and the 2010 American Community Survey.
[4] Detailed Languages Spoken at Home by English-Speaking Ability for the Population 5 Years and Over: 2011.

It is not language in itself that is a impeding factor but the social origin of its speakers, as Catalan sociolinguist L.V. Arancil showed some time ago.[5]

The second explanatory factor is the "linguistic distance" between the speaker's native language and the English language. The closer one's native language to the natural organization of the English language (in terms of syntax, morphology, vocabulary, and cultural references), the more naturally it comes to speak English "well." That linguistic proximity may be either natural—between Slavonic, Romance, or Germanic European languages[6]—or cultural: Thus the communities issued from the former British Empire and whose school system or socialization use English do not find it difficult to speak English "well."[7]

In fact, the more recent the immigrant community, the more difficult it is for its members to master the English language. Quite logically, linguistic integration takes time. On the other hand, the larger the immigrant community, the lesser the mastery of the English language, as if too high an integration in a community practically made independent because of its numbers was an obstacle to insertion of the English language. That is particularly striking about the two larger linguistic communities—Spanish and Chinese. The circulation of language skills at school—what we call a didactic approach of the contact between languages—is therefore a major challenge.

As a last preliminary step, we need to define what we call "linguistically close" languages as opposed to "linguistically remote" languages. This is important so as not to imagine the notion of "language groups" as watertight and opposed to the historically dominant group that is English. First, the idea

---

[5] Lluís V. Aracil, «Conflicte lingüístic i normalització lingüística a l'Europa nova», 1965, *Papers de sociolingüística*, Barcelona, La Magrana, 1982, 23-38.

[6] Among the 135 000 speakers of Scandinavian languages 1,7% say they don't speak English well, and 0,1% say they don't speak it at all. However, among the 213 000 Cambodians 29,5% think they don't speak English well, and 6,6% say they don't speak it at all.

[7] Schooling and Language Socialization are clearly major factors in the mastery of languages, of English and of multilingualism (English + mother-tongue + another language) as evidenced by the two large linguistic communities from countries where English was or is the language of schooling and an official language for administration. Only 6.5% of the 650,000 Hindi-speaking Americans speak a little or no English; the figure is 10.7% for the 374,000 Urdu-speaking Indians (the language of Indian Muslims and the official language of Pakistan).

that each language is a homogenous[8] linguistic block must be dispelled. Second, the perception of the linguistic remoteness of a language is relative. I met a young Chinese student at the San Francisco airport once and asked her where on earth she had learnt the beautifully fluent French she spoke. "In Warsaw," she said. That struck me dumb. For a European, Polish and French are two seriously different languages. "Of course not!" she said, "as seen from China, Polish and French are quite similar: same alphabet, same syntax, and a vocabulary based on the same linguistic roots."

This Chinese student reminds us that the languages of European immigration all belong to the same family. Her experience confirms that we could quite effortlessly transfer our language skills from one European language to the other and thus enter the realm of what we will henceforth call the "intercomprehension of related languages."

We can enter an unknown language, or a foreign language—as they used to be called at school in particular—for the very reason that we already know and speak one language: our own. But we can do so also because that language belongs to a far wider group of languages that form a *family*. Intercomprehension consists in understanding how a family of languages works in order to learn one or several specific languages. It relies on the notion of interlinguistic transfer.[9] In the United States, while the languages spoken are probably almost innumerable, they can be reduced to a few large families. Besides English, which is by far the most dominant language spoken as an only language by a little more than 230 million Americans, and after Spanish, which is spoken also by more than 37 million people, the most widely spoken languages are the Romance languages, used by nearly 3.5 million people.

---

[8] The Chinese community uses several distinct languages. Mandarin is the main language, although divided into eight dialects from the West to the North of China, but other languages coexist on the Chinese mainland, especially in the densely populated South-East: Wu (around Shanghai) and Cantonese especially in the far-South.
[9] Of which he spoke as early as 1923 in his article «The influence of first-year Latin upon the ability to read English», *School and Society*, 17, 1923, 165-168.

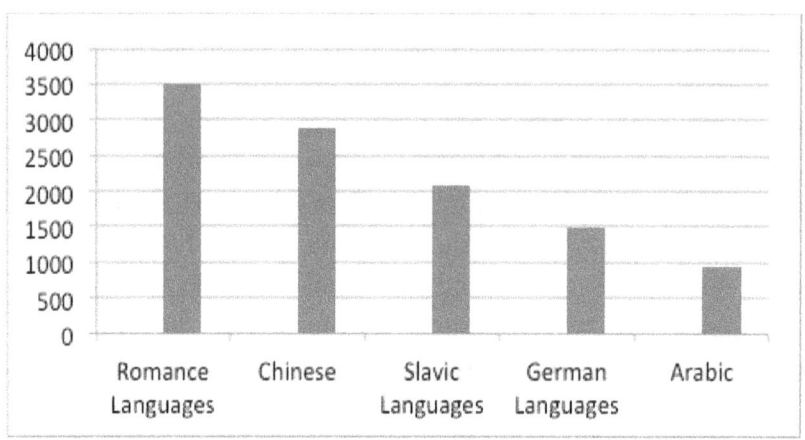

Figure 2

English is the most Romance of the Germanic languages, notably through its lexicon. Spanish speakers have natural abilities that merely need to be didactically organized for them to enter other Romance languages with ease and understand the circular, transparent phenomena that connect English, Spanish, French, Italian, or Portuguese. Similarly, the 230 million monolingual English speakers could find it useful to enter Romance languages—including Spanish, French, and Italian, which have been present on American soil for so long and are historical languages, in some places, just like English.

Let's reflect on the stakes and the benefits of such a didactic approach. First, it would enable individuals to master some languages spoken by the vast majority of American citizens. Second, for the country as a whole, intercomprehension would make it possible for all the official languages of the American continent: English, Spanish, French and Portuguese—to interact. After all, they are spoken by nearly one third of the world population.

2. A FEW HISTORICAL CONSIDERATIONS

Learning a language without taking other languages into consideration is a rather recent approach. Of the 500 million citizens of the political Europe 97 percent speak languages derived from three large families: 42 percent speak a Romance language (French, Spanish, Portuguese, Italian, Romanian, …), 39 percent speak a Germanic language (English, German, Dutch, Scandinavian languages), and 16 percent speak a Slavonic language (Polish, Czech, etc.).

Figure 3: The word for bear *in various European languages*[10]

These three families share a tremendous part of their vocabulary. The more "specialized" the words—chemistry, mathematics, nuclear physics—the more our languages seem close, at least wordwise. To this day, the 42 percent speakers of Romance languages have the feeling that they speak languages that are a little different, but not really foreign, for all their languages—to which one should add non-national languages such as Occitan, which was the language of the first European poets and of Literature Nobel Prize-winner Frederic Mistral, or Catalan, which is very close—are Romance languages. In short, as we all speak bad Latin, we all understand each other!

This practice of intercomprehension is both scholarly and intuitive. As a scholarly activity it was defined for the first time in the Renaissance. In the 16th century, curious volumes were printed for the likes of tradesmen, the new elite who did not speak Latin and took Europe and the world by storm through the commerce of ideas and goods. These books were called *Colloquia*, or conversation textbooks.[11] This was a time when vernacular languages

---

[10] http://www.businessinsider.com/european-maps-showing-origins-of-common-words-2013-11.

[11] Cf. Sandrine Caddéo and Béatrice Charlet-Mesdjian, «Latin et intercompréhension», in *Didactiser le contact des langues en milieu scolaire: convergences, intégration, intercompréhension*, Actes du Colloque «Unité et diversité des langues. Théorie et pratique de l'acquisition bilingue et de

soared in royal administration and in the Catholic Church,[12] thanks to the newly invented printing press. About one hundred of these dictionaries for merchants and travelers were published until the 18th century in the highly active merchant zone of the Netherlands, through Flanders, France, Spain, and England, in the large pivotal cities of European trade.

In the 19th century, the invention of philology gradually revived a form of comparative language studies. Romance philology is the most dynamic and fruitful of them all. Many German and French scholars pointed out word transparency, parallel morphology, and syntactic fluidity among all Romance languages. In 1888, a renowned dictionary of pedagogy advises the study of other Romance languages—Occitan, Spanish, Italian—for a better learning and understanding of the way the French language works.

Scholarly knowledge gives birth to intuitive practices illustrated by the literature of many centuries. This letter written by Racine to La Fontaine in 1661 marks the two authors' discovery of the existence of an *other* Romance language (Occitan) in a political sphere now largely centralized around Paris.

> We went on the Rhône for two days. (…) From Lyon I had begun not to understand the language of the country very much, and not to be understood myself. (…) I swear that I am as badly in need of an interpreter as a Moscovite would be in Paris.

What does Racine do? To understand and make himself understood, he uses languages belonging to the same family:

> However, I am beginning to realize that it is a language mixed with Italian and Spanish, and as I understand both languages rather well, I sometimes resort to them to understand others and to make myself understood.[13]

---

l'intercompréhension», Toulouse, directed by P. Escudé, Paris, Editions des Archives Contemporaines, 2014.

[12] As early as 1492, Spanish grammarian Nebrija said that «La lengua es compañera del Imperio», and French became the sole language of the royal administration (1512-1539); Bembo normalized a central «Italian» (1525); Luther spread the translation of the Bible in a German dialect that was to become standard German as we know it (1522-1534).

[13] Letter from Jean Racine to Jean de la Fontaine, Uzès, 11 November 1661. The letter ends with the Occitan salutation *adioussias*.

Closer to our times, Italian author Mario Rigoni Stern's *Storia di Tönle* (1921–2008) tells the story of a simple shepherd from Asiago, between Italy and Austria, who, because of his poverty, his nomadic life, and his central geographic location, has more language skills in 1914 than any ordinary European of his times.

> Other than Cimbre, he spoke Austrian and German dialects as well as Bohemian Romani, Hungarian, Croatian and Italian.[14]

What this means is that for this man, who has never been to school, the daily intercourse with speakers of other languages has given him language skills in numerous dialects and Germanic languages (Cimbre, Austrian, German), Slavonic languages (Bohemian, Croatian), Romance languages (Italian), and even in Hungarian, which belongs to none of these families.

Jules Ronjat, a French linguist and the editor of Ferdinand de Saussure's *General Linguistics Course*, gave a name to this practice for the first time in 1913—he called it *intercomprehension*. This practice means that ordinary or scholarly speakers alike can lead a sustained conversation although they are not aware of belonging to the same language. To be able to do that, the first requirement is that there be a need for them to exchange: Speaking and understanding make sense only if meaningful and purposeful. That is how the speakers will notice the differences but most of all the resemblances between the languages:

> The differences in pronunciation, morphology, syntax and vocabulary are not such that a person mastering one of our dialects to near perfection could not talk in that dialect to another person speaking a different dialect that she masters to near perfection too.[15]

For these differences are less important than the numerous similarities. A sustained practice of co-construction will lead to the *awareness* of a *common language*.

---

[14] Mario Rigoni Stern, *Storia di Tönle - L'anno della vittoria*, Einaudi, 1978. In a footnote, Stern explains that Cimbre is a Germanic language spoken by the population of the high Italian plateaus—now an extinct language.

[15] Jules Ronjat, *Syntaxe des parlers provençaux modernes*, Mâcon, Protat frères, 1913, p. 13.

> One clearly has the feeling of a common language, pronounced a little differently; the context makes it possible to grasp sounds, forms, phrases and words that would puzzle if they were isolated. You ever so seldom have to ask for a word to be explained or repeated, or to change the turn of a sentence to be better understood.[16]

That says it all. Through intercomprehension you belong to a family of languages if you master one language of that family. Ronjat takes the study of languages and their didactic approach from philology (where each language is studied in its singularity) to linguistics (the science that studies what languages have in common, whether universal or specific). Ronjat was the editor of Saussure whose *General Linguistics Course* propelled language studies into modernity. For Saussure,

> In every human collectivity two forces are always working simultaneously and in opposing directions: individualism or provincialism [esprit de clocher] on the one hand and intercourse—communications among men—on the other.[17]

This truth is particularly useful when dealing with language learning. There is hardly any doubt that for Ronjat, the saussurian "force of intercourse" is intercomprehension, which enables the global unity of language beyond dialectal particularisms.

But this was written in 1913 when states all over Europe had built their identities as monolithic nations around a single common language. National education systems enforced a standardized, purified version of the national language with the idea that bilingualism and the contact between languages is necessarily detrimental. Navigating between languages was henceforth seen as a mistake or a fault and duly punished as such.

Our language learning system is generated by our political vision of languages: When we are taught that languages are *foreign*, we are taught to beware of them and to beware of *false friends*. Once we rediscover that these

---

[16] Ibid. p. 15.
[17] Ferdinand de Saussure, *Cours de Linguistique générale*, Paris, Payot, 1916, édition Tullio de Mauro, p. 481.

languages belong to the same family, that they are not foreign but rather linked by a natural continuum that is historical and also cultural and linguistic, we can integrate intercomprehension as an effective and dynamic didactic practice. This became possible only after the nationalisms had ended after WWII and after the emergence of the notion of a political Europe, minutes before globalization.[18]

In the 1970s the great French linguist Claire Benveniste established the idea that in French, spoken language is not a lesser version of written language, but a different form of linguistic logic and expression that says the same things but differently. Having introduced the notion of a form of duality within something that had previously been considered whole and indivisible, Benveniste could then fling wide the gates for linguistic practices of intercomprehension.[19] However, it took another generation for these "plural practices" to finally appear in our curricula.

3. EUROMANIA: AN EXAMPLE OF INTERCOMPREHENSION AS PART OF SCHOOL PRACTICE

From 2005 to 2008 I conducted a university program[20] that created the first European textbook for pupils aged 8 to 11. All resources are free online on the website www.euro-mania.eu: a textbook in the seven Romance languages, a recording of all the texts in the textbook, a teacher's manual, a forum, etc. We based our work on the observation that in Europe, every Romance language school system—in France, Spain, Italy, Portugal, and Romania—provides its pupils with monolingual textbooks to teach subjects that are common to all the countries. We therefore invented a principle by which pupils would learn a common knowledge or know-how (for instance, building an electric circuit, understanding numeration, etc.) through documents and texts in various languages that all belong to the same family of languages.

---

[18] Cf. Pierre Escudé, «Histoire de l'éducation: imposition du français et résistance des langues régionales», dans Georg Kremnitz, *Histoire sociale des langues de* France, Presses Universitaires de Rennes, 2013, p. 339-352.

[19] Cf. Elisabetta Bonvino's contribution, this volume.

[20] With a subsidy of 270 000 € (360,000 USD), this program involved fifteen linguists, didacticians and pedagogs from France (Toulouse), Spain (Valladolid), Italy (Roma), Romania (Bucarest) and Portugal (Leiria) over a period of three years. We worked «in intercompréhension», each one of us speaking his own language, with French and Spanish as a common language.

Thus pupils acquire the notions on the curriculum while learning to understand the way their own language works and building multilingual skills. The didactic economy of the project that teaches those three things—cognitive, metalinguistic, and multilingual skills—over a single class period is based on four types of integration.

3.1 *Integrating languages together*

The first step was about the linguistic aspect. We sifted through language elements that are common to all our languages. That step was made easier by numerous published works on Romance philology.[21] We selected two kinds of comparative elements: on the one hand, what we call "bridges," and on the other hand, a number of morpho-syntaxic elements.

Bridges are tiny variations in the way the same word is written in various languages. These variations sometimes prevent us from perceiving the lexical transparency between languages: They indicate (or sometimes they do not) phonological changes that have taken place in Romance languages over the years.

Latin	Portuguese	Spanish	Catalan	Occitan	French	Italian	Romanian	*English*
castănĕa	castanha	castaña	castanya	castanha	châtaigne	castagna	castană	*chestnut*

Their accumulation renders texts more opaque and increases the impression of foreignness. However, if given the following words to look at simultaneously, pupils will quickly guess that it is in fact the same form written differently in different languages: the same, but different. The system is global and coherent, and it hinges on variations. Pupils will learn to organize their observations like this:

---

[21] *Grammaire des langues romanes,* F. Diez, Paris, Franck, 1874; *Eléments de linguistique romane,* E. Bourciez, Paris, Klincksieck, 1910; *Manuel pratique de philologie romane,* P. Bec, Paris, Picard, 1970; *Manuel de Linguistique romane* de J. Allières, Paris, Champion, 2001. Famously comparativist publications such as *Pratique des langues romanes,* S. Reinheimer & L. Tasmowski, Paris, l'Harmattan, 1997; *De una a cuatro lenguas. Del español al portugués, al italiano y al francés* by our colleague C. Hernández-González, Madrid, ArcoLibros, 2001 and *Comprendre les langues romanes. Méthode d'intercompréhension,* P. Teyssier, Paris, Chandeigne, 2004, also helped us.

Latin	PT	ES	CA	OC	FR	IT	RO
-ně-	-nh-	-ñ-	-ny-	-nh-	-gn-	-gn-	-n-

This parallelism works with words that have the same etymological form. Thus the French words *montagne* (mountain), *pigne* (pine cone), *gagner* (to earn but also to gain), *vigne* (vine) or *vignoble* (vineyard), *signaler* (to signal), *ligne* (line) can be "decoded" by Spanish or Portuguese pupils once they have identified the following "bridge": [gn FR = ñ ES = nh PT]. The bridge is not a law,[22] but rather a tool that sometimes enables one to clarify opacities, to play around with the shape of the words, and to observe that the key to the meaning often lies in the variations of the written form.

The same group of words yields another parallel:

Latin	PT	ES	CA	OC	FR	IT	RO	EN
ca-	ca-	ca-	ca-	ca-	châ-	ca-	ca-	che-

Over this continuum one may observe a gap with French, then with English, as if the Romance lexicon of the English language were grafted onto the Romance continuum through French and Occitan. Other forms need to be observed in order for a new bridge to appear:

Latin	PT	ES	CA	OC	FR	IT	RO	EN
capreă	cabra	cabra	cabra	cabra	chèvre	capra	capră	*goat*
cămīsĭa	camisa	camisa	camisa	camisa	chemise	camicia	cămașă	*shirt*

Henceforth, pupils will be able to decode a [ca-] in all other Romance languages whenever they read a [ch-] in French.

When pupils observe the following words:

---

[22] The forms in PT / ES / IT are: montanha / montaña / montagna; pinha / piña / pigna; ganhar / ganar / guadagnare; vinha / viña / vigna; assinalar / señalar / segnalare; linha / línea / linea.

Latin	PT	ES	CA	OC	FR	IT	RO	EN
dignitas	dignidade	dignidad	dignitat	dignitat	dignité	dignità	demnitate	*dignity*

they immediately create the bridge [-dad ES = -té FR]. Once they get used to manipulating repetitive forms and to observing parallels, pupils will be able to conceive the missing forms in the grid:

Latin	PT	ES	CA	OC	FR	IT	RO	EN
	parcialidade							
		opacidad						
			particularitat					
				libertat				
					fraternité			
						discontinuità		
							securitate	
								humanity

This means that the regularity of the formal repetition of forms is the way to create *predictability* (= predictibilidad/prédictibilité) among learners. This fundamental skill is the capacity (= capacidad/capacité) to create meaning in new forms, to invent language—insofar as inventing means finding something that already exists. This capacity of invention gives pupils some control over their learning process. After they have discovered about 20 of those bridges, pupils gain security, pleasure, and ease in entering related languages. Learners soon find that texts are clearer, and the reoccurrence of identified forms strengthens their understanding of the global system. Because they have learnt to navigate between languages and transfer meaning, their understanding of words, forms, and meaning grows exponentially.

The second language element studied in this procedure concerns morphosyntactic features—i.e., what is involved in either syntactic agreement or government. Every language has ways to deal with notions of singular and plural; gender; closeness and remoteness; present, past, and future, etc. We proceeded the same way as for the bridges and defined 20 morphosyntactic entries.[23] The idea is not for pupils to become experts in each language, but to understand the global architecture of these languages and to grasp them as they are and reword content in their own language.

After that, we distributed one bridge and one morphosyntactic entry in each of the 20 modules of the textbook. We wrote texts with easily identifiable occurrences of forms that included the said bridge and morphosyntactic entry each. Guiding pupils through the observation and the manipulation of these forms helps them to build skills and confidence in the global system of Romance languages.

The only remaining difficulties lie in occasional snags in the parallelisms (contrary to other Romance languages, French requires a subject before the verb—just like English!); diacritics (the circumflex in French, as in *château* or *châtaigne*, where other Romance languages—and English—use an –*s*; the Portuguese *tilde* on the â or on the ô); the absence of the –s to indicate the plural in Italian and Romanian, etc. Each snag in the parallelism indicates the entrance in a language's specific territory.

Pupils enter the new languages through full texts, never through isolated words or lists of words. These texts must be coherent, authentic, and they often provide cultural awareness that is seldom found in strictly "communicative" approaches. The final portfolio, module 21 in the textbook, reorganizes all linguistic entries and offers exercises in scanning, listening, manipulating, and writing. It introduces lexical units in a systematic way that follows the linguistic and geographic continuum of *Romania* in which French holds a specific place as it connects the Romance languages to English within the Romance arch.

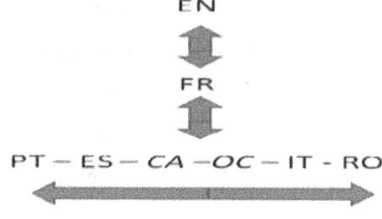

Figure 4

---

[23] See the *Portfolio* on the website www.euro-mania.eu.

3.2 Integration of languages and subject matters

Integrating languages and subject matters makes it possible to work with texts that have a meaning and bear a pragmatic intention. Understanding the text makes it possible to understand what one *must* do or understand in class. Reciprocally, the subject *sustains* the interest and meaning of the text. Language ceases to be described as an object (as in a grammar lesson), or merely imitated (as in a communicative situation), but as the core of the work at hand: The text needs to be entered, manipulated, questioned, and scrutinized for it to make sense. That sense is induced by the math, science, or history lesson. Moreover, each lesson is organized around at least five texts or documents, each in a different Romance language, which echo each other and help build the core knowledge or know-how that is expected in the curriculum.

That method is also called Content and Language Integrated Learning. Form is not dissociated from content. That is why language works as a global and spatial text and not as a linear addition of isolated words: Even if one word—or several words—does not make sense immediately, the text as a whole can still serve a global intention. Just like in a television news program when the anchorperson utters a word that does not immediately resonate for me, I still understand a whole, an intention. I don't stop because of a lexical unit unknown to me, I don't give up because of an opacity, I remain engaged in an active and global quest for meaning.

The themes of the 20 modules were thus selected because they are common to the curricula of the five national education systems. The interest of the technology lessons is that teachers and pupils can immediately validate the understanding of instructions: For instance, if the "water-rocket" takes off at the end of module 5, it means that pupils have understood how to build it, thanks to the explanations given in each of the Romance languages.

The principle that lies behind the textbook is that of the "experimental approach." The starting point is an "epistemological obstacle,"[24] a problem-situation that needs solving. Pupils must form hypotheses about the situation and suggest ways to solve the problem. The next step consists in observation

---

[24] "All knowledge is in response to a question. If there were no question, there would be no scientific knowledge. Nothing proceeds from itself. Nothing is given. All is constructed". Gaston Bachelard, "Epistemological obstacles", in *The Formation of the Scientific Mind*, Paris, Vrin, 1938.

and research based on two pages of five to seven diversified documents each written in a different language. The simultaneity of these five, six, or seven documents in distinct languages but with the same "bridge" and morphosyntactic element is fundamental: The eye can move from one text to the next, look out for clues, formulate hypotheses, and validate them. The reasoning and the explaining that follow are conducted in the pupils' own language—the language used in the classroom—and based on the documents that helped them make their hypotheses in the first place. The first part of the module ends with a final written summary, a synthesis of conclusions written in the classroom language—just like with a monolingual textbook.

In the second part, the subject as such is set aside and the work centers on language and specifically on the two items that were strewn across the scientific or technical documents but that are now rendered explicitly in texts with a specific cultural content. The experimental method also applies to these texts: Pupils are invited to observe and organize their observations through the grids at hand before re-using the forms in the exercises or in the portfolio.

3.3 Integration of understanding and producing skills and of oral and written activities

A preliminary observation is that teaching/learning is essentially a matter of language. Mathematics, history, and science are also, and perhaps crucially, languages. The whole process of observing the problem-situation, validating or invalidating scientific hypotheses, or questioning one linguistic point or another in an "unknown" text are as many moments when pupils enter other languages to assimilate them and make them yield meaning. That impregnation is fundamental and corresponds to what Ronjat calls "language storing,"[25] a phase of internal comprehension that the teacher will make explicit by asking the pupil to reword in the classroom language.

However, each class contains students with multilingual language histories. In that case, pupils can at last develop the latent skills that in most cases are never activated and often not even considered as skills. Rewording is an opportunity to structure bridges, transfers, elements of linguistic complicity and of a construction of a global language system. Besides, the construction

---

[25] Jules Ronjat, *Le Développement du langage observé chez un enfant bilingue*, Frankfurt, New-York: Peter Lang, 2013.

of a scientific or historical object is never limited to one language. Constructing this knowledge through several languages places it at a distance where it can be questioned and examined in all its depth and to rediscover it later on as it is in reality. Grammar and communicative methods tend to divide the globality of language into large—and sometimes watertight—chunks: writing here, listening there, understanding first, speaking later. But this grid, useful as it may be for teachers to assess pupils' skills and progression, hides the fact that language is a whole.

	Understanding	Production
Oral	1- Listening comprehension	2- Speaking 3- Conversation
Written	4- Reading comprehension	5- Writing

Intercomprehension adds one dimension to this grid. Assessing reading comprehension in a given language (for instance, Italian for a French speaker) will be conducted through a speaking activity in French. Of course, intercomprehension classwork mainly relies on reading comprehension activities, for the simple reason that only the written form allows several linguistic objects to remain indefinitely accessible for simultaneous observation.

Activities \ Levels	A1	A2	B1	B2	C1	C2
Reading comprehension						
Listening comprehension						
Writing						
Speaking						

Comparing, transferring, and predicting accelerate and reinforce the acquisition and understanding process. Over a relatively short period of time, pupils become rather highly competent at reading comprehension in languages of the same family, which then drives the other skills forward in a more autonomous and confident way.

3.4 Curricular integration

What we have just developed may seem obvious and fascinating, but it turns out to be hardly practical in our school system based on compartmentalized knowledge where integration is not welcome. The general organization of our education systems follows a horizontal separation and a vertical hierarchy of languages and contents. Teacher training, when there is such a thing, prepares teachers to accept this and work that way. No teachers would dare to use intercomprehension unless they mastered all the skills in all the languages.

The common misconception behind that is the idea that intercomprehension is another word for polyglossia. But no! The idea is *not* to learn five, six, or seven languages. The idea is to get an understanding of the globality of these languages. To learn to learn languages. To grasp the fact that each and every one of us has the potential ability to make connections between languages that are only arbitrarily and artificially defined as foreign. To enter the reality of our multilingual, complex world.

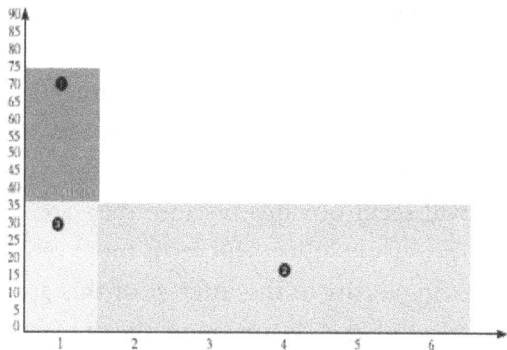

Figure 5

The graph above[26] visualizes how complementary "traditional" language teaching (left, the darker rectangle 1 + 3) and the intercomprehension method (right, the lower, longer rectangle 1 + 2) are. Where traditional language teaching aims to give pupils as rich and comprehensive a set of language abilities as possible (75 percent ability in a "foreign" language), intercomprehen-

---

[26] Cf. P. Escudé & P. Janin, *L'intercompréhension, clef du plurilinguisme*, Paris, CLE International, 2010, p. 55.

sion favors a more modest and more restricted set of skills (35 percent language ability) applied to a larger number of languages. At the end of the day, the one gives highly precise skills in one given language. The other opens a wider space of comprehension (35 percent over 6 languages opens a space that is three times as wide as 75 percent over one language). Moreover, intercomprehension builds ties between the first language—English or Spanish in the United States—and languages belonging to the Romance family, and to a certain extent, with English. That interconnection appears as the small pale rectangle on the left in our graph. That zone is the zone of metalinguistic skills which is the real driver of an in-depth understanding of the way languages work.

For the time being, *Euromania* is the only textbook based on an intercomprehension approach. It is as such a kind of laboratory. We have deliberately targeted the youngest age-group—between 8 and 11—for the children have enough reading skills but also because primary school is still multidisciplinary: A single teacher is in charge of teaching the main language, a foreign language, scientific subjects and other subjects. The textbook offers written documents that have all been recorded and are accessible on the web site for class use and oral practice.

The textbook does not set a language progression for this does not mean anything in a multilingual space. Within one language, there is a progression from simple notions to more complicated ones. But in a language family, some characteristics will seem obvious because they are very close or similar to English or to Spanish, while others will seem more remote or less frequent. This permanent relativity is part of the interest of this approach. The teacher organizes the progression of the class around the subjects as needed. In any case, the linguistic aspects studied in modules 1, 8, or 20 will also appear in the other modules, even if they are not specifically highlighted there. For language is a global unit from the start.

Such an approach requires a little risk-taking. Even with help from the teacher's book, the teacher may sometimes not be able to explain this or that linguistic phenomenon. Far from a pedagogy consisting in the imitation of a single, vertical but non-transferable model, the approach is collaborative. What the teacher does master is the scientific content of the subject. The rest builds on the active participation of the class, driven and moderated by the teacher.

Intercomprehension places a bet on the intelligence of the pupils, on their ability to link, connect, manipulate and explain the global and the specific organization of a set of languages. We tell pupils the truth: This is a multilingual world, and the only way to gain access to that world is to build a true multilingualism. The only remaining issue is the didactic engineering process that will enable the transfer of efficient methods[27] adapted to each level, from primary school to university.

---

[27] The team directed by Clorinda Donato and Markus Muller at the California State University Long Beach has been placing that enthusiastic bet with our help since 2009.

BIBLIOGRAPHY

Allières, J. (2001). *Manuel de Linguistique romane,* Paris: Champion.

Aracil, L. V., (1982). Conflicte lingüístic i normalització lingüística a l'Europa nova, *Papers de sociolingüística,* (pp. 23–38). Barcelona, La Magrana,

Bachelard, G. (1938). Epistemological obstacles, in *The Formation of the Scientific Mind,* Paris: Vrin.

Bec, P. (1970). *Manuel pratique de philologie romane,* Paris: Picard

Bourciez, E. (1910). *Eléments de linguistique romane,* Paris: Klincksieck

Caddéo, S. and Charlet-Mesdjian, B. (2014). Latin et intercompréhension, in Escudé, P. (ed.) *Didactiser le contact des langues en milieu scolaire: convergences, intégration, intercompréhension,* Actes du Colloque «Unité et diversité des langues. Théorie et pratique de l'acquisition bilingue et de l'intercompréhension», Toulouse. Paris: Editions des Archives Contemporaines.

de Saussure, F. (1916). *Cours de Linguistique générale,* edited by Tullio de Mauro, Paris: Payot.

Diez, F. (1874). *Grammaire des langues romanes,* Paris: Franck, 1874

Escudé, P. (2013). Histoire de l'éducation: imposition du français et résistance des langues régionales, in G. Kremnitz, (ed.) *Histoire sociale des langues de France,* (pp. 339–352). Rennes: Presses Universitaires

Escudé, P. & Janin, P. (2010). *L'intercompréhension, clef du plurilinguisme,* Paris: CLE International.

Hernández-González, C. (2001). *De una a cuatro lenguas. Del español al portugués, al italiano y al francés,* Madrid: ArcoLibros

Reinheimer, S. & Tasmowski, L. (1997). *Pratique des langues romanes,* Paris: l'Harmattan

Ronjat, J. (2013). *Le Développement du langage observé chez un enfant bilingue,* Frankfurt, New-York: Peter Lang.

Teyssier, P. (2004). *Comprendre les langues romanes. Méthode d'intercompréhension,* Paris: Chandeigne

Integrating Plurilingualism into Curriculum Design: Toward a Plurilingual Shift in Higher Education

Barbara Spinelli

1. INTRODUCTION

In the past few decades, language departments, among others, in colleges and universities in North America have been facing challenges posed by both the conditions created by the world's increased globalization—such as the emergent new technology practices, mobility, and migration processes—and the climate of accountability and austerity in academia.

It is widely believed that to respond effectively to these challenges language departments need to thoroughly revise their mission and educational goals. This thinking was recently endorsed by a report published by the MLA Foreign Languages ad hoc committee (2007).[1] The committee was charged with examining the current language crisis that has occurred as a result of 9/11 and with considering the effects of this crisis on the teaching of foreign languages in colleges and universities. The members claimed that the current structure of foreign language programs is inadequate. The 2007 MLA report called for a complete overhaul of FL curricula. According to the committee one of the main goals of these language curricula should be the development of the student's translingual and transcultural competence, which "places value on the ability to *operate* between languages."

In the past decade, many scholars invoked *literacy* as a way to address the issues highlighted in the MLA report. The proposals these scholars put forward, while not identical, share many notions and generally align with Cope and Kalantzis (1993) and the New London Group's (1996) notion of a pedagogy of multiliteracies. Cope and Kalantzis and the New London Group advocate an understanding of language as a socioculturally situated semiotic system (Halliday, 1978), with meaning-making as a form of design or active and dynamic transformation (Cope and Kalantzis, 2000, 2009). They emphasize

---

[1] See http://www.mla.org/flreport

the *multiplicity of languages*, of genres, and of modalities present in any given social context, particularly "driven by technological innovations mainly in the field of media and information and communication technology" (Blommaert 2010, p.13), and advocate a pedagogy that puts this *multiplicity* at the center of the curriculum.

This essay describes a classroom project that aimed at developing these multiliteracies and plurilingual competences in an Intensive Elementary Italian language course for Romance language speakers at a college and university in New York City. The Intensive Elementary Italian course was a hybrid course that included the use of the authoring tool "Wiki" to build a multilingual electronic space. This paper describes the challenges encountered when integrating such an instructional approach into a more "traditional" classroom. Qualitative data are examined in order to analyze students' response to this approach, and further practical applications for language teaching are suggested.

2. Multilingualism in North American Higher Education: A Basis for Redesigning The Curriculum

In the language departments of North American colleges and universities, teachers work increasingly in multilingual classrooms where students' language practices include multiple languages (García and Sylvan, 2011; García and Flores, 2013; Kramsch, 2012; May, 2014). The international composition of language classes, and the presence of Anglophone learners who are themselves users of more than one language in everyday life, call for a teaching literacy that has to move toward a flexible model of multiliteracies. This model includes the use of all the students' linguistic repertoire and the employment of multimodalities—visual, aural, and textual multiplicity of semiotic resources—that allow construction of different dimensions of meaning (New London Group, 2000; Kress, 2000, 2003; Saravanan, 2012, Spinelli, 2015). In this multilingual and multicultural context, language plurality is seen as a source of positive learner attributes, such as higher cognitive flexibility; linguistic, cultural, and conceptual transfer; and enhanced capacity for abstract, divergent, and creative thinking (Piccardo, 2013; Boekman, Aaalto, Atanasoska and Lamb, 2011).

This multilingual challenge has implications in both research and practice.

First of all, it has many implications in Second Language Acquisition (SLA). The traditional notion of language learner as a *deficient non-native speaker* originated by his/her comparison with an ideal native speaker perceived as an abstract, homogeneous and fixed entity can be replaced by the notion of a plurilingual speaker who can *use* her/his linguistic resources to navigate among communicative obstacles (Kramsch, 2012, p.108). Additionally, studies on Third Language (or additional languages) Acquisition (TLA) highlight differences in L3/Ln and L2 students' language learning processes (Cenoz, 2013). The former has the experience of acquiring a second language and some degree of communicative competence in the second language besides the first language. This prior experience needs to be taken into consideration in language learning and teaching. Third-language learners can progress faster because they are experienced learners with more developed language strategies and they can refer to two or more linguistic and communicative systems while learning an additional language (even though this progress is more evident when L2 and L3/Ln are closely related such as Spanish and Italian). The TLA, therefore, stresses the importance of using this previously acquired language knowledge and skills.

Piccardo (2013) underlines that the perception of moving from a monolithic view of language proficiency "that occurs independently of *linguistic repertoires and trajectories of learners and teachers*" to a more dynamic vision is becoming more and more popular in higher education practices.

A direct implication of this perception can be seen in the wider offering of courses provided by the foreign language programs of the universities and colleges of North America. For instance, the educational programs of many Romance language departments include intensive language courses for students who know at least another Romance language besides the target language or courses to preserve their heritage languages (e.g., Italian, Spanish). This offering seems to underline the value of studying other languages, considering learner's language experiences, and developing awareness of his/her mother tongue by collocating it within his/her plurilingual spectrum.

However, if we look closely at the foreign language policy and requirements of the North American academia and at most foreign language department programs, it appears that language learning goals are still focusing on the "language per se" and on the development of appropriate communicative skills, which allow speakers to function in the future "monolingual environment" of the target language. The emphasis of this approach is still on "one language at time" (Gorter and Cenoz, 2011, p. 443), on differences between languages rather than on links and similarities, which can facilitate language learning.

Another important aspect that seems often to be missed is the role that the language plurality can play in a learner's identity construction (Pavlenko, 2011; Kramsch, 2009, 2012; Norton, 2013, among others). Plurilingual learners negotiate their identities through languages, and the latter play a crucial role in the development of the "language-learner persona."

De facto, the relevance of studying languages seems to be highlighted by the data of MLA survey, which took place in 2009. The data concerning language courses enrollment shows that the interest in language learning is undoubtedly growing (see Figure 1).

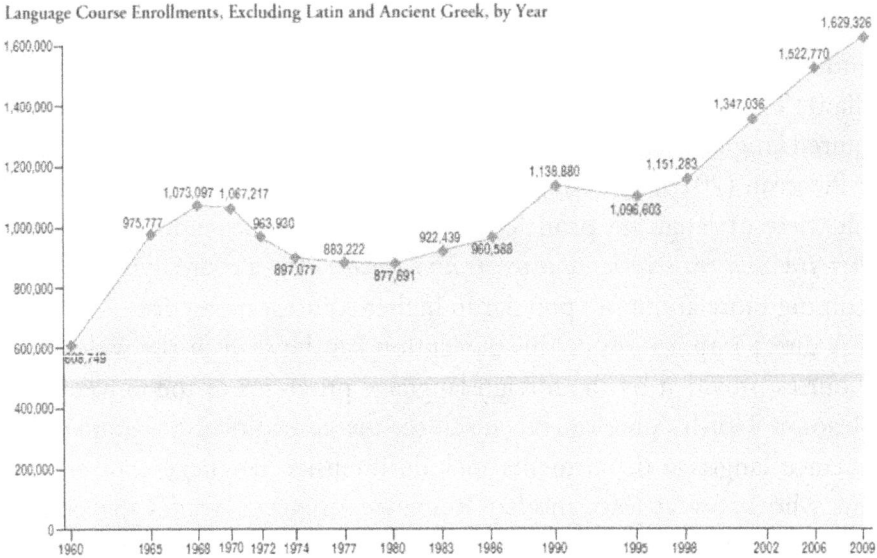

Figure 1. Language course enrollments

This growth is evident for several languages, for instance for the Italian language and culture, which is included within the spectrum of the 12 languages most studied in United States (see Figure 2).

Table 5
Enrollments in the Twelve Leading Languages, Excluding Latin and Ancient Greek, in Selected Years

Enrollments	1960	1970	1980	1990	1995	1998	2002	2006	2009
Spanish	178,689	389,150	379,379	533,944	606,286	656,590	746,267	822,985	864,986
French	228,813	359,313	248,361	272,472	205,351	199,064	201,979	206,426	216,419
German	146,116	202,569	126,910	133,348	96,263	89,020	91,100	94,264	96,349
ASL	–	–	–	1,602	4,304	11,420	60,781	78,829	91,763
Italian	11,142	34,244	34,791	49,699	43,760	49,287	63,899	78,368	80,752
Japanese	1,746	6,620	11,506	45,717	44,723	43,141	52,238	66,605	73,434
Chinese	1,844	6,238	11,366	19,490	26,471	28,456	34,153	51,582	60,976
Arabic	541	1,333	3,466	3,475	4,444	5,505	10,584	23,974	35,083
Russian	30,570	36,189	23,987	44,626	24,729	23,791	23,921	24,845	26,883
Hebrew[1]	3,834	16,567	19,429	12,995	13,127	15,833	22,802	23,752	22,052
Portuguese	1,033	5,065	4,894	6,211	6,531	6,926	8,385	10,267	11,371
Korean	168	101	374	2,286	3,343	4,479	5,211	7,145	8,511
Total	604,496	1,057,389	864,463	1,125,865	1,079,332	1,133,512	1,321,320	1,489,042	1,588,579

Figure 2. Twelve leading languages studied in the United States.[2]

---

[2] Data highlighted by the author.

However, the data concerning the language enrollments at the advanced level of competence provide evidence that there is a loss of undergraduate students, particularly for Italian. In this case, only one student out of 10 continues to study the language (see Figure 3).

Table 7a
Comparison of Introductory and Advanced Undergraduate Course Enrollments in the Top Fifteen Languages in 2009

	Introductory Enrollments	Advanced Enrollments	Ratio of Introductory to Advanced	All Enrollments	Advanced Enrollments as % of All Enrollments
Spanish	711,032	141,749	5:1	852,781	16.6
French	172,573	39,605	4:1	212,178	18.7
German	76,317	17,432	4:1	93,749	18.6
ASL	83,450	7,487	11:1	90,937	8.2
Italian	72,403	7,574	10:1	79,977	9.5
Japanese	59,892	12,825	5:1	72,717	17.6
Chinese	47,676	12,291	4:1	59,967	20.5
Arabic	29,650	4,651	6:1	34,301	13.6
Latin	27,273	4,309	6:1	31,582	13.6
Russian	19,850	6,437	3:1	26,287	24.5
Greek, Ancient	12,812	3,046	4:1	15,858	19.2
Portuguese	8,112	2,821	3:1	10,933	25.8
Hebrew, Biblical	4,848	3,868	4:3	8,716	44.4
Korean	6,010	2,153	3:1	8,163	26.4
Hebrew, Modern	6,354	1,536	4:1	7,890	19.5
Other languages	31,998	6,356	5:1	38,354	16.6
Total	1,370,250	274,140	5:1	1,644,390	16.7

Figure 3. Advanced course enrollments.

These data call for a curriculum reform that takes into account the rapidly increasing linguistic diversity in U.S. classrooms and the need to incorporate plurilingual competences and the multiplicity of communication channels provided by the new technology into the language teaching practices. As mentioned above, such an approach, which optimizes learning through transferability of knowledge and skills across a learner's language repertoire, can increase his/her motivation and self-esteem and develop awareness of the role that languages assume in his/her emotional, affective, and intellectual growth. A dialogue among language departments should be incremented in order to facilitate students' transition in the multilingual context of academia, which through internationalization is becoming more and more a "global village."

2.1 Rethinking pedagogy in the multilingual language classroom

In a multilingual classroom, where speakers with different linguistic and cultural backgrounds interact using a target language, many variables can occur that affect language learning. Seidlhofer (2009, p. 62) affirms that this process is "a dynamic locally realized enactment of a global resource," that is ethnolinguistic, social, cultural, political, and emotional diversity of individuals affects ways of meaning-making and language use within this "ecosystem" (Leung, 2014). If this is true for any classroom because learners are individuals with different backgrounds, it is even more complex in a multilingual setting.

The main goal of language teaching/learning in this context is to capitalize plurilingual[3] individuals' diversity and to empower plurilingual speakers "to use language in ways that might differ from those of monolingual speakers" (Kramsch, 2012, p. 116).

In a plurilingual system, languages are intertwined, and their boundaries are dynamic and fluid, therefore languages "mutually affect each other over time" (Van Geert, 1994, p. 50).

Jessner (2013) argues that this plurilingual system is able to adapt and change according to the communicative needs of the plurilingual individual and that plurilingual speakers develop skills and competences that cannot be found in monolinguals. For instance, a plurilingual speaker while interacting with a monolingual speaker is more likely to use just one language and more languages when interacting with plurilingual speakers (Gorter & Cenoz, 2011). As mentioned above, plurilingual speakers can also choose the appropriate language that is linked to a specific context and for a specific goal. However, language practices in a multilingual environment are more complex than this. Increasing awareness of this complexity of plurilingualism can have practical results in language teaching.

---

[3] In the European context the notion of plurilingualism (Council of Europe, 2001; Escudé & Janin, 2010, among others) emphasizes the dynamic and fluid borders between languages that an individual can use. Multilingualism, instead, refers to the presence in a geographical area, large or small, of more than one "variety of language". In the USA the term multilingualism is used in a broader sense. In this paper these terms are used taking into consideration these distinctions.

Plurilingual approaches focus and develop pedagogical techniques based on these plurilingual practices, such as: translanguaging,[4] codeswitching, codemeshing, cross-linguistic influence, cross-linguistic interaction or language transfer. All these practices provide evidence of possible intersection among languages.

It goes without saying that, in this multilingual environment, the learner's personal language biography and experience play a crucial role. In the classroom, languages interrelate and interconnect both at the societal level of the class community and at the level of the individual.

Consequently, plurilingual practices and a more dynamic learner's participatory engagement in knowledge construction need to be enhanced (May, 2014, p. 5).

Plurilingual speakers and their plurilingual repertoires need to come into contact through practice in actual communication to develop a more complex language awareness and borrow reciprocal resources to communicate meaningfully. In the United States, SLA debate on multilingualism emphasizes this practice-based use of language and competences talking about *performative competence* (Canagarajah, 2014), *usage-based linguistics* (e.g., Bybee, 2010; Ortega, 2014) *translanguaging* (García, 2009), and *participatory involvement* (Leung, 2014).

Additionally, it is worth noting that language is only one aspect of actual communication, particularly if this communication occurs in an electronic environment where multiple codes and channels can be used to convey meanings. Learners, therefore, need to develop not only plurilingual competences and strategies but also multimodal ways to communicate successfully.

In this respect, the capacity to communicate requires, as mentioned above, the development of learner's multiliteracies, which can facilitate his/her interaction in a more fluid, dynamic, and complex context and emphasize the importance of his/her participatory involvement. Leung (2014) argues that this *proactive notion* of language is fundamental to understand the nature of communicative competence in the current society. Kramsch and Whiteside (2008) add the concept of "symbolic competence" for which the learner is

---

[4]The term translanguaging refers to a pedagogical practice in which students are asked to select languages feature from their repertoire for communicative use (see García &Kano 2014; García & Sylvan 2011 among others).

not only capable of reproducing what he/she has learned in order to communicate appropriately but also to play with different languages and shape new uses, for instance while speaking and writing.

In multiple-language-learning environments, therefore, learners' plurilingual personal trajectories become one of the main resources for teaching. Teachers should value their local setting, and their pedagogy should be tailored to each group of students' backgrounds and needs.

In the 1980s, the notion of *learner-centered curriculum* (Nunan, 1988) already pointed out this participative aspect of learning and need of collaboration between teacher and students. However, new technologies and the huge resource of information the Internet provides contributed to enhancing the learner's agency making him/her more and more independent from teacher's knowledge.

Additionally, in the multilingual classroom, where, in many cases, also teachers can bring their plurilingual and pluricultural background (and their "symbolic competence"), multidirectional processes in language practices are multiplied, and the negotiation among participants can be particularly effective. Wei (2014, p. 169) defines this process *co-learning* that is the "process in which several agents simultaneously try to adapt to one another's behavior so as to produce desirable global outcomes."

Plurilingualism, therefore, challenges the goals of Foreign Language teaching and learning in tertiary education to enable learners to perform in a more universal communicative context (Kramsch, 2012, p. 109), which, in most of the cases, is still not contemplated in educational programs.

3. INTEGRATING PLURILINGUAL PRACTICES INTO A TRADITIONAL CURRICULUM: AN OPPORTUNITY FOR MOVING FORWARD?

As mentioned above, the contemporary globalized society with its dynamic dimension, mobility, internationalization processes, and migration flows has generated multilingual realities at the local level in North American academia.

For instance, according to the data available in the site of the academic context described in this paper, almost 28 percent of the population is represented by foreign students. Additionally, according to the recent data provided by the Census Bureau's American Community Survey,[5] New York City is a "polylingual" city, which embraces around 800 different languages, and where the 49 percent of the population speaks a language other than English at home.

Such a context should have a big impact in educational programs and call for new perspectives in language education. However, as stated above, although some signs of these changes can be found in language courses offered, in academia the structure of language curricula still mirrors a monolingual view of language learning or, using Pennycook's (2010, p. 12) words, "a pluralization of monolingualism."

The course and project described in this paper are an attempt, a first step, in breaking this logjam.

This is a pilot project aimed at adopting a holistic approach that integrates plurilingual practices into a more traditional classroom. The main project goal is to investigate students' reaction to such an approach in order to examine if there are solid foundations for proposing a new plurilingual approach-based language course at the departmental level.

The nature of a "traditional classroom," in this circumstance, is meant as a pedagogical context in which the main focus of language learning and communicative interaction is still the target language although many plurilingual practices and activities are used (i.e., code-switching, code-meshing, cross-linguistic comparison, language transfer, etc.).

There are different plurilingual approaches that provide teaching/learning resources and tips. Plurilingual approaches differ from "singular" approaches because they involve several languages and not only one in isolation (Candelier et al., 2007, p. 7). Candelier et al. (2007, 2011) identify four main plurilingual approaches: *awaking to languages, intercomprehension of related languages, integrated didactic approach, and intercultural approach.*[6] *Awaking to languages* focuses on the value of being exposed to many languages, the language of education and any other language, which is in the process of being learnt. *Intercomprehension* concerns languages of the same linguistic family, which are studied in parallel focusing particularly on receptive skills. *Integrated didactic approach* aims at establishing links between the languages learnt,

---

[5] See http://www.census.gov/acs/www/
[6] See http://carap.ecml.at/CARAP/tabid/2332/language/en-GB/Default.aspx

for instance the first language to study the second one and the latter to study the third one. The *intercultural approach* is probably the most well known and aims at developing knowledge of different cultures and awareness on their differences and similarities.

Against this classification, these approaches share common plurilingual practices and techniques, which can be transferable and combined according to the specific teaching and learning context, as occurred for the course and project described in this paper.

Additionally, taking into account the broader notion of communication and the need to develop learners' multiliteracies, new technologies can provide effective tools to empower the plurilingual environment, as mentioned above. One of these electronic resources is the authoring tool Wiki. This tool can provide a common ground to sustain and develop the plurilingual environment. It can extend language learners' opportunities for meaningful, creative language processing, such as plurilingual learning, using multiple representational modes (e.g., video, images, audio, etc.). In fact, this electronic device enables learners to creatively design their own learning environment on the basis of their previous knowledge and skills (Spinelli, 2015). In this specific learning setting, Wiki can allow for creating a multimedia and multimodal space in which multiple languages can simultaneously be represented.

As already stated, the main goal of the project described in this paper is to use all these resources in order to explore if such holistic approach and learning environment can provide valid arguments for language curriculum developments and changes.

4. Developing the "Plurilingual Board" project in a first year Italian classroom

4.1 *Description of the course and project*

The "Plurilingual Board" project was conducted in an Italian Intensive Elementary course offered at a college and university in the city of New York. The Italian Intensive Elementary is an accelerate course that covers two semesters of elementary Italian in one and prepares students to move into Intermediate Italian. The knowledge of at least another Romance language (the level of proficiency is not specified) is required to attend this course. The project was developed in two different semesters: during the spring semester

2013 and 2104. The class met three days a week (for one hour and 50 minutes) for 14 weeks. The course syllabus (learning objectives and language contents) was planned according to the descriptors of the Common European Framework of Reference (Council of Europe, 2001) and the "Profilo della lingua Italiana" (Spinelli and Parizzi, 2012) to reach an A2+ level of language proficiency. The materials of the course were created by the instructor, and the textbook was used only as a grammar of reference and as an outline for the selection and sequence of the domains and themes of the syllabus (for instance "Public domain," theme "Leisure"). Due to the multilingual dimension of these classes the project has been incorporated into the syllabus to empower learners' plurilingual competences and skills and consequently to optimize their target language learning. The main objectives of this project were to:

1. raise leaners' critical awareness of their plurilingual repertoires
2. use different strategies to establish linguistic proximities or distances among the languages of the individual and collective plurilingual repertoire
3. facilitate reading by developing intercomprehension skills (e.g., using the knowledge and skills already mastered in other languages together with reading strategies to decode the meaning of a text)
4. make cross-cultural comparisons
5. communicate in a plurilingual group taking into account the language repertoire of peers and various languages and modes of communication (e.g., using code-switching to negotiate meanings).[7]

---

[7] These learning goals were identified through the FREPA framework for pluralistic approaches (Candelier et al., 2012)

4.2 Participants

Fourteen students participated in this project during spring semester 2014. They were nine female and five male students between the ages of 18 to 33. Amongst them, one was a non-traditional student[8] and one was a Ph.D. student. During the spring semester 2013 the class consisted of 16 students, 11 females and five males, between the ages of 17 and 25.

The multilingual dimension of these two classrooms varied in terms of learners' plurilingual repertoires, language experience, and background (see Appendix 1).

4.3 Instructional procedures and materials

The "Plurilingual Board" project was developed during the spring semester 2013 on a trial basis, and consequently students' participation was not mandatory. In order to increase their participation, extra credits were offered. During the spring semester 2014, instead, this participation was compulsory and the project work was assessed as 10 percent of students' final grade. The instructional steps for the project were carefully designed, incorporating plurilingual activities proposed by the pedagogy of pluralistic approaches into the more traditional syllabus.

These activities have been integrated into the syllabus according to the theme, lexical area, and grammatical structures introduced each week.

Figure 4 shows some examples of linking the traditional syllabus to the plurilingual techniques used in the electronic space.

---

[8] Non-traditional students are adults who decide to go back to school after the traditional college age of 18-24.

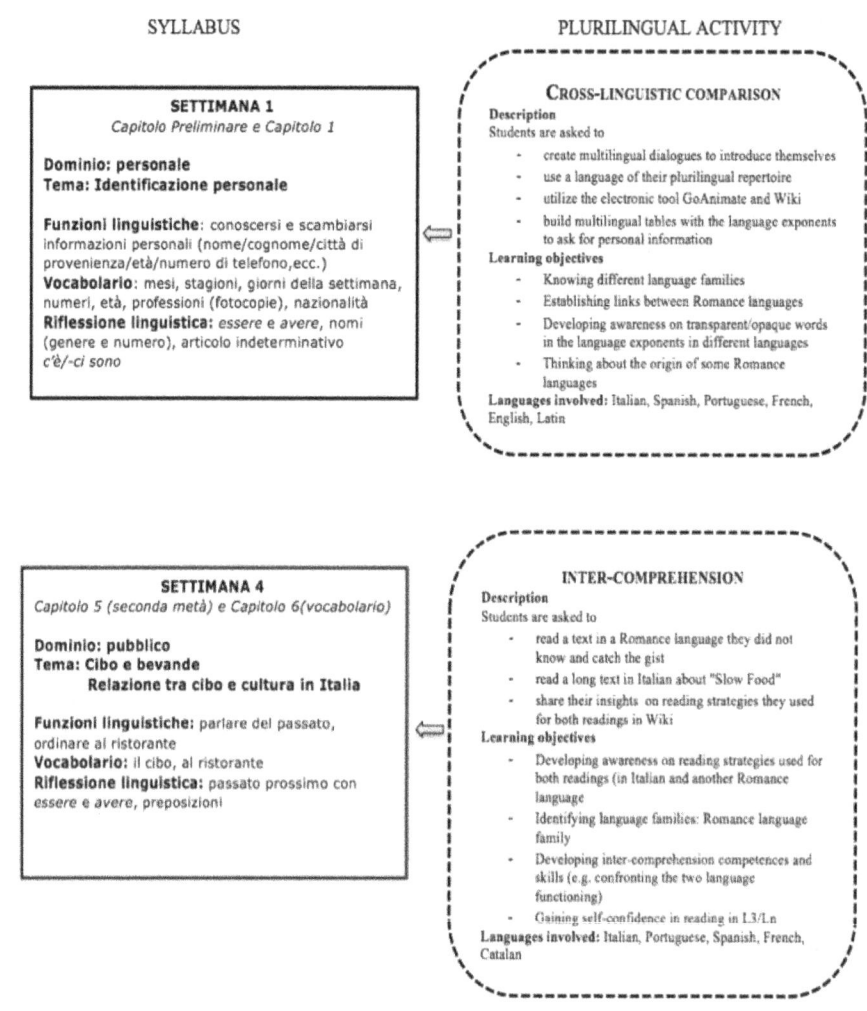

Figure 4: Example of plurilingual activities incorporated into the traditional syllabus

Based on a view of learning as a sociocultural practice (Lave and Wenger, 1991; Vygotsky, 1997; Lantolf, 1994, 2000), the project mainly incorporated collaborative working processes (e.g., peer-editing, peer-learning/teaching, peer-scaffolding) along with teacher instruction. Students were asked to work together to create multilingual scripts and vocabulary and cross-linguistic and cross-cultural tables in the Wiki environment.

The project included four main phases: 1) familiarizing with the key concepts of plurilingual approaches, individually, through extracts from online articles in the field and online activities aimed at noticing links among languages of the same family; 2) sharing in Wiki, as a class, language experiences and backgrounds to develop awareness of individual and collective plurilingual repertoires through a preliminary task; 3) discussing in the classroom, in a plenary session, the results of phases 1 and 2; 4) building in Wiki, in groups, plurilingual materials through different tasks and activities.

The project also included evaluation and assessment procedures. At the beginning of the course students were asked to fill in a questionnaire in order to collect information about their language profile, motivation, and awareness of their plurilingual skills. Halfway through the semester students took a traditional reading test, which included readings of incremental complexity. This test was designed to investigate if plurilingual activities had contributed to improve students' reading skills.[9] Students were also asked to fill in a post-reading self-assessment questionnaire to examine their learning process, particularly the impact that plurilingual activities had on their reading progress. Finally, students completed a final questionnaire organized around four main aspects: the frequency of the access to the plurilingual space; the development of plurilingual skills; the usefulness of the authoring tool Wiki in building this space; and students' suggestions for further improvement.

Some of the plurilingual techniques and activities used in this electronic space and their learning objectives are described in detail below.

5. Reflective learning: familiarizing with individual and collective plurilingual biographies

The qualitative data collected during the project (through initial, post-reading, and final questionnaires) highlighted the fact that a decisive and vital pivot of plurilingual approaches is conscious and reflective learning. Plurilingual learners must develop awareness on the multilingual dimension of their linguistic and cultural experiences (Moore and Castellotti, 2008; Le Pichon Vorstman, 2008; Piccardo, 2013). The identification of the classroom's "biodiversity" is an essential key to focus on the plurilingual practices that can occur in the specific learning environment and to design pedagogical materials.

---

[9] See Spinelli, forthcoming.

García and Sylvan (2011, p.391) point out that the "instruction is plurilingual, in the sense that each student's languaging is recognized and the pedagogy is dynamically centered on the singularity of the individual experiences that make up a plurality." This statement highlights the dynamic nature of the plurilingual pedagogy that enables students to learn from each other as well as from their teacher and vice versa (that is what was defined above as "co-learning").

As Jessner suggests (2013, p. 1) the plurilingual aspect of the complex language practices of individuals has a chronological and emotional dimension. In the life-span development of the multilingual experiences the chronological factor does not necessarily affect the definition of L1 as the "dominant language." In the personal long-life trajectory, for instance, L1 might become an L2 or L3 at later phase due to some changes of the individual's linguistic needs. In this perspective, the emotional dimension plays a crucial role and makes this classification even more complex. According to Pavlenko (2005, p. 154), language learning is characterized by two main processes: the *conceptual development* and the *affective linguistic conditioning*. The first process focuses on the *denotative* meaning of words and the second on the *connotative meaning* the words can gain due to the affective conditioning of personal and emotional memories and experiences, which make this process unique at the individual level.

The plurilingual language learning environment, therefore, "provides an interesting opportunity for co-participants to think further about who they are, what they know, and what they can learn from others" (Wei, 2014, p. 187).

In this encounter, new ideas of identities can emerge. The development of these co-learning processes is, de facto, the main objective of the preliminary task of the "Plurilingual Board" project, which is described in this section.

In order to accomplish this task, students were asked to describe their language biography as a multi-sensorial experience considering their intercultural encounters, which were relevant for their linguistic and cultural grow. Namely, students were asked to focus on the affective dimension of their language learning by associating the languages of their plurilingual repertoires to a specific part of their "body." This sensorial link was crucial to recall the emotional meanings interconnected to every single language experience.

Figure 5 shows one of students' narratives, which highlighted the relationship between language, action, thinking and their emotional experience in multiple cultural contexts.

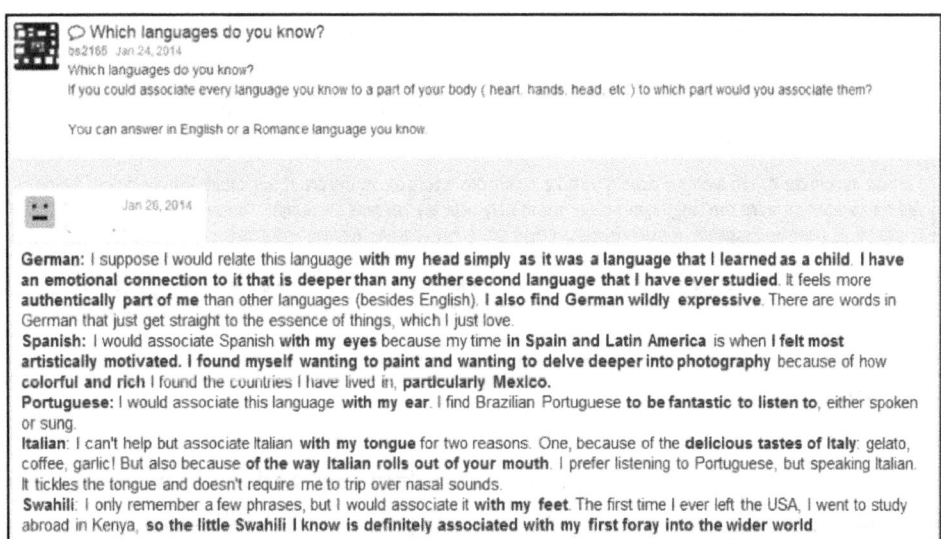

Figure 5. Student's narrative (1)[10]

By becoming aware of the multiple layers of acquired linguistic systems drawing upon several cultural experiences learners can familiarize with their several and sometimes conflictual identities—this learner seems to feel "more authentic" while speaking German and English, her original bilingual voices, than other languages—and, at the same time, "to draw strength from living in between" (Kramsch, 2012, p.116). In fact, her sensorial experience in multiple cultural contexts seems to enrich her "plurilingual-learner persona."

As Stavans suggests (2001, p.251) "a language is a set of spectacles through which the universe is seen afresh." This "image" seems to emerge out of the description above and the other students' narrative. Another student's narrative (see Figure 6), for instance, highlighted the nature of multilingualism at the age of globalization.

---

[10] Main ideas highlighted by the author.

> English is my native tongue, so I would associate it with my brain. It is a necessary, logical, rational means of communicating. Whether it's taking a standardized test, reading road signs, or explaining how to give directions, English always does the job. However, I don't want to reduce English to mere function. I love writing and I enjoy telling stories. **My comfort with the English language allows me write and speak creatively and freely.** Though the brain is often associated with logic, it can also be equally imaginative and artistic.
>
> **I took Spanish from Kindergarten** through my senior year of high school, and I would probably have to **associate it with my feet.** During my **junior year, I travelled to the small town of Requena in Valencia and lived with a host family.** That period of traveling around Spain with my classmates resulted in some the most formative experiences of my life. Spanish makes me want to move and explore. **When I walk through New York and hear Spanish spoken on the street, my mind always goes back to that memorable trip.**
>
> I would associate Italian with my eyes. I've take numerous courses on the art of the Italian Renaissance, which led me to want to learn the language. I travelled to Italy with my parents the summer before I came to Columbia, and I have never been **so inspired by such beauty.** Italian art, in my opinion, remains unparalleled in the mastery of painting. I look forward to reading and responding to Vasari's The Lives of the Artists in its native language. **I cannot wait to visit Padua to see Giotto's Scrovegni Chapel and express my feelings about it to native speakers.** Italian aesthetics have had a major influence on my time as an art history student, and I look forward to being able to speak the language.

Figure 6. Student's narrative (2)

Borders of speech communities are so fluid that walking in a multilingual city like New York can evoke a previous experience in a different cultural setting through the simple sounds of a language. This narrative also pointed out another important aspect: the sociolinguistics of multilingualism (Clark, 2012). The student perceived the need to know an additional language (Italian) to gain access to the local culture (Italian art) and to share feelings about it with the local people (Italians). On one hand, this perception highlighted the social construction of multilingualism. Plurilinguals in different contexts can use their plurilingual repertoire according to their social, academic, and professional practices and the related needs. In this respect, as mentioned above, plurilingual speakers use languages that might differ from monolingual speakers and they can exploit the semiotic potential of code-switching. On the other hand, it seems that the student's perception of himself as Italian language speaker is still as a *deficient-non-native speaker* who needs to reach the competence of an ideal and recognizable authority, the *native speaker*. This equation is typical of "one language at time" approach to which students are used to in academia. In this respect, the plurilingual pedagogy should reflect the complexity of students' linguistic repertoires and everyday practices focusing on the fluid dimension of this plurality. The pedagogical techniques described below aimed at reaching this goal.

6. Multilingual scripts and Multiliteracies Pedagogy

In order to design the first task adopted in this course, some of the pedagogical features proposed by the pedagogy of multiliteracies (New London Group, 1996) were taken into consideration. This pedagogical framework was conceived to enhance learner agency, creativity, and collaboration. It includes some steps—i.e., Situated Practice (SP), Overt Instruction (OI), Critical Framing (CF), and Transformed Practice (TP). The SP takes into consideration all the resources students can retrieve from their lived experiences. The OI refers to the intervention of the teacher who can provide scaffolding to develop students' metalanguage awareness and control of their resources. CF enables students to use critically what they have learned in relation to a specific context. Finally, the TP happens when students utilize the resources of the context of SP for their own purposes through the application of the understandings learned in OI and CF. According to the New London Group, these steps are not linear. They may have interrelated components that may occur simultaneously and can be revisited at different stages.

This specific task was incorporated (see Figure 4 for learning objectives) into the first week of the classroom syllabus. Students were divided into groups with different plurilingual repertoires. They were asked to write multilingual scripts to introduce themselves and to provide biographical information following teacher's instruction (see Appendix 2) and utilizing the electronic tool GoAnimate.[11] Every member used a language of his/her own repertoire. Students used their plurilingual repertoire as a starting point (SP) and created collaboratively their dialogue (TP), thinking critically about decisions to be made (CF)—i.e., using the appropriate register—according to the input provided by the teacher (OI). They had to use all the tools provided by GoAnimate to create the appropriate setting for their storyboard (see Figure 7).

---

[11] GoAnimate (https://goanimate.com) is an electronic tool which allows creating animated videos. It provides a spectrum of customized characters with all the right moves, different settings, voice recording, music track, and sounds effect.

Figure 7. Extract from students' multilingual dialogues

Afterwards, students were asked to accomplish sub-tasks aimed at finding similarities and differences between linguistic exponents (OI) retrieved from these dialogues (see Appendix 3) and to discuss it in a plenary session on Wiki. Some extracts from students' comments are the following:

> LYNN:[12] The Latin seems to be the root for most of the languages, even sometimes for English, which *I found surprising given that I did not think many words from English would have much in common with the other languages.* [...]. In addition, *it's interesting to think about how some words change so much, like anniversarius becomes anniversaire or aniversario in French and Portuguese, but in Spanish and Italian it's cumpleaños and compleanno.* These kinds of differences are more interesting to look at to me than which ones sound exactly like the Latin because then their origins are more questioned.

---

[12] Fake names are used and main ideas highlighted by the author.

KATHRYN: I must admit I was not very surprised by the results of this activity. [...]. Obviously *there are some interesting distinctions: while "anniversaire" means "birthday" in French, in other romance languages "anniversary" or "anniversario" has a broader meaning.* Clearly there are not across the board similarities between all words in all romance languages: for instance, *Spanish has significant influences from Arabic,* given the historical presence of Arab populations pre-inquisition/re-conquista. But overall, this demonstrates the merits of a plurilingual approach to language study: *knowing one romance language would clearly help intuit words in another.*

In the plenary discussion, students focused on different aspects. For instance, Lynn focused more on similarities in terms of word form both in Romance language and English while Kathryn seemed to be interested in differences of word meaning. Additionally, the latter student highlighted the importance of historical reasons that may have impact on the development of languages that belong to the same family generating differences. In this context, peer-scaffolding and co-learning occurred for meanings construction.

These tasks and sub-tasks enabled students to develop metalanguage awareness and plurilingual competences. As mentioned above, the transfer of this knowledge and competences can facilitate the learning of other additional languages as the student herself pointed out ("*knowing one romance language would clearly help intuit words in another*").

This type of work was enhanced during the semester through other tasks, as the one described in the section below.

7. INTERCOMPREHENSION AND INDIVIDUAL/COLLECTIVE READING AWARENESS

The starting point of the intercomprehension is the *continuum* in which languages of the same family are distributed (Escudé and Janin, 2010; Caddéo and Jamet, 2013; Conti & Grin, 2008, among others).[13] Because of this continuum, the intercomprehension is grounded on the notion of *transferability*,

---

[13] See also the other papers in this book.

that is extending the comprehension skills among languages of the same family (and later of different families as well) on the basis of linguistic similarities and language transfers, for instance, through lexical and syntactical transparencies. The intercomprehension, therefore, "fonctionne par affinité, proximité géolinguistique"[14] (Escudé and Janin, 2010, p. 37). Consequently, the *comparison* becomes a language learning instrument (Blanche-Benveniste, 2008, p. 43), particularly for receptive skills like reading. The intercomprehension techniques are mainly based on bottom-up processes, which enable students to make inferences and guess meanings by means of linguistic links and similarities. However, also top-down processes are important for reading, for instance the familiarity with the topic, which can facilitate the reader in catching the gist. It goes without saying that one of the main aspects of this approach is the participatory involvement of the learner's plurilingual repertoire, which becomes pivotal for the development of plurilingual competences and reading skills.

The task described in this section was incorporated into the syllabus during week 4 (see Figure 4 for learning objectives). The main topic and lexical area covered by the syllabus were respectively the "Relationship between food and culture in Italy" and "Food and drinks."

This task included four main phases, which asked students to: 1) read a text in a Romance language they did not know[15] about a familiar topic and answer reading comprehension open-ended questions (see Appendix 4); 2) fill in a self-evaluation questionnaire to identify which plurilingual competences and strategies, developed through the plurilingual activities, turned out to be useful for that reading; 3) read a text in Italian on a different topic (related to the unit of the syllabus), answer the reading's open-ended questions, and think about which of those competences and skills they had used for the reading in

---

[14] Author's translation: "operates through geo-linguistic affinity and proximity"
[15] This reading was in Portuguese. The instructor proposed an adapted version of a reading used in the "Janua Linguarum" project (Andrade et al., 2002). See: http://jaling.ecml.at/english/welcome_page.htm
 For those students who knew Portuguese, a reading on the same topic found in Internet was provided in Catalan.

the target language; 4) share, in a Wiki plenary discussion, their insights about these two reading experiences.

The input for the online discussion covered the following points:

1. How was the reading of these two texts?
   Very easy; easy; pretty easy; difficult.
2. Which reading and plurilingual strategies did you use? Briefly describe them providing some examples (you can use the examples from your personal self-evaluation questionnaire)
3. Read your peers' comment. Are there any strategies they used that you did not utilize? If yes, which ones?

Students' comments provided very interesting information about cross-linguistic comparisons and language transfers they used while reading as well as cognitive processes involved in both readings (bottom-up and top-down processes). Examples of processes recalled by students are described in the following comments:

RACHEL: 1. Il Catalano: Facile. Per me, credo che il catalano era più facile che il italiano forse perché catalano ha più in comune con spagnolo. Il Italiano: abbastanza facile.
2. Per me, è molto importante leggere il titolo perché posso pensare al tema e lo che già so del tema. *I think that I use transparent words a lot, but generally transparent not between English and Catalan/Italian but between Spanish and those languages which I think is less likely to lead to false cognates. Even with words that weren't cognates, the other romance language knowledge helped.* For example, in *Spanish ambos means both. In Catalan amb, as it appeared in the sentences, clearly did not mean both, but I was able to figure out that it meant "with" which certainly conceptually has a relationship with "both." Sentence structure certainly helps* as well when looking at romance languages as they are structured more similarly than say German or even original Latin. *It's generally relatively easy, even without understanding the way plurals are formed or what not, to tell which words are modifying which because they are physically next to one another. Context can be quite helpful as well, one of the sentences in my Catalan text began with "abans" which*

could have meant before or after, but when skimming through the rest of the sentence and finding reference to the word "precedents" it became clear that the word meant before [...].

STEPHANE: 1. As línguas românicas sua origem: questo testo era abbastanza facile perche conoscevo il soggetto e potevo dedurre di che cosa parlava. La rivoluzione con il cibo: questo testo anche era abbastanza facile perché di nuovo conoscevo un po del soggetto.
2. *I read the texts very quickly in order not to get stuck on individual words* or expressions that i did not know and I relied on the flow of the sentence in order to help me understand where the text was going. *Like Rachel i also used transparent words* in order to better understand the text and I found that usually I could derive the meaning. *For example, the word culture is pretty much the same in all languages as is conquistados for conquered. In addition, the "parole connettive"*(come/queste) were very useful in allowing me *to make assumptions in my reading.* I also thought *it was helpful to "assume" that I understood the text which, again, allowed me not to worry about the little details* but focus more on *the overall message of the text, the big picture, the flow.*
3. Like Rachel, I felt that the title was very helpful in setting me on my way to understanding the text as were the individual expressions that I could relate to: if I did not understand a word or a phrase, the rest of the sentence would generally help me figure it out. *Sentence structure also, as Rachel points out, which is similar to sentence structure in French, helped me to understand the otherwise complex sentences.*

These qualitative data show that the two students shared some common reading strategies but also focused on different reading features activating different cognitive processes. Both of them used their plurilingual competences. One student focused on transparent words recalling her Romance languages knowledge, particularly the Spanish knowledge. The words "amb" in Catalan and "ambos" in Spanish are semi-transparent words[16] (the form is similar but the meaning even if it is close is not identical). In this case, the latter facilitated the semantic mediation. The other student, instead, made cross-linguistic comparison between languages of different families (Romance languages and English, e.g., conquistados/Portuguese and conquered/English). Both students used the same reading strategy (skimming) in order to answer their questions, however while Rachel seemed to rely more on text features, (activating particularly bottom-up processes), Stephane referred also to paratextual information (e.g., the picture that came along with the text) and topical knowledge, activating top-down processes. In order to have "the big picture," Stephane particularly focused on syntactical transparency and connective words to construct reading meanings. Also Rachel activated top-down processes when she referred to her general knowledge, particularly to the chronological text structure (together with bottom-up processes using text clues such as the Catalan words "abans" and "precedents") and while making inferences from the title to familiarize with the topic of the reading.

Providing students with regular opportunities of self and collective reflection is a crucial aspect for multiliteracies-based and plurilingual instruction. In this discussion, co-learning and peer-scaffolding took place.

Some examples of successful co-learning are highlighted by the following students' statements:

JAQUELINE: [...] I think Ariana's point about *using the sections titles is important, and not something I thought of* [...]
ELLA: [...] *I am going to try to specifically use of Ashley's strategy of* reading without analysis in order to ease my understanding [...]

MICHAEL: [...] *I hadn't thought about it* (using the title of the article to make inferences and cognates)[17] *consciously* until I read Robert's comments above [...] I am often obsess over English grammar and word order.

---

[16] Castagne (2007) identifies three main dimensions of lexical transparency: 1) transparent word, 2) semi-transparent word, 3) and opaque word. For a summarizing table of this classification see Caddéo & Jamet (2013).
[17] Author's note.

These data showed that individual reading trajectories and experiences became strategic to reach global goals. Students' comments highlighted that peer collaboration was beneficial for mutual language learning: from local/individual to the central/societal level and vice versa (Wenger, 1998; Lave and Wenger 1991). Data also highlighted that the reflection phase was crucial to develop students' awareness of their plurilingual and multiple resources and ways to make them operative for successful language learning.

DISCUSSION

In this section the answers of the final questionnaire of both experimental stages (2013 and 2014)[18] of the "Plurilingual Board" project are analyzed and confronted.

The outcomes of questionnaires were grouped around four main topics: 1) students' awareness of their plurilingual repertoire; 2) curiosity about the unfamiliar languages of their peers' plurilingual repertoire; 3) focus on the main features of the collective plurilingual system; 4) suggestions for plurilingual teaching/learning improvement.

In both experimental phases of the project, plurilingual and reflective learning increased students' awareness of their plurilingual repertoire, as their feedback pointed out:

(2013): "It helped me to *organize all my languages* in my head. It helped me *to separate Spanish, Portuguese and Italian* in my mind. It's interesting to see how Latin transformed across the continents. *And it never hurts to have a basic knowledge of an unknown language.*"

(2014): "[…] how many similarities exist between the Romance languages that *I knew in theory but I did not really realized before.*"

"It taught me how to *see the connections between languages and really helped me with my reading I never thought that I could read Portuguese* and understand *as much of it as I did.*"

---

[18] The main and substantial difference between these two phases was that in 2013 students' contribution in the project was voluntarily while in 2014 their participation was mandatory and evaluated.

"It was helpful because it helped us understood new things *based on the concepts we already learned.*"

"I learnt that *using a method that separates languages* while you are learning a new language *is not the best method. There are more benefits* (especially with closely related languages) *than the possible disadvantages* for confusing the languages."

"A plurilingual approach *involves taking a language that you know and using it* as a means to learn more about another language. *It does not need to be perfect but knowing basic similarities* among Romance languages can *be quite helpful.*"

"Because it *allows you to compare visually information that you may be aware of* subconsciously but it *allowed me to actually know these.*"

These qualitative data showed that the plurilingual approach helped student to turn their attention to their plurilingual system and to internally systematize its languages. The operational aspect of finding similarities and connections between languages of the same family had evident benefits in learning not only the target language but also an additional language even if partially. On the basis of their prior knowledge of other Romance languages and the implementation of their plurilingual competences students were surprised to discover their partial competence in another language ("*I never thought that I could read Portuguese and understand as much of it as I did*"). One student's statement about imperfect and basic knowledge ("*it does not need to be perfect but knowing basic similarities among Romance languages can be quite helpful*") evokes the notion of the "droit à la approximation"[19] (Blanche-Benveniste, 1990, 2007; Escudé and Janin, 2010) that, in a plurilingual system, turns out to be a fruitful help to optimize language learning. This partial competence is no longer seen as deficiency in plurilingual learning but rather a useful resource to comprehend texts in unfamiliar language. Additionally, students' awareness increased their curiosity about additional languages. The following comments pointed out this aspect:

---

[19] Author's translation: "right to approximation." This notion emphasizes the benefit of the "imperfect knowledge" of words, which can facilitate, instead of impeding, the comprehension between languages of the same family, catching the gist of a text.

(2013): "(The project) helped me to understand how the Romance languages work in general but *it was very interesting for me to see Portuguese because I do not know Portuguese.*"
(2014): "I learnt how languages are both very similar and very different and *I am curious now to better understand their genealogy.*"
"It was useful not only to improve my Italian but also *learning the basics of the other languages.*"

Students' awareness and curiosity emerged while plurilingual activities gradually brought to light the main features of their plurilingual repertoire. Students identified the fluid nature of its borders as they highlighted in the following feedback:

(2013): "(In Wiki) *languages were placed side by side and that helped us to compare them. I learnt that they are more similar* than I have never thought. I think that plurilingual approach is useful because *it highlights a central language among the others.*"
(2014): "It was very interesting to join my peers and *find together similarities across languages.* That was very useful because *when you know several languages you can get confused between them.*"

It is worth noticing that having languages "side by side" students noticed their continuum and had the "big picture" of the landscape of languages in which, as Escudé and Janin (2010, p. 59) point out "chaque langue trouve sa place au milieu des autres langues, son autojustification naturelle"[20] (*"a central role among the others"* see student's comment above).

Although students' general response to the project was positive, their participation was not equal during the two experimental phases. In 2013, participation was not mandatory, and only eight out of 16 students accomplished the online plurilingual tasks. However, 13 out of 16 students highlighted, in their final questionnaires, the need to make this project mandatory. Additionally, two students did not participate because they did not know Romance languages, but they were accepted by the program because they had

---

[20] Author's translation: "Every language finds its place among the other languages, its self-justification."

been previously exposed to the Italian language. As mentioned above, in the academic context described in this paper the multilingual dimension of classroom can vary a lot. The features of this environment affect instructional decisions and practices, which need to be adapted to every single "ecosystem." In the 2013 project five out of eight students participating in the project realized that the participatory involvement of their peers and a more structured design were crucial components for the success of the project:

"*Make sure that all students participate* […] talking about their experiences because I think it is very interesting […]"
"[…] *More structured activities and roles assignment.*"
"[…] *More exercises for the online project* than the regular exercises of the LabManual and Workbook."

By following those students' suggestions a holistic approach was adopted in 2014 integrating an updated design online project into the syllabus, as described above. In the section devoted to feedback on the project improvement, five out of 14 students participating in the 2014 project highlighted a missing linkage between the online and the classroom work as the following comments pointed out:

"Clearly the *wiki involved a more multilingual approach* while most of our *exercises in class were only in Italian.*"
"I would only *have the plurilingual stuff in class.*"

Although some plurilingual online activities were discussed in class, these five students highlighted the need to foster connections between the classroom work and the plurilingual learning mainly based on the Wiki activities.

The perception of this missing linkage may be due to different reasons, as students themselves pointed out:

"*Do exercises more often than once a week.*"
"I would assign *WIKI related homework more frequently* but have them be smaller, *more specific assignments*. That way the *multilingual approach will be even more integrated into our experience learning Italian.*"

"Maybe it would be better to explain a bit more about the theory in which this work is based, I know we did it, but *I am not sure that all students of our class really got it."*

According to these comments, a more systematic and interconnected work between the materials of the course and the plurilingual instruction is needed if a hybrid course is designed. Most importantly, as one of the students pointed out above, they need not only to develop awareness of their plurilingual repertoire but to deeply understand the value of this plurality in a globalized world in which the boundaries of speech communities are no longer so clearly delineated *("it would be better to explain a bit more about the theory in which this work is based")*. By adopting a plurilingual approach the biggest challenge is, therefore, to move students away from an atomistic and traditionally monolingual perspective on their language learning. This change cannot be done by sporadic and isolated instructional experiences, but it may call for a more general curriculum innovation.

9. Conclusion

This paper described a tentative holistic approach, which has been adopted in a multilingual classroom and aimed at incorporating plurilingual instruction into a more traditional syllabus.

Qualitative data collected during two different phases showed that there were evident advantages in adopting this approach. Through the accomplishment of plurilingual activities students became aware of the plural dimension of their language competences and identity. These activities enabled students to position themselves as plurilingual language users (Kramsch, 2012) rather than "incomplete" world language learners (Kumagai et al., 2015) by using their multiple linguistic resources and exercising their agency.

Through a reflective learning, students were able to develop awareness of those plurilingual competences and to use them in order to optimize their learning. From the point of view of a multiliteracy pedagogy, which aims at developing multiple literacies (not only the multiple use of languages but also new literacies such as using the different codes and channels offered by the new technology to create their own texts), students could use the Wiki tools in order to create their multilingual materials (TP) following teacher's instructions (OI), making decisions and providing personal insights about the collective plurilingual repertoire (CF), and sharing previous language experiences (SP).

However, the data also highlighted that there is still a long way to go. There is the need to further integrate plurilingual activities and practices into the current curriculum. As Kramsch (2010, p.107) points out, we need to "draw on students' multilingual competences, even if they are learning a single language."

By taking into consideration the outcomes of this exploratory study and the current language policy of most universities in North America, many questions can arise: Do we really need to find this type of compromise for our instructional decisions while working in a multilingual context? Do we need a more radical change and innovation in the traditional curriculum selecting students through more specific requirements (for instance, creating courses for plurilinguals who share the knowledge of languages of the same family? Or clearly stating in the course description that a plurilingual approach and practices will be adopted, etc.)? Is this a feasible choice considering that most of our students attend these courses to fulfill language requirements?

Even though the outcomes of this project can provide evidence for the necessity of a radical change in the language curriculum in multilingual contexts, further investigation is needed to answer the above questions, and most importantly the discussion needs to be taken from a local to a broader administrative discourse level, which may involve all the concerned language departments.

BIBLIOGRAPHY

Blanche-Benveniste, C. (1997). *Eurom 4. Méthode d'apprentissage simultané de quatre langues romanes.* Firenze: La Nuova Italia Editrice.

Blanche-Benveniste, C. (2007). Formes des compréhension approximative. In E. Castagne, *Les Enjeux de l'intercompréhension* (pp. 167–179). Reims: Èpure-éditions et presses universitaires de Reims.

Blanche-Benveniste, C. (2008). Comment retrouver l'expérience des anciens voyageurs en terre de lngues romanes. In V. Conti, & F. Grin, *S'entendre entre languages voisines* (pp. 53–77). Genève: Georg éds.

Blommaert, J. (2010). *The Sociolinguistics of globalization.* Cambridge: Cambridge University Press.

Boekman, K., Aalto, E., & Atanasoska, T. &. (2011). *Promoting plurilingualism: Majority language in multilingual settings.* Graz: Council of Europe Publishing.

Bybee, J. (2010). *Language, usage and cognition.* Cambridge, UK: Cambridge University Press.

Caddéo, S., & Jamet, M. (2013). *L'intercompréhension: une autre approche pour l'ensignement des langues.* Paris: Hachette.

Canagarajah, S. (2014). Theorizing a Competence for Translingual Practice at the Contact Zone. In S. May, *The Multilingual Turn Implications for SLA, TESOL and Bilingual Education* (pp. 78–102). New York: Routledge.

Candelier, M., de Pietro, J., Facciol, R., Lõrincz, I., & Pascual, X., (2011). *CARAP-FREPA A framework of reference for pluralistic approaches to languages and cultures.* Strasbourg: Council of Europe Publishing.

Castagne, E. (2007). Trasparences lexicales entre langues voisines. n E. Castagne, *Les Enjeux de l'intercompréhension* (pp. 155–166). Reims: Èpure-éditions et presses universitaires de Reims.

Cenoz, J. (2013). Third Language Acquisition. In C. Chapelle, *The Encyclopedia of Applied Linguistics* (pp. 1–5). Malden, MA and Oxford: Wiley/Blackwell.

Conti, V., & Grin, F. (2008). *S'entendre entr languages voisines.* Genève: Georg éds.

Cope, B., & Kalantzis (Eds.). (2000). *Multiliteracies: Literacy Learning and the design of Social Futures.* London: Routledge.

Cope, B., & Kalantzis, M. (1993). Introduction: How a genre approach to literacy can transform the way writing is taught. In B. Cope, & M. Kalantzis, *The power of literacy: A genre approach to teaching writing* (pp. 1–21). London: The Falmer Press.

Cope, B., & Kalantzis, M. (2009). "Multiliteracies": New literacies, new learning. *Pedagogies: An International Journal*, 4(3), 164–195.

Council of Europe. (2001). *The Common European Framework of Reference for Languages: Learning, teaching, assessment.* Cambridge: Cambridge University Press.

Escudé, P., & Janin, P. (2010). *Le point sur l'intercomprhénsion, clé du plurilinguisme.* Paris: CLE International.

García, A., & Sylvan, C. (2011). Pedagogies and Practicies in Multilingual Classrooms: Singularities in Pluralities. *The Modern Language Journal*, 95(iii), 385–400.

García, O. (2009). *Bilingual education in the 21st century: A global perspective.* Malden, MA and Oxford: Wiley/ Blackwell.

García, O., & Flores, N. (2013). Literacy in Multilingual Classrooms. In C. Chapelle, *The Encyclopedia of Applied Linguistics* (pp. 1–7). Malden, MA and Oxford: Wiley/Blackwell.

García, O., & Kano, N. (2014). Translanguaging as Process and Pedagogy: Developing the English Writing of Japanese Students in the US. In J. Conteh, & G. Meier, *The Multilimgual Turn in Language Education* (pp. 258–277). Bristol: Multilingual Matters.

Gorter, D., & Cenoz, J. (2011). A Multilingual Approach: Conclusions and Future Perspectives: Afterword. *The Modern Language Journal*, 442–445.

Halliday, M. K. (1978). *Language as social semiotics: The social interpretation of language and meaning.* London: Edward Arnold.

Jessner, U. (2013). Complexity in Multilingual System. In C. A. Chapelle. Malden, MA and Oxford: Wiley/Blackwell.

Kramsch, C. (2009). *The Multilingual Subject.* Oxford: Oxford University Press.

Kramsch, C. (2012). Authenticity and Legitimacy in Multilingual SLA. *Critical Multilingualism Studies*, 1(1), 107–128.

Kramsch, C., & Whiteside, A. (2008). Language Ecology in multilingual settings: Towards a theory of symbolic competence. *Applied Linguistics*, 29(4), 645–671.

Kress, G. (2000). Multimodality. In B. Cope, & M. Kalantzis (Eds.), *Multiliteracies: Literacy learning and the design of social futures* (pp. 182–202). South Melbourne: Macmillian.

Kress, G. (2003). *Literacy in the new media age.* London: Routledge.

Kumagai, Y., Konoeda, K., Nishimata, M., & Sato, S. (2015 in press). Fostering Multimodal Literacies in the Japanese Language Classroom. In Y. Kumagai, A.

López-Sánchez, & S. Wu, *Multiliteracies in World Language Education*. New York: Routledge.

Lantolf, J. (2000). Introducing sociocultural theory. In J. Lantolf, *Sociocultural theory and second language learning* (pp. 1–26). Oxford: Oxford University Press.

Lantolf, J., & Appel, G. (1994). Theoretical framework: an introduction to *Vygotskian approaches to second language research*. In J. Lantolf, Vygostkian approaches to second language reserach (pp. 1–32). London: Ablex Publishing.

Lave, J., & Wenger, E. (1991). *Situated Learning: Legitimate Peripheral Participation*. Cambridge: Cambridge University Press.

Le Pichon Vorstman, E. (2008). Coscience méta-cogntive et competence plurilingue. In D. Moore, & V. Castellotti, *La compétence plurilingue: Regards francophones* (pp. 129–146). Bern, Switzerland: Petere Lang.

Leung, C. (2014). Communication and Participatory Involvement in Linguistically Diverse Classrooms. In S. May, *The Multilingual Turn Implications for SLA, TESOL and Bilingual Education* (pp. 123–146). New York: Routledge.

May, S. (2014). Introducing the Multilingual Turn. In S. May, *The Multilingual Turn Implications for SLA, TESOL and Bilingual Education* (pp. 1–6). New York: Routledge.

Moore, D., & Castellotti, V. (2008). *La compétence plurilingue: Regards francophones*. Bern Switzerland: Peter Lang.

New London Group. (1996). A pedagogy of multiliteracies: Designing social futures. *Harvard Educational Review, 66*(1), 60–92.

New London Group. (2000). A pedagogy of multiliteracies. Designing social futures. In B. Cope, & M. Kalantzis (Eds.), *Multiliteracies. Literacy learning and the desugn of social futures*. London: Routledge.

Norton, B. (2014). "Identity, Literacy, and the Multilingual Matters." In S. May, *The Multilingual Turn* (pp. 103–122). New York: Routledge.

Nunan, D. (1998). *The learner-centred curriculum: A study of second language teaching*. Cambridge, UK: Cambridge University Press.

Ortega, L. (2014). Ways Forward for a Bi/Multilingual Turn in SLA. In S. May, *The Multilingual Turn Implications for SLA, TESOL and Bilingual Education* (pp. 32–53). New York: Routledge.

Pavlenko, A. (2005). *Multilingualism and emotions*. Cambridge: Cambridge University Press.

Pavlenko, A. (2011). *Thinking and Speaking in two languages*. Bristol: Multilingual Matters.

Pennycook, A. (2010). *Language as local practice.* New York : Routledge.

Piccardo, E. (2013). Plurilinguism and Curriculum Design: Toward a Synergic Vision. *TESOL Quartely*, 47(3), 600–614.

Saravanan, V. (2012). Curriculum design, development, innovation and change. *Social and Behavioral Sciences*, 47, 1276–1280.

Seidlhofer, B. (2009). Orientations in EFL research: Form and function. In A. Mauranen, & E. Ranta, *English as lingua franca* (pp. 37–59). New Castle, UK: Cambridge Scholar Publishing.

Spinelli, B. Forthcoming. Pedagogy in Multilingual Classroom: Investigating L3/Ln Learners' Reading/Writing Relationships.

Spinelli, B. (2015). In press. Empowering Students in the Italian Classroom to Learn Vocabulary through a Multiliteracies Framework. In Y. Kumagai, A. López-Sánchez, & S. Wu, *Multiliteracies in World Language Education*. New York: Routledge.

Spinelli, B., & Parizzi, F. (2010). *Il Profilo della lingua Italiana Livelli del QCER A1, A2, B1, B2*. Firenze: La Nuova Italia.

Stavans, I. (2001). *On Borrowed Words*. A Memoire of Language. New York: Penguin.

van Geert, P. (1994). A dynimic system model of cognitive and language growth. *Psychological Review*, 98, 3–53.

Vygotsky, L. (1997). *Thought and Language*. Cambridge, MA: The Massachusetts Institute of Techonology.

Wei, L. (2014). Who's Teaching Whom? Co-Learning in Multilingual Classrooms. In S. May, *The Multilingual Turn Implications for SLA, TESOL and Bilingual Education* (pp. 167–190). New York: Routledge.

Wenger, E. (1998). *Communities of Practices*. Cambridge, UK: Cambridge University Press.

Appendix 1

Students' Plurilingual Repertoires in the 2013 and 2014 Project

Italian Intensive Elementary 2013

Students' L1: ENG, SPA, CHI, BUL, RUS, GER, IND

Students' L2/L3/Ln: ENG, SPA, PORT, BENG, JAP, FRE, LIT

Italian Intensive Elementary 2014

Students' L1: EN, FRE, SPA, GER

Students' L2, L3, Ln (excluding Latin and Ancient Greek): GER, FRE, SPA, PORT, RUS, EBR, ARAB, CHI

Appendix 2

Task Week 1:
Teacher's instruction for multilingual scripts (using GoAnimate)

GROUP 1
- build a video with your peers (4 characters) asking information about: GREETINGS (INFORMAL), NAME, NATIONALITY, WHERE YOU COME FROM
- identify the context in which this dialogue will take place
- speak the language assigned by the teacher
- send your script to your teacher by […] for feedback

GROUP 2
- same instructions but different information: GREETINGS (INFORMAL), NAME, PROFESSION, AGE

GROUP 3
- same instructions but different information: GREETINGS (INFORMAL), PROFESSION, DATE OF YOUR BIRTHDAY

GROUP 4
- same instructions but different information: GREETINGS (FORMAL), WHERE YOU LIVE, PROFESSION

Script for video EXAMPLE 1 (in WIKI):
- Ciao mi chiamo Anna, sono italiana, sono di Roma
- Hola, me llamo Soledad y soy de Madrid, encatada
- Piacere!
- Lui si chiama Daniel
- Salut, je m'appelle Daniel et je suis de Paris

APPENDIX 3

TASK WEEK 1:
ACTIVTIES

A. Ascolta i dialoghi in più lingue e completa la tabella seguente (se non trovi la parola, lo spazio rimane vuoto):

ITALIANO	dove	buongiorno			io	come	Mi chiamo		bene		quando
FRANÇAIS		mon		enchanté	je						
ESPAÑOL									todo		
PORTOGÛESE											
ENGLISH	where		hello		I am	–		–		years	birthday

B. Guarda la tabella: quali delle parole sopra deriva dal latino? Fai una lista come nell'esempio:

MEUS	Mon, ...
ANNIVERSARIUS	....
PLACERE	....
EGO	....
TOTUS	....
QUOM	....
BENE	....
SUM	....

C. Write whatever you notice about the words of the table (i.e. similarities/differences). <u>Please write your comments on the Wiki page "SCAMBIO INFORMAZIONI" under the table in "COMMENTS"</u>). You can write in English or a Romance language you know.

Appendix 4

Task Week 4:
Reading Activities

1. Leggi questo testo in portoghese. Anche se è una lingua che non conosci cerca di capire il <u>senso generale</u> (di che cosa parla e NON parola per parola). Aiutati con la conoscenza delle altre lingue che conosci. Poi fai l'attività 2.

As línguas românicas
Sua origem

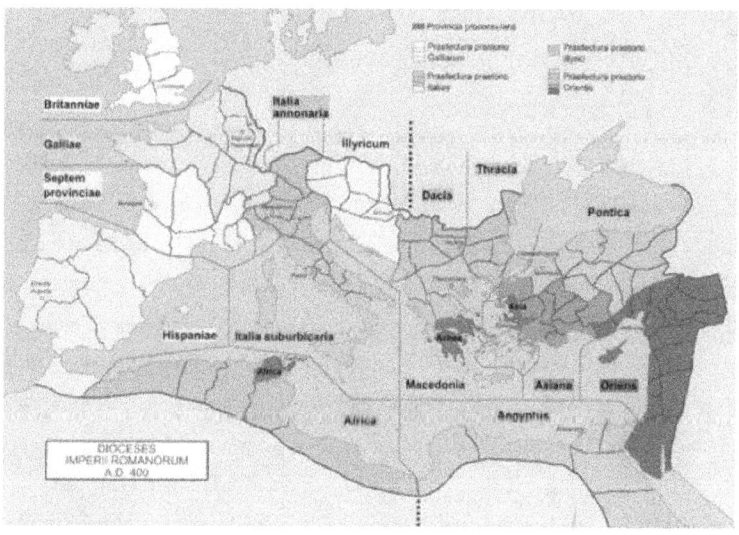

Roma sendo o resultado das culturas Etrusca e Grega (Magna Graecia), começou a estabelecer-se quando finalmente a Grécia e a Macedónia se tornaram províncias Romanas. Levados pelo seu espírito dominador o povo romano fundou um dos maiores impérios da Antiguidade, que se estendia desde o Atlântico ao Índico e do Mar do Norte aos montes desertos do Norte de África (desde Espanha até à Grã-Bretanha, Norte de África e actual Iraque). Apesar de não mostrarem interesse particular em divulgar a sua língua, o latim depressa se difundiu pelos territórios conquistados, sendo vista como a língua dos conquistadores, veículo da cultura e da organização romana.

Para isso muito contribuíram os Portugueses e Espanhóis (os quais tinham sido sucessivamente subjugados pelos Fenícios, Gregos, Romanos, Visigodos e Mouros) aquando das descobertas ao chegarem ao Novo Mundo, levavam as suas línguas e a fé. Cristã até às populações nativas, onde ainda hoje se encontram vestígios da sua presença.O latim surgiu assim de uma língua mais antiga, já evoluída, e prolonga-se largamente sob a forma de línguas–filhas que são a línguas românicas.

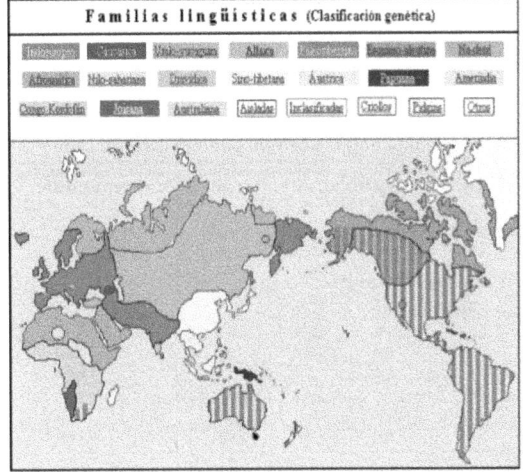

Família linguística

Quando as línguas evoluíram de uma única língua original podemos afirmar que se trata de uma família linguística. "na metáfora normalmente utilizada, diz-se que o latim é a língua mãe, e o romeno , o sardo, o italiano, o francês, o catalão, o espanhol e o português as línguas filhas" (Ruhlen, 1996). Não podemos limitar o papel do Latim na história linguistica da Europa ao de ser origem das línguas românicas, uma vez que ao ser adoptada pela igreja como língua própria continuou a ser uma língua viva, apesar de toda a estrutura política que a apoiava se ter desfeito. É devido a este facto que hoje podemos reconstituir toda a história da família românica, pois são vastos os registos escritos existentes desde a sua origem. Através de estudos efectuados por linguistas tem cada vez mais força a tese de que as línguas da Europa têm uma origem comum, sendo esta designada por Indoeuropeia, "o indo-europeu é pois uma língua reconstruída teoricamente pelos linguistas a partir da comparação das línguas cuja existência pôde ser certificada" (Walter, 1994).

Esta classificação deveu-se sobretudo à descoberta de palavras, que apresentam semelhanças no som e no significado apesar de pertencerem a línguas diferentes. O que levou à conclusão de que estas semelhanças não são "obra do acaso," só o conhecimento das estruturas lingüísticasfacilita a aprendizagem destas línguas irmãs.

1. Rispondi alle domande (nella lingua che vuoi anche in inglese).
    a. Di che cosa parla il testo che hai letto? Qual è l'argomento principale? Descrivilo brevemente.
    b. Quali delle seguenti strategie hai usato per capire il testo? Può essere più di una.

- Le immagini che accompagnano il testo mi hanno aiutato a capire l'argomento trattato
- La conoscenza dell'argomento trattato nel testo
- Il titolo del testo mi ha aiutato a capire l'argomento trattato
- ho usato le parole trasparenti (ad es. Resultado PO- risultato IT- result EN- resultado SP- résultat FR o sendo PO e essendo IT) se sì quali? Fai alcuni esempi.
- Alcune informazioni grammaticali (ad es. accordo estudos efectuados, o articoli come uma familia linguistica), puoi fare qualche esempio?
- Alcune parole connettive (ad es. como, o, esta, o pronomi come "línguas–filhas que são a línguas românicas"), puoi fare qualche esempio?
- La struttura della frase (soggetto –verbo – oggetto)
- facendo inferenze e capendo il significato di una parola dal contesto in cui è, puoi fare un esempio?
- Altro

Ora leggi il seguente testo in italiano che parla di un argomento completamente diverso e rispondi alle domande sotto il testo (in inglese o nella lingua che preferisci)

La rivoluzione con il cibo

Tutto comincia nel 1986. Siamo in Italia e la catena di fast-food "McDonald's" sta per installare un nuovo ristorante a Piazza di Spagna, sito storico di Roma. È in quel momento che interviene Carlo Petrini (sopra nella foto) che, indignato per l'avanzare della cattiva nutrizione, convince con intelligenza e umorismo, un gruppo di intelletuali e artisti italiani a "mettere le mani in pasta."

Il concetto di Slow Food è dunque, all'inizio, un semplice appello ai gastronomi per ricordargli le origine filosofiche e umoristiche del cibo. In seguito, l'idea si è fatta strada ed è diventata un vero movimento, con una sua filosofia descritta nel "Manifesto Slow Food per il gusto e la biodiversità," che ha coinvolto, nel 1989, un'organizzazione internazionale a scopo non lucrativo. Il movimento si fonda sul principio di "eco-gastronomia" che riconosce la relazione tra il nostro piatto, il nostro territorio e il nostro pianeta invitando tutti a riappropriarsi dei piaceri della tavola con gli amici e la famiglia. Mangiare diventa, quindi, un momento di condivisione e di scoperta. Ognuno è invitato a rinnovare le tradizioni o a scoprire delle nuove culture culinare senza, allo stesso tempo, danneggiare l'ambiente.

La missione principale di questa organizzazione è, quindi, di risvegliare in un largo pubblico il gusto per un'alimentazione di qualità e di mettere in relazione i produttori e i consumatori (attraverso l'organizzazione di numerose manifestazioni) per sviluppare una conoscenza migliore dell'origine degli alimenti e delle loro condizioni di produzione. Essa dà particolare importanza agli alimenti di natura artigianale e crede che il patrimonio umanitario e l'ambiente siano messi in pericolo dall'industria agroalimentare che propone prodotti su larga scala per soddisfare rapidamente il nostro appetito. Allo stesso modo, essa vuole trovare soluzioni ai problemi di sotto-alimentazione del Sud e di malnutrizione del Nord. Per questa ragione promuove una migliore conoscenza delle diverse culture alimentari e di una più equa divisione delle risorse del nostro pianeta. Per questo i "slow foodisti" pensano che sia necessario rallentare il ritmo della vita: prendersi del tempo per scegliere gli alimenti, conoscerli, cucinarli e sentirne il gusto.

« È inutile forzare i ritmi della nostra esistenza. L'arte di vivere consiste nell'imparare come dedicare il tempo ad ogni cosa. » (Carlo Petrini, fondatore di Slow Food)

a) Di che cosa parla il testo che hai letto? Qual è l'argomento principale? Descrivilo brevemente.

b) Quali delle strategie sopra menzionate hai utilizzato per capire il testo in italiano? Fai una lista e se possibile qualche esempio.

THE FLORIDA STATE UNIVERSITY EXPERIENCE: DESIGN, DEVELOPMENT, AND IMPLEMENTATION OF ITALIAN FOR SPANISH SPEAKERS COURSES

FABRIZIO FORNARA AND IRENE ZANINI-CORDI

1. WHY ITALIAN FOR SPANISH SPEAKERS?

How can we boost enrollment in Italian classes at a moment when our AP program is threatened and colleges and universities are heavily shifting their emphasis and funds away from the Humanities and into STEM? In a state like Florida, with a steadily fast-growing Spanish speaking population, setting up special classes of Italian language geared toward native, heritage, or even fluent speakers of Spanish is a simple but brilliant idea. The successful California State Long Beach (CSLB) program of Italian and French for Spanish speakers offered a blueprint for The Florida State (FSU)'s experiment.

The potential of this project for boosting the FSU Italian Program was immediately clear. A similar program, Portuguese for Spanish speakers, has been thriving for a few years in our Department of Modern Languages and Linguistics, and our colleagues in Portuguese have more students than they can accommodate. Relying on Professor Clorinda Donato and her colleagues' experience in setting up such a program at CSLB, we started our first course of Italian for Spanish speakers in Fall 2012.

Housed in the Modern Languages and Linguistics Department, the FSU Italian Studies Program is quite large and active. It offers the only Italian Studies MA program east of University of Texas at Austin and south of the University of Georgia. Each semester, undergraduate classes total over 600 students, excluding those students attending the year-round classes in the FSU program in Florence. Unfortunately, the university does not have a system in place to track minors, but our major, double-major, and co-major numbers hover around 45 per academic year. Since its recent beginnings in the year 2000, our Italian MA program has awarded degrees to 40 alumni, and can boast a 100 percent placement rate either in prestigious Ph.D. programs, in Florida high-schools and colleges teaching Italian language, or in the job market in general. Graduate students are awarded teaching assistantships and have a teaching load of three courses per academic year. The program can support up to 13 graduate students on teaching assistantships and research fellowships. On average, every year there are 8–10 graduate students in the program: Some come from our undergraduate program but the majority are out-of-state students. Our full-time faculty is numbered at five and one-half.

In order to decide how to best tailor the Italian for Spanish speakers classes to the needs of the target students and our Italian program, we needed to understand if and how these students differed from the others. More than with other Romance languages, when Italian and Spanish interact the principle of intercomprehension becomes self-evident. The incidence of vocabulary, syntax, and structure overlap is great enough that the Italian and Spanish speakers can usually understand each other and communicate on a basic level–in particular through reading and writing–simply by using their native language. Most of us have experienced this situation as tourists, but as language teachers we have all encountered it in the classroom. We might have witnessed the Spanish speaking student getting impatient in the first semester of Italian because the learning pace is too slow for her, while we might have tried to prevent the passionate one from monopolizing the conversation in the higher levels. If this ease in intercomprehension is especially true in the case of Italian and Spanish, it is however valid for all Romance languages, as Claire Blanche-Benveniste's studies on *Intercompréhension* have shown (Blanche-Benveniste and Valli, 1997). But what kind of language students are these? What are their possible strengths and weaknesses in language acquisition?

According to the observations of Professor Frédéric Latty, Teaching Supervisor at the Institut de Français in Villefranche, France (personal communication, September 4, 2013), students learning French, whose first language is Latin based, often share similar profiles, with common traits in the following order of relevance:

1. A comprehension that is dominant
2. An oral expression characterized by great ease and fluidity
3. An average, or even weak, correction in oral expression

4. An auditory acuity quite similar to students coming from other language groups (notably Germanic languages)
5. Average pronunciation skill

One of the most relevant problems, in Latty's view, is that since for these students comprehension is very easy from the start they may become impatient during class time. While it is the main feature of intercomprehension and an ability that we wish to exploit in our classes, this advantage in comprehension may also entail two major issues. The first is an all too easy fluidity of expression (the student is likely to think, "I understand well so I can also speak … I just need to say the same thing I would say in my language but 'in the Italian way' ") and, consequently, a poor degree of correction. The student loses the feeling that she needs to make an effort to produce correct sentences in the target language. It is then the instructor's task to make students aware of these issues. The instructor should not stifle the students' enthusiasm and output with an overwhelming emphasis on grammar and correction (Krashen, 1997), but she should try to infuse in them a passion for the target language, which goes hand in hand with the satisfaction of being able to understand and to communicate fluently in that language. However, since some of our students will become language teachers and will pursue graduate studies, it is necessary that instructors monitor their accuracy in output from the beginning.

To understand not only the viability but also the potential impact of classes of Italian for Spanish speakers on the FSU Italian Program it suffices to look at data reflecting the composition of both Florida's population and FSU's student body. According to 2013 Census Bureau figures, more than one out of four Floridians speak a language other than English in their homes, with Spanish or Spanish Creole being the most common. Florida's overall population is 19.3 million people, and there are about 3.6 million Spanish-speakers out of Florida's 17.9 million residents over the age of 5. Florida's population is 22.5 percent Hispanic, mostly Cuban-Americans, Puerto Ricans, and South Americans. In contrast with the West Coast or Southwest United States, the Mexican-American presence is quite small.

As of spring 2014, the total FSU student body was 39,878 persons. Of these students, 6,125 recognized themselves as Hispanic, the second-largest campus group by ethnicity. In the past four years, the median growth of Hispanic students on campus has been of about 400 per year. Although, unfortunately, it is not possible to know the percentage of Spanish-speaking students on campus, these data on ethnicity reflect the Census data of a growing Hispanic population, with a large first-generation component.

2. ADVERTISING STRATEGIES

FSU requires three semesters of language courses–or equivalent competence–for students in the College of Arts and Sciences. Spanish-speaking students, however, are often exempted from the language requirements because they can demonstrate proficiency in a foreign language other than English. Thus, those who enroll in Italian language classes are usually highly motivated and intelligent individuals who wish to add another language and cultural experience to their CV. This also means that Spanish-speaking students are an untapped source of potential Italian language students, and, given the right incentives, they could easily become Italian minors and majors.

By adding Italian for Spanish speakers classes to our offerings we managed to lure some students from this group into a class specifically tailored to their intercomprehension ability. We thus raised our general language enrollment by attracting students who would probably not take a demanding language course otherwise. The program is now in its fifth semester, and we have already started to notice an increase in the minor and major enrollment numbers. Moreover, many more graduate students enroll in these classes than in regular language classes. One of the main reasons is probably the reduced contact time. While our normal language classes during the semester are part of a four-credit hour course and meet Monday through Thursday for 50 minutes, the Italian for Spanish speakers classes meet only three times a week for 50 minutes–and are worth three-credit hours. These classes are taught Mondays, Wednesdays, and Fridays: Although the Friday class might appear to be a deterrent, it does not seem to pose a big problem. We also schedule these classes during the most popular time slots, which range from 10:00am until 1:00pm.

However, in order to be able to offer these classes only three times a week we had to use a different class code–FOL 3930 instead of ITA1120. The major drawback of using this different code, which groups together Modern Languages and Linguistics courses, was that it made the class less visible to students on the registrar's system at the time of enrollment, and many students were unaware of its existence. This code also confused students who wondered if the class was the equivalent of a "normal" ITA class and if it counted toward their language requirements and/or minor/major course work. After the second semester, we tried to remedy both of these problems through a stronger advertising campaign.

The first class, in Fall 2012, had only 13 students enrolled. In Spring 2013 we were able to offer two classes, one corresponding to the first-semester Italian and one corresponding to the second semester, each with 10 students. The university's minimum enrollment threshold is 12, but since some graduate students were enrolled, we managed to keep both classes open. In light of the low numbers, in Fall 2013 we decided to offer only the first-semester class. It was clear that in order to make this experiment work we needed to better publicize the class. So, during the summer we:

1. Emailed flyers with the class description to all undergraduate advisors on campus
2. Invited all students enrolled in the Fall ITA1120 classes to switch into FOL3930 if they were fluent in Spanish
3. Emailed all Spanish majors, co-majors, and those taking the Spanish for Heritage Speakers classes, advertising this class
4. Emailed the Hispanic students' organizations on campus
5. Emailed previous students asking to promote the class among their friends
6. Advertised the course with colleagues in the Spanish Program
7. Plastered catchy posters (featuring the image of Pitbull —a popular singer from Miami) at the Students' Union, at the International Students' Global Center, around dining areas, etc.
8. Debated about posting an ad in the students' newspaper, but decided against it because of its cost.

As a result of the advertising campaign, the Fall 2013 Italian for Spanish Speakers 1 class had 20 students enrolled, and the Spring 2014 class had 18. We also know that word-of-mouth advertising has started to work: Students are enrolling because their friends already took the class and loved it.

3. COURSE LOGISTICS

Our objective is to be able to offer all three language levels each semester. At that point, we will request a permanent ITA code for the class and will be ready to adopt a specific textbook. At the moment, FOL3930 classes use the same textbook as the regular language classes, and the syllabus covers the same grammar structures as the basic Italian program–Elementary Italian I (ITA1120) and II (ITA1121), although the pace of the FOL3930 courses is a little more accelerated. We edited the syllabi of both FOL3930 courses to fit this reduced schedule. Usually, Spanish speakers need less time than their fellow monolingual speakers to understand, practice, and master a structure that is similar in Spanish and Italian. For example, Spanish speakers already know how to use the *indicativo imperfetto* (e.g., "comía" in Spanish, "mangiavo" in Italian), a past tense that exists in Spanish and Italian but not in English. The instructor of FOL3930 is free to customize content, exercises, and assignments to the needs of the students and to devise quizzes, exams, and written and oral tests. The final exam is the same for the FOL3930 courses and their corresponding basic Italian courses.

We decided to model the syllabi of FOL3930 courses on the syllabi of the basic Italian courses to facilitate the transition of students from one type of course to another (Appendix B). So far, we have been able to offer only one section of Italian for Spanish Speakers 1 and one section of Italian for Spanish Speakers 2 per semester. Unfortunately, this does not offer an option to students who are interested in one of these courses but are not able to take it because of scheduling conflicts. At the end of the semester, students can switch from the first level of FOL3930 to the second of the basic Italian program, and vice versa, and complete their language requirements either by taking FOL3930 Italian for Spanish Speakers III, when offered, or ITA2220 Reading and Conversation, the third level of the basic Italian program. Usually, Spanish speakers tend to choose FOL3930 over a basic Italian course not only for the experience of learning Italian through Spanish, but also to have fewer weekly meetings and pay for fewer credit-hours.

During the first year of implementation and until we are able to consistently offer Italian for Spanish Speakers in the first three levels, we decided to write the syllabi of FOL3930 following a mixed communicative and intercomprehension approach. Students of the basic Italian courses study vocabulary and grammar at home, where they also complete written exercises–

mostly non-communicative drills. In class, they practice these structures through communicative activities and by engaging in meaningful interactions. The Italian for Spanish Speakers courses follow the same model but integrate these practices with activities based on the Intercomprehension approach.

4. Intercomprehension Approach

The intercomprehension approach emphasizes the similarities among languages to facilitate the comprehension of a foreign language (Doyé, 2004). According to this approach, the active or passive knowledge of one or more languages of the same family of the target language helps learners to easily understand and acquire its lexical, phonetic, morphological, and syntactic aspects. When reading a text in the target language, a learner makes meaning of its linguistic features through metalinguistic and meta-communicative adjustments, a constant negotiation with other learners, and a collaborative reformulation of the meaning of the text (De Carlo and Anquetin, 2011). These activities foster the collaborative construction of the meaning of a text (Bonvino, Caddeo, Vilagines Serra, and Pippa, 2011), encouraging learner-content, learner-teacher, and learner-learner interaction.

FOL3930 students complete intercomprehension activities in class and at home, either individually or in groups. In class, each student introduces to her classmates a news article of her choice. Students read the text and answer a set of questions in groups. At home, students access the Facebook page of the course and complete activities based on written, audio, and audio-visual texts. They usually have to complete these activities individually, but they can ask other classmates and the instructor for clarifications and help. Due to the accelerated pace of the course and the reduced class time, the practice on Facebook makes up the majority of the intercomprehension activities.

5. Facebook for Language Learning

Facebook is the most popular social networking site among American college students (Junco, Heibergert, and Loken, 2011). On Facebook, users usually express themselves and engage in social interactions that are similar to the ones that language instructors try to reproduce in class to foster language acquisition (McBride, 2009). We decided to create a Facebook page for FOL3930 students to increase their exposure to the target language and to provide a familiar, informal environment where students can access authentic material and interact in the target language.

Facebook users usually connect to Facebook more than once a day to update their profile, interact with other users, browse the news feed, and access the material posted by their friends or the pages that they follow. At the beginning of the course, we invite the FOL3930 students to "like" the Facebook page using their personal account. Every time we post new material, FOL3930 students who "liked" the page can see it in their news feed. Students thus have access to the learning activities at every moment of the day and everywhere they are. Through the Facebook page, the target language overcomes the logistic barriers of the class and becomes part of students' daily life.

So far, all the FOL3930 students used their personal Facebook account and did not express any concern related to privacy. Students do not have to be connected with the instructor or the other classmates (i.e., Facebook friends) to interact on the page. As Facebook users, students also control the degree of information disclosed on their profile to friends and non-friends. In an academic context, this greatly reduces the risk for privacy issues.

5.1 *Language Learning Activities on Facebook*

The activities on Facebook do not substitute for but integrate other language learning activities. FOL3930 students learn new vocabulary and grammar at home, read passages from the textbook, and complete online exercises. They then practice the recently acquired language features in class and on Facebook, where they also complete the intercomprehension activities devised by the instructor.

The Facebook page is organized in two main sections, the Wall and the Event pages. On the Wall we post most of the intercomprehension activities and other relevant content, including the links to the Event pages. The activities of each event are built around the lexical topic of the current unit. For example, in the "Presentations" event students practice how to introduce themselves and other basic structures of the Italian language, while in the "Food" event they further explore vocabulary related to this topic and practice the grammar structures covered in the same unit. All activities are based on authentic material retrieved from the Internet. Students access online sources (i.e., web pages, images, videos, audios), search for information, or answer a set of questions in the target language.

Students' activities on Facebook–both on the Wall and the Events–are graded. For every interaction students receive a participation point, regardless of its correctness. Every week students can receive a maximum of four points that combine with the six points of the in-class participation, for a total of 10 points. The participation grade counts for a 12 percent of the final grade (Appendix B).

5.2 Intercomprehension Activities on Facebook

As we mentioned above, FOL3930 follows a mixed communicative and intercomprehension approach. The class time for intercomprehension activities is, however, limited. We develop our own intercomprehension activities following the principles and practices of the most important resources in the field (i.e., EuRom5, Galanet, EuroComRom, InterRom, Interlat). These activities are, at the same time, theoretically sound, based on consolidated practices, and tailored to our specific context and audience. For example, we select a news item or video related to the topic covered on the current Facebook event and develop an activity following the EuRom5 model. When the students complete this activity, they not only get input in the target language but they also come into contact with authentic and meaningful cultural information about Italy.

Developing these activities from scratch, posting them regularly on Facebook, monitoring students' answers, and providing the necessary feedback are time consuming. However, we consider it an efficient way to integrate an already dense syllabus with practices whose goal is: to improve students' comprehension of the language; to actively engage them in the learning process; and to boost their perception of self-efficacy in their skills in the target language. Any language instructor in any educational setting can follow a similar model provided that she is willing to invest the time in the development and monitoring of the activities.

On Facebook, we propose two different types of intercomprehension activities, based on written or aural texts. In both cases, we select an online text in Italian and post its link on Facebook. Following consolidated intercomprehension practices, on a "post," we present the title of the text translated in Spanish, a vocabulary "box" with the less comprehensible words and expressions of the text translated in Spanish, and a set of questions. The students access the text–on a different browser tab if it is a written text and on the same page if it is a video, refer to the vocabulary box for clarifications, and answer the questions in Italian using the "comment" feature.

Since the answers appear in chronological order, from the oldest to the newest, it is not possible to control whether the students who post later are actually offering their own answers or just slightly modifying the answers of their classmates. This is of little concern to us since we are more interested in their participation effort. In any case, students do not always give the same answers, in fact very often they word them quite differently. They may read the answers of their classmates but, in most cases, even if they do, it appears that they actually read the text before completing the activity.

Intercomprehension activities are not mandatory, but students complete them to receive four out of 10 weekly participation points. During a week, we post an average of eight to nine activities on the Wall and the current Event page, three to four of which are aimed at fostering students' comprehension skills. Students usually interact only in four or five of these posts; only about half of the class usually completes a specific intercomprehension activity.

5.3 *News and Other Texts.*

The majority of the texts that we select for the intercomprehension activities are online news. These activities are modeled on EuRom5 and aim at fostering students' intercomprehension skills while at the same time exposing them to some aspects of Italian society and culture. We select news pertaining to Italian culture, chronicle, sport, technology, and entertainment. We always provide the direct link to the original text without modifications. At the beginning of the course we explain to students that they should not expect to understand every word in the text in order to complete the activities; what is important is that they grasp the general meaning of the sentences. According to the intercomprehension approach, Spanish speakers are able to figure out by themselves the meaning of most of the Italian words that have a common root with a Spanish word of the same lexical family. Moreover, in the vocabulary box, we also offer the Spanish translation of the less clear words and expressions in the text, in order to facilitate the overall comprehension of the text.

The FOL3930 are basic Italian courses. Students who enroll in the first-semester course usually have little or no prior reading experience in the target language. For this reason, we usually select short, catchy news so as not to overwhelm or scare students. Because we need to pay attention to the length of the news item, our sources are usually not the most important online Italian newspapers (i.e., *La Repubblica*, *Il Corriere della Sera*, Huffington Post Italia) but rather Italian news agencies' websites (i.e., ANSA, ASCA, AGI), or Internet-based news aggregators (i.e., Yahoo! News) (Appendix A). We also try to alternate the sections from which we choose the news and to diversify the topics, in order to present different aspects of Italian society and cover ample vocabulary. Finding a short, interesting, and appropriate article can be tricky, but, given the wide array of news sites, it usually does not take more than 10 minutes.

Once we have the article, we create a post with the link and the Spanish translation of the title, to give students a better idea of the article's topic (Figure 1). We then devise a set of questions–usually four or five–to assess and stimulate students' understanding of the text. Most of the time the questions require a short answer that can be found directly in the text or can be easily inferred. For example, we can ask students for the name of a place or the price of a product mentioned in the article or to deduce from the given information the effects of a heavy snowfall on city traffic. Students answer these questions in a post's comment box and, when necessary, they receive feedback from the instructor. This feedback can simply be in the form of a "like" when the answers and the language are correct, or it could appear as a comment on the student's post by using the "reply" feature. Feedback is usually provided at the end of the week when all students have had the chance/opportunity to complete their assignments. Sometimes students use the comment feature to ask for clarification on the meaning of parts of the text or to express personal opinions on the news–usually in Spanish or English. The rest of the class tends not to engage with these comments, but the instructor always does, when it is appropriate.

Figure 1. Intercomprehension activity on Facebook: News.

We also create intercomprehension activities based on online texts that correspond to the same topic as the current Facebook Event. For example, for the "City" event, we search for a short text that describes an Italian city and then create an intercomprehension activity following the news model (Figure 2). We then add the activity on the event along with the other language learning activities on the same topic. It may not always be easy to find a text that is relevant, understandable, and short enough for our purposes. We usually find these texts on thematic websites (e.g., on tourism, recipes, fashion) or in blogs. Varying the sources of the articles is advisable in order to expose students to different communication and writing styles.

Italian for Spanish Speakers, Fall 2013
September 9, 2013

Leggi il testo e rispondi alle domande:

LE PIÙ BELLE CITTÀ D'ITALIA

Venezia, per la sua caratteristica unica di città "acquatica", conta il più elevato flusso di turisti in Italia. Dichiarata nell'anno 1987 dall'Unesco, patrimonio dell'umanità accoglie i visitatori in ogni periodo dell'anno.
Venezia è famosa anche per il suo Carnevale che attira milioni di visitatori nel periodo di febbraio e marzo.
Milano è la capitale della produzione d'Italia ma soprattutto un centro d'arte e di cultura: qui ci sono famosissimi teatri, edifici storici quali il Duomo e il Castello Sforzesco, gallerie d'arte, boutiques di moda.
Senza dimenticare la città dei sette colli, Roma, un vero e proprio museo a cielo aperto: in tutti gli angoli, dal Vaticano al Colosseo, dal Lungotevere al Pantheon, la capitale regala fiabesche atmosfere, legate alla storia della nostra nazione che si perde nella notte dei tempi...
(Adattato da http://www.regioni-italiane.com/belle_citta.htm)

Attira = atrae
Senza dimenticare = sin olvidar
Angoli = rincones
Fiabesche = de fábula
La notte dei tempi = la noche de los tiempos

Quale città italiana ha il flusso di turisti più elevato?
Cosa si celebra a Venezia a febbraio?
Qual è la capitale commerciale d'Italia?
Dov'è il Lungotevere?
Dov'è il Castello Sforzesco?
Quale città italiana ti piacerebbe (te gustaría) visitare?

Like · Comment · Share · 💬 4

Figure 2. Intercomprehension activity on Facebook: Online text on the current lexical topic.

5.4 *Videos and Audios.*

The other type of intercomprehension activity on Facebook is based on aural text (i.e., audio and video recordings). These activities have the same structure as the news. Students access a posted video or audio recording and answer a set of questions. We mostly post videos in Italian in order to provide authentic linguistic inputs, offer snapshots of Italian society and culture, and focus on "an Italian point of view." The topics of the videos and audio files need to be suitable for an academic environment and should provide a simple plot and authentic dialogues that are relatively understandable for beginning language learners. These videos are mostly short films that we find on YouTube and are no longer than six to eight minutes.

Another valuable source is cartoons that are either Italian or dubbed in Italian. Since they are mostly aimed at a younger public, they generally use a simple language, and the characters tend to repeat the key words of the episode often. One of our favorite animations is *Peppa Pig*, a famous British cartoon chronicling the life and adventures of a 5-year-old pig-child and her family and friends. Each episode lasts five minutes and presents a main topic (e.g., grocery shopping, public transportation, school) that we can use for vocabulary input. We select an episode related to the topic currently covered in class, post its link on the current Facebook Event, and create a set of questions. Questions normally focus on some words that students already know and that are mentioned in the episode (i.e., "What does Peppa buy?" "What is George eating?"). However, questions can be a bit more challenging and thread on unfamiliar vocabulary because videos offer added visual clues for comprehension. Students can, then, be asked to look up vocabulary or expressions that they don't know but that are present in the episode. Other sources that we use are *Pimpa*, an Italian cartoon narrating the adventures of a puppy dog who behaves like a child, and episodes from famous Walt Disney cartoons. We also create intercomprehension activities from Italian movie clips, advertisements, songs, cooking recipes, radio advertising, and brief interviews.

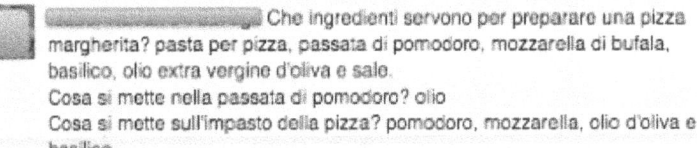

Figure 3. Intercomprehension activity on Facebook: Italian recipe video.

Following Chapelle's (1998) suggestion, we have recently started to provide a transcription of the oral texts highlighting the linguistic features on which we want students to focus attention. This is a time-consuming task for the instructor but it allows us to offer comprehensible input rather than just input, with evident potential benefits on students' learning.

Finally, sometimes we also use videos and audio recordings from language learning sources such as textbooks and websites. These sources provide specific and simplified input and usually focus on a single topic (i.e., job interviews, presentations, leisure activities). Even if this material is easier to use in a language learning setting, we prefer to use authentic material and provide comprehensible input when it is necessary. Indeed, engaging students with authentic online material promotes its use beyond the boundaries of the course, prompting students to become autonomous and lifelong learners (Garrett, 2009).

6. CLASS ACTIVITIES

Although class time for intercomprehension practice is limited, we start each class with an intercomprehension activity modeled on the practices described in EuRom5. Every day a different student presents an item from the Italian news. Following our instructions, she selects an online news story from one of the suggested news agency websites and posts the link on Facebook, along with a set of questions in Italian for her classmates. In class, the presenter projects the news and introduces it, translating the title in Spanish. Her classmates read the news and, in groups of three or four, negotiate the meaning of the text and answer the questions. When they cannot understand a word or expression, they ask the presenter for clarifications. At the end, the groups share their answers with the class. This activity benefits both the student who presents and the rest of the class. The presenter has to consult different sources in Italian in order to select a text that is appropriate for the level of the class, while the other students have regular opportunities to read in Italian and develop their intercomprehension skills. Furthermore, this is a good starting exercise for the class, as it makes students actively participate from the very beginning of the session.

7. Outcomes

In general, FOL3930 students appear to be more proactive learners than students in regular Italian language classes. They especially appreciate the intercomprehension approach and engage in constant comparisons between the languages and cultures. They particularly like to practice their intercomprehension skills on Facebook, where they can access a great amount of authentic information on Italian culture in a friendly and familiar environment. According to an informal survey that we conducted with FOL3930 students (N=38) during the past two semesters, students like to conduct intercomprehension activities (62 percent). They usually read the news on Facebook (80 percent) and understand most of the information (75 percent). They also stated that the vocabulary box helps them to better understand the written texts (78 percent) and that when they see or hear a grammar structure or vocabulary that they have already encountered in class they usually recognize it (49 percent). The same percentage of students claimed that they can understand a great deal of written Italian. They believe that accessing written and aural texts in Italian helps them learn Italian better (67 percent). Finally, they would like to continue reading Italian news and to complete other intercomprehension activities on Facebook in their next FOL3930 class (67 percent).

The activities that we described here can be easily adapted in different teaching settings, both at the high-school and college level, as they supplement and enhance a regular curriculum. For example, the practices that we carry out on Facebook can be proposed on other educationally oriented platforms, such as learning management systems (e.g., Blackboard, Moodle) or social learning platforms for teachers (e.g., Edmodo). These activities are particularly appropriate for an exploratory stage of course development, given that administrative constraints and fear of innovation often prevent visionary instructors from offering a full-blown intercomprehension course.

BIBLIOGRAPHY

Blanche-Benveniste C., Valli A. (1997). L'intercompréhension: le cas des langues romanes. *Le Français dans le monde-Recherche et Applications*, 33-37

Bonvino, E., Caddeo, S., Vilagines Serra, E., & Pippa, S. (2011). *EuRom5, leggere e capire 5 lingue romanze*. Milano, Italy: Hoepli.

Census Bureau. Retrieved November 8, 2013, from http://www.census.gov/.

Chapelle, C. (1998). Multimedia CALL. Lessons to be learned from research on instructed SLA. *Language Learning & Technology, 2*(1), 22-34.

De Carlo, M., & Anquetin, M. (2011). L'intercomprensione: da pratica sociale a oggetto della didattica. In M. De Carlo (Ed.), *Intercomprensione e educazione al plurilinguismo* (pp. 27-97). Porto Sant'Elpidio, Italy: Wizarts editore.

Doyé, P. (2004). A methodological framework for the teaching of intercomprehension. *Language Learning Journal, 30* (1), 59-68.

Garrett, N. (2009). Computer assisted language learning trends and issues revisited: Integrating innovation. *The Modern Language Journal*, 93 (Focus Issue), 719-740.

Junco, R., Heiberger, G., & Loken, E. (2011). The effect of Twitter on college student engagement and grades. *Journal of Computer Assisted Learning, 27*(2), 1-13.

Krashen, S. D. (1997). *Foreign language education the easy way*. Language Education Associates.

McBride, K. (2009). Social-networking sites in foreign language classes: Opportunities for re-creation. In L. Lomicka & G. Lord (Eds.), *The next generation: Social networking and online collaboration in foreign language learning* (pp. 35-58). San Marcos, Texas: CALICO.

Shih, R. (2011). Can web 2.0 technology assist college students in learning English writing? Integrating "Facebook" and peer assessment with blended learning. *Australasian Journal of Educational Technology, 27*(5), 829-845.

Appendix A

VALUABLE ONLINE SOURCES

This is just a small sample of the wealth of resources that can be retrieved on the Internet to create Intercomprehension activities.

News
- Italian news agencies' websites:
  - ANSA: www.ansa.it
  - ASCA: www.asca.it
  - AGI: www.agi.it
- News aggregator: Yahoo! Notizie Italia: http://it.notizie.yahoo.com/
- Newspapers:
  - La repubblica: www.repubblica.it
  - Il corriere della sera: www.corriere.it
  - Huffington Post: www.huffingtonpost.it
  - La stampa: www.lastampa.it

Other websites
- Tourism. Italia.it: www.italia.it
- Sport.
  - La gazzetta dello sport: www.gazzetta.it
  - Tuttosport: www.tuttosport.com
  - Corriere dello sport: www.corrieredellosport.it
- Music.
  - Rolling Stone: www.rollingstonemagazine.it
  - Extra!: www.xtm.it
- Television. TV Sorrisi e Canzoni: www.sorrisi.com
- Fashion.
  - Vogue: www.vogue.it
  - Vanity Fair: www.vanityfair.it
  - Glamour: www.glamour.it
- Recipes.
  - Giallo zafferano: www.giallozafferano.it
  - Misya: www.misya.info
- Science.

- - Focus: www.focus.it
  - Le scienze: www.lescienze.it
- Technology.
  - Wired: www.wired.it
  - BitCity: www.bitcitymagazine.it
- Women.
  - Cosmopolitan: www.cosmopolitan.it;
  - Donna moderna: www.donnamoderna.com;
  - Al femminile: http://www.alfemminile.com
- Men. Max: http://max.gazzetta.it

Videos

YouTube (www.youtube.com) and Vimeo (www.vimeo.com) are our go-to sites for videos, especially cartoons, movie clips, advertisements, and songs.

Appendix B

FOL3930 Syllabus Sample
General Information

The format of this class is based on the premise that the best way to learn a foreign language is through repeated, meaningful exposure to the language along with opportunities to interact with others, in class and online. Class consists of short presentations by your instructor and a lot of interaction among you and your classmates along with the instructor. In order to help you reach the goals of the course, most of the instruction will take place in Italian. Your instructor will also use Spanish as a bridge to Italian to promote your comprehension of Italian and accelerate the acquisition process. You must try to express yourself in Italian from the beginning using your expanding vocabulary and lots of gestures. Be especially careful with words/verbs/expressions that are similar in Italian and Spanish! While you can easily understand them, you may often reproduce them in Spanish instead of Italian.

Course Components and Grading Scale

You must earn a final grade of 70 percent (C-) in order to pass this course and continue on to the next level. Students taking this course for a grade of S/U must earn a minimum of 70 percent (C-) in order to receive a grade of S. Your final grade will be determined from the following components:

In-class and online participation (12)	12%
Homework	18%
Daily (Workbook/Textbook/Lab)	*4%*
Cultural activities (4)	*6%*
Writing assignments (Temini) (4)	*8%*
Unit Exams (4)	28%
Mid-Unit Quizzes (5)	10%
Final	20%
Oral exams (2)	12%

Participation and Preparation
Of your final grade, 12 percent is devoted to participation and preparation.

Although your attendance is expected (see *Attendance Policy* above), it is not enough to simply "show up" to earn these points. Research has shown that people learn languages best when they are actively engaged in the process. If you miss class, no participation points can be awarded for that day. Each day (except exam days) your instructor will make a mark in his/her grade book regarding your participation and will assign you a daily grade.

Daily participation will be graded according to the following scale:

2 points
- Arrived on time, attended full class, and participated in all activities.
- Brought all necessary material (including textbook) to class.

1 point
- Arrived less than 10 minutes late to class and/or left early.
- Did not participate and/or did not pay attention. Used cell phone or laptop improperly.
- Displayed behavior deemed inappropriate by instructor.

0 points
- Absent or arrived more than 10 minutes late.
- Repeated improper use of cell phone and laptops.

Additionally, you are supposed to actively participate in the online activities on the Facebook page of the course (your instructor will give you specific instructions during the first week). Every week your instructor will assign you a grade according to your participation. Weekly participation will be graded according to the following scale:

4 points
- Actively participate on the proposed activities during different days, upload material, comment on material uploaded by the instructor and other classmates (4+ interactions on different days)

3 points
- Participate on the proposed activities during different days, upload material, comment on material uploaded by the instructor and other classmates (3 interactions on different days)

2 points
- Sporadic participation on the proposed activities or concentrated in a unique session (2 interactions on different days or 2+ interactions on only one day)

1 points
- Only one interaction on the proposed activities.

0 points
- Null participation on the proposed activities.

COURSE SCHEDULE – SAMPLE

TERZA SETTIMANA	
Lunedì 20 gennaio Presentazione di una notizia alla classe. **Unità 1,** *Parliamo italiano!* **La geografia:** • Guarda il video "Italia Much More" e scrivi il nome di tutti i termini geografici che riconosci. Compara la tua lista con quella di un compagno. • In gruppo, guarda la cartina dell'Italia e rispondi alle domande dell'esercizio 1.2. • Di dove sei? Presentati a un compagno e digli di dove sei ("Mi chiamo… Sono di…"). **Il sostantivo singolare e l'articolo indeterminativo:** • Maschile o femminile? Aggiungi l'articolo alle parole della lista dell'esercizio 1.10. • In gruppo, abbina le figure con le parole della lista e aggiungi l'articolo corretto (fotocopia).	(DUE by 11:59pm yesterday) **Esercizi online (Quia).** Unità 1, *Parliamo Italiano!* - Workbook: Attività 1, 2, 6. - Lab: Attività 1, 2.
mercoledì 22 gennaio Presentazione di una notizia alla classe. **Unità 1,** *Parliamo italiano!* **La città:** • Leggi le parole della lista e abbinale alle figure (fotocopia). • Guarda il video "Milano – Italy" e, in gruppo, descrivi il centro di Milano. **I pronomi soggetto, il verbo essere, il negativo:**	(DUE by 11:59pm) - **Composizione culturale** 1. Leggi le istruzioni su Blackboard → Materiale del corso → Composizioni culturali, e completa l'attività. (DUE by 11:59pm yesterday) **Esercizi online (Quia).** Unità 1, *Parliamo Italiano!*

• I pronomi soggetto e il verbo essere: completa le frasi dell'esercizio 1.26. • Il negativo: Scrivi due frasi su di te (sobre ti) e due frasi sulla tua città, una positiva e una negativa.	- Workbook: Attività 3, 4, 5. - Lab: Attività 3, 4.
venerdì 24 gennaio Presentazione di una notizia alla classe. Unità 1, *Parliamo italiano!* **L'articolo indeterminativo singolare:** • Maschile o femminile? Aggiungi l'articolo alle parole della lista dell'esercizio 1.30. **I mesi e le stagioni:** • Leggi il testo "Le quattro stagioni" e, in gruppo, rispondi alle domande (fotocopia). • Completa le frasi dell'esercizio 1.34. **Il verbo avere:** • Guarda le figure della fotocopia e scrivi che cos'hai e cosa non hai.	(DUE by 11:59pm yesterday) **Esercizi online (Quia).** Unità 1, *Parliamo Italiano!* - Workbook: Attività 8, 9, 11. - Lab: Attività 5. **Facebook.** Attività sull' home page e l'evento *La città*.
QUARTA SETTIMANA	
lunedì 27 gennaio Presentazione di una notizia alla classe. Unità 1, *Parliamo italiano!* **Le espressioni idiomatiche con avere:** • Guarda le tre pubblicità e descrivi che cos'hanno (freddo, fame, ecc…) i protagonisti del video. **Le preposizioni semplici:** • Scrivi dove abitano le persone famose dell'esercizio 1.45. • Guarda la foto proiettata e, in gruppo, rispondi a questa domanda: dove sono i gatti? **La data:** • In gruppo, rispondi a queste domande: Che giorno è oggi? E domani? E l'altro ieri? E fra una settimana? E il mese scorso? E fra un anno?	(DUE by 11:59pm) - **Temino 1.** Leggi le istruzioni su Blackboard → Materiale del corso → Temini, e completa l'attività. (DUE by 11:59pm yesterday) **Esercizi online (Quia).** Unità 1, *Parliamo Italiano!* - Workbook: Attività 10, 12. - Lab: Attività 6, 7.
mercoledì 29 gennaio Presentazione di una notizia alla classe. Unità 1, *Parliamo italiano!* **La data:**	(DUE by 11:59pm yesterday) **Esercizi online (Quia).** Unità 1, *Parliamo Italiano!* - Workbook: Attività 14, 17.

• Leggi il testo "Le festività italiane" e rispondi a queste domande: che giorno è Natale? E Santo Stefano? E Capodanno? E l'Epifania? Che giorno è Ognissanti? E Pasqua, quest'anno? Che giorno è l'anniversario della liberazione italiana? E la festa della Repubblica? E la festa del lavoro? **Il presente indicativo dei verbi della prima coniugazione:** • Completa le frasi dell'esercizio 1.55 con il verbo corretto. • Guarda il video "Verbi in –are" e scrivi una frase per ognuna delle azioni che fai abitualmente. Chiedi poi a due compagni cosa fanno loro.	- Lab: Attività 8.
venerdì 31 gennaio Presentazione di una notizia alla classe. **Unità 1, *Parliamo italiano!*****L'ora:** • Guarda le immagini della fotocopia e, in coppia, rispondi a questa domanda: che ora è? • Leggi il testo "Le abitudini degli italiani" e rispondi a queste domande: A che ora fanno colazione/pranzano/cenano di solito gli italiani? A che ora vanno al lavoro? A che ora vanno in pizzeria? A che ora vanno a dormire? **Ripasso per l'esame 1.**	(DUE by 11:59pm yesterday) **Esercizi online (Quia).** Unità 1, *Parliamo Italiano!* - Workbook: Attività 18, 20, 21; Lab: Attività 9. (Due by 11:59pm Sunday) **Facebook.** Attività sull' home page e l'evento *Quando? A che ora?*

The "French/Italian for Spanish Speakers Project": From Idea to Permanent Program

Markus Muller
California State University, Long Beach

1. Introduction

The following report summarizes the development of the "French/Italian for Spanish Speakers Project" as it has evolved over the last nine years in the Department of Romance, German, Russian Languages and Literatures (RGRLL) at California State University, Long Beach (CSULB). Particular attention will be given to the administrative and curricular context of this project, our deepening understanding of the Intercomprehension Teaching Method as it was developed in Europe, and finally the progress that we made in our efforts to enhance our students' foreign language learning experience by combining the Intercomprehension Method with the Communicative Teaching Approach. I will also touch upon the NEH grant's impact on the project and how it has allowed us to expand the idea of teaching French/Italian to speakers of Spanish. This report will address both the challenges as well as the benefits of this ongoing project from an administrative, curricular, and pedagogical perspective.

Over the years, my colleagues and I have presented our research, our classroom experiences, and the data derived from student surveys involved in this project at workshops and conferences in the United States and abroad. In particular, we presented at ACTFL in 2009, 2011, 2012 and 2013, at the John D. Calandra Italian American Institute in New York in September 2013, and in various language and literature departments at universities in and outside of California. Two recurring reactions by the audience should be mentioned here as they anticipate numerous points I will address later in this report. First, teachers of Romance languages such as French, Italian, and Portuguese in high schools and colleges alike have noticed the steadily growing number of Spanish-speaking students in their classrooms. This is due primarily to the growing number of heritage Spanish speakers but also to the fact that many non-Hispanic students study Spanish as a second language in high school or college. Second, the recognition of this demographic trend is rarely followed by curricular and/or administrative actions. While many of our colleagues feel overwhelmed by the difficult task of addressing the linguistic needs and learning styles of these students without any institutional help, others have taken matters into their own hands by developing their own curriculum and teaching materials. While a growing interest in heritage speakers in general, and Spanish heritage speakers in particular, has led to a considerable body of research, the establishment of heritage speaker resource centers, as well as curricular innovations in this field at many institutions of higher education, nonetheless emerging research on multilingual and multicultural students and how they fit into the paradigm of the "communicative" foreign language classrooms has not entered mainstream discussions among language educators yet.[1] It is fair to say that the initial focus of our research and curricular innovation evolved around the Spanish-speaking students for whom we sought to develop a more efficient and effective approach to learning another Romance language. We quickly realized, however, that the overarching issue of having students with multiple language and cultural backgrounds in our classrooms would have to transcend our more narrowly defined initial approach. We hope, therefore, that our project will contribute to a sustained national discussion on how we can improve the teaching of foreign languages to account for this new demographic paradigm.

2. INSTITUTIONAL CONTEXT OF OUR PROJECT

The Department of Romance, German, Russian Languages and Literatures is a mid-size multilanguage and literature department with currently 16 full-time faculty in four MA programs in French, German, Italian (a recently approved MA, which welcomed its first cohort of graduate students in Fall 2014), and Spanish. The department also offers a Minor in Russian and a two-year lower-division language course sequence in Arabic. One of the largest universities in the California State University system, CSULB is a Hispanic-serving institution embedded in an urban environment with a Hispanic/Latino population of approximately 40 percent.[2] It was the steadily in-

---

[1] Claire Kramsch has published a number of enlightening studies on this subject).
[2] http://quickfacts.census.gov/qfd/states/06/0643000.html

creasing number of Hispanic surnames on the class rosters in our lower-division French and Italian language courses that first led us to inquire about the actual "linguistic make-up" of the students, and we discovered that classes in both languages were comprised of upward of 50 percent of Spanish heritage speakers. In addition to these heritage Spanish speakers, we found a significant contingent of non-Hispanic students who had studied Spanish in high school or had acquired it by other means. Not to pay attention to this development would have been a disservice to these students, and the idea of finding a more suitable teaching approach to accommodate their learning needs was born. It is important to point out that the value of this project is independent of the students' ethnic, economic, or social background and only considers their pre-existing linguistic competence in Spanish as a selection criterion for enrollment purposes. It has always been our explicit goal to provide a more efficient and more effective way for students to build on their existing linguistic knowledge when they learn another Romance language. That such a project is, on the other hand, of particular academic, professional, and personal value to the large Hispanic student body on our campus is a significant outcome of our efforts and will be discussed later.

2.1 *First steps*

Limited to the teaching of a single section of "French for Spanish Speakers," the origin of this project can be traced to the year 2005 and a visit by the cultural attaché of the French Consulate in Los Angeles to our department, which was followed by the French Consulate giving a small grant to French and Italian professor Dr. Clorinda Donato that the department has been using to fund scholarships for Spanish-speaking students studying French. The value of this initial recognition of the French for Spanish Speakers project by the French government cannot be underestimated as it established not only the financial basis for this project, but also led to a closer intellectual collaboration between us and French experts in the field of European (French) intercomprehension studies and teaching methodology that continues to this day. A defining moment of our collaborative efforts occurred in Spring 2009 when two specialists in this field, Pierre Escudé and Pierre Janin, visited our campus. Their considerable knowledge and experience in this area[3] has led to a sustained collaboration with Pierre Escudé from the University of Toulouse, who has visited our campus twice since 2009. More recently, Elisabetta Bonvino, a researcher and teacher of the Intercomprehension Method at the Università degli Studi Roma Tre, has joined the growing number of specialists such as Kim Potowski and Claire Kramsch who contributed to the project.[4]

To move from student support through scholarships to teaching French to only Spanish-speaking students was the next logical step in the project and presented us with two concrete obstacles. Initially, we had no means to separate our non-Spanish-speaking from the Spanish-speaking students prior to the start of the semester, and we were forced to recruit students into a single designated section of French for Spanish Speakers by personally visiting all sections of our first-semester French course during the two-week open enrollment period at the beginning of each semester. This somewhat cumbersome process of recruiting students into the designated French (and later also Italian) for Spanish Speaker sections at the beginning of the semester remained with us until we created the necessary new courses with their own catalog numbers and titles. But even as we managed to have separate course numbers and titles, small problems presented unexpected obstacles. For instance, we initially called the courses "French (or Italian) for Hispanophones." Because students were confused by or simply did not know what "Hispanophones" meant or what level of Spanish they were required to have to enroll in these courses, they enrolled in the regular French or Italian language courses. Consequently, we changed the course titles to "French (or Italian) for Spanish Speakers." To make things even clearer, footnotes in our online course schedule now provide the students with basic information explaining the nature of these courses, prerequisites, and/or an enrollment recommendation.

Even the numbering of the course had to be adjusted. We first numbered our French/Italian for Spanish Speakers courses 102A and 102B to parallel the numbering for our regular courses (101A and 101B). Many of the Spanish-speaking students told us that they enrolled in the regular course (101A) instead of 102A because they thought the higher course number required a

---

[3] http://www.csulb.edu/misc/inside/?p=3763
[4] See Also Donato, this volume

more advanced knowledge of French (or Italian). We finally settled on 100A and 100B for French and Italian for Spanish Speakers, and despite our best efforts to be as clear as possible, we still experience some enrollment fluctuation at the beginning of the semester, but the initial enrollment is strong enough in all sections to protect them from course cuts. Success and a growing awareness on campus (through centralized advisers, publicity, and events) of the existence of our project have also contributed to making our enrollment management and staffing of these courses more predictable.

As of Fall 2014, we have the following courses in place:

- French/Italian 100A and French/Italian 100B: Elementary French/Italian for Spanish Speakers (4-unit courses each). These two courses mirror our regular French/Italian 101A and 101B courses in the sense that they are taught with the same textbook and an only slightly modified syllabus. The difference lies in the fact that we introduce substantial intercomprehension elements (referred to as "bridges") into the lesson plans on a regular basis that allow Spanish speakers to almost "naturally" pick up grammatical features in the target language (French or Italian) with which they are already familiar (the use of reflexive verbs, for instance) in their native or acquired language (Spanish). We have been creating these materials over several years of studying and working with Intercomprehension materials and by trying to "couple" them in the most effective manner with the Communicative Approach. I will return in more detail to the pedagogical aspect of this project later.
- French/Italian 200: Intermediate French/Italian for Spanish Speakers (6-unit intensive course taught in hybrid format; four traditional face-to-face hours plus two hours on online work). Just like the 100A and 100B courses, French/Italian 200 are taught parallel to our existing second-year courses with the difference that they combine two semesters' worth of materials into a single semester.

The following chart provides a timeline and lists the various course titles/numbers starting in 2009 when they first appeared in the class schedule. Prior to this date, we taught "French for Spanish Speakers" in specially designated sections of our regular "French 101A and 101B: Fundamentals of French" (first and second semester) courses. The corresponding second-year course did not appear until 2012. At this point, it is also helpful to state that all language courses in our department have been scheduled twice a week (either Monday/Wednesday or Tuesday/Thursday) in blocks of two hours (for four credit hours per course).

CATALOG #	TITLE	FROM	TO
ITAL 102	Fund. of Italian for Hispanophones	Fall 2009	Spring 2011
ITAL 102A/B	Fund. of Italian for Hispanophones	Fall 2011	Spring 2012
ITAL 100 A/B	Fund. of Italian for Spanish Speakers	Fall 2012	Present
ITAL 200	Int. Italian for Spanish Speakers	Fall 2012	Present

CATALOG #	TITLE	FROM	TO
FREN 102	Fund. of French for Hispanophones	Fall 2009	Spring 2011
FREN 102A/B	Fund. of French for Hispanophones	Fall 2011	Spring 2012
FREN 100A/B	Fund. of French for Spanish Speakers	Fall 2012	Current
FREN 200	Int. French for Spanish Speakers	Fall 2012	Current

Changing course numbers and titles was a largely administrative issue and only had the above-mentioned minimal effect on student enrollment that was solved by personal invention and through curricular changes. What remained was the problem of providing students with a smooth path through the course sequence into the second year and hopefully into upper-division courses leading to a minor or major in French and Italian. While any multi-section language program can offer a variety of days/times for its sections of the same level, we could offer only one section of 100A, 100B, and 200 each semester for each language. Finding a day/time for these sections that would assure maximum enrollment thus amounted to a guessing game despite our efforts to gauge the students' scheduling preferences through polls that we conducted in all French/Italian sections. Even after a number of attempts to change the days/time blocks (8–10am or 10am–12pm or 12–2pm), we could not establish any predictable enrollment pattern and resorted to scheduling the French/Italian for Spanish Speaker courses during the most popular times (10am–12pm or 12–2pm). As a result of the restricted number of sections we can offer, we still "lose" Spanish speakers to our regular French or Italian sections due to their scheduling conflicts. Our recent efforts in creating online language courses might solve the scheduling conflict, and we are in the process of evaluating the feasibility of French/Italian for Spanish Speakers courses that are completely online.

3. THE IMPACT OF THE ECONOMIC CRISIS

The financial collapse of 2007–2008 and the ensuing economic crisis went largely unnoticed in terms of overall student enrollment in our department as student numbers in all language programs remained fairly stable through 2011. The shrinking budget forced us, however, to serve the same number of students with significantly fewer sections. In other words, we were asked to raise our enrollment caps significantly. Fewer sections also meant less flexibility and fewer options for students. The situation for us became even more unpredictable and perilous when the university implemented an enrollment cap policy of 13 units during the first months of enrollment. This cap of 13 units is not lifted until approximately three weeks prior to the start of the semester. Consequently, non-language majors try to cover their major-specific courses or other requirements before they contemplate enrolling in a language course and, to make matters worse, are frequently advised not to study languages and to concentrate on a timely graduation instead.

To counter the negative effect of these policies on our programs, we provide our students with a maximum of flexibility for their scheduling needs and allow them to switch from the "traditional" to the "Spanish Speakers" course sequence during the first year (see explanation and chart below). For example, students are allowed to enroll in "Italian 100A: Fundamentals of Italian for Spanish Speakers" during the first semester and continue with the regular "Italian 101B: Fundamentals of Italian" in the second semester before enrolling in "Italian 200: Intermediate Italian for Spanish Speakers" in the third semester of their language study sequence.

The creation of our two intensive and hybrid format French/Italian 200 courses was primarily a pedagogical response to our observation that the students in the French/Italian for Spanish Speakers courses reached, on average, a higher level of competence compared to the students in our regular courses. This higher level is particularly noticeable in the students' speaking and reading skills. For instance, we observe high levels of reading comprehension already during the very first semester (in comparison to the regular courses) and an increasing willingness to communicate in both Spanish and the TL as the students advance through the course sequence. Consequently, we wanted to produce a course that would adequately address their learning needs with the additional benefit of also offering them a faster path toward upper-division course work and ultimately the minor and major in one of the languages. In hindsight, this pedagogically inspired move had an administrative benefit that we could not anticipate when I first started writing the Standard Course Outlines for the intensive and hybrid format French/Italian 200. By the time French/Italian 200 were officially included into the university catalog in Fall 2012 (see chart above), the budget crisis had reached its height in both the CSU and UC systems. While we saw a signification drop in enrollment numbers in language courses in our department and consequently had to cut the number of sections offered, the reduction of units in a lower-division language course was welcomed by the administration because the single-semester 6-unit course not only saves students two units compared to the usual eight units over two semesters, it also saves students a full semester. The impact of this cannot be underestimated in an environment where timely graduation policies seem to dictate our students' enrollment patterns.

As we slowly emerge from the economic crisis and return to a more "normal" operational mode, we observe that its impact on our project and the department overall is multifaceted. On the one hand, it is clear that the shrinking number of sections in language courses has made it very difficult for us to maintain the complete sequence of courses (as a case in point, we had to cancel a low-enrolled section of French 100B: French for Spanish Speakers in Spring 2014), and significant enrollment fluctuations are still possible. At the same time, we witnessed significant stability if not growth in the Italian for Spanish Speakers sequence, where we have been able to schedule and fill two sections of Italian 100A for Spanish Speakers for a third semester in a row.

The chart below compares the two tracks that our students can use to advance through the lower-division sequence and illustrates how they can save units and time. The right column in Semester 4 shows, for instance, that students in the Spanish Speaker sequence can enroll in an upper-division course and thus earn units toward their minor or major while the students in the other sequence are finishing their last lower-division language course.

	Traditional Course Sequence	Italian for Spanish Speakers Sequence
Semester 1	French 101A (4 hours)	French 100 A (4 hours)
Semester 2	French 101B (4 hours)	French 100 B (4 hours)
Semester 3	French 201A (4 hours)	French 200 (6 units)
Semester 4	French 201B (4 hours)	Any upper-division course in French
Total cr. hours	16 units	14 units

One of the most recent developments in our ongoing efforts to provide a streamlined access to the minor and major in Italian can be seen in the chart below. In contrast to the French program where we currently offer the 6-unit hybrid course in the Spanish Speakers sequence, Italian has eliminated the traditional 201A and 201B sequence completely from its schedule and only offers the 6-unit hybrid courses at the intermediate (second-year level).

	Traditional Course Sequence	Italian for Spanish Speakers Sequence
Semester 1	Italian 101A (4 hours)	Italian 100 A (4 hours)
Semester 2	Italian 101B (4 hours)	Italian 100 B (4 hours)
Semester 3	Italian 200 (6 hours)	Italian 200 (6 units)
Semester 4	Any upper-division course in Italian	Any upper-division course in Italian
Total cr. hours	14 units	14 units

3.1 *Two distinct benefits for students:*

Many of the benefits of our new approach to teaching French and Italian were known only intuitively to us in the beginning and emerged over the years through trial and error and through student questionnaires, surveys, testimonials, our improving knowledge with the intercomprehension method and finally our growing experience to integrate intercomprhension teaching modules in our communicative language teaching.

    a. Learning community. What was described above as a disadvantage, namely the fact that we normally offer only one section of French/Italian for Spanish Speakers, has developed into an advantage from a student learning perspective. The benefit of "traveling" through the first- and second-year courses in a community of students who share the same interest cannot be underestimated, especially in a discipline such as language studies. These learning communities contribute to a significant lowering of the affective filter, on the one hand, and create a motivational and interactive learning environment on the other. We rarely see such learning communities develop on a large scale in traditional multisectional language programs where students normally meet just two or three of their peers when they move to the next level in the language course sequence. The positive effects of "traveling" and experiencing language learning with a larger and relatively unchanged group of students was not obvious to us until we had developed and taught all three courses in the French/Italian for Spanish Speakers sequence. We realized at one point that once students reach the 200 level of French/Italian for Spanish Speakers courses they display, by comparison with their peers in the traditional 201A/201B sequence, a greater willingness to speak in front of others and, in general, have better communicative skills. Consequently, they feel empowered and find a greater level of satisfaction in their learning experience. Once they have completed the entire sequence, they are also more likely to pursue their language studies with a minor or even a major in French or Italian.

b. Hybrid courses: Our 6-unit hybrid courses (four traditional face-to-face classroom hours and two hours of online interaction with both the instructor and classmates) have had a significant impact on our recruitment efforts. Several developments contributed to the creation of the 200-level hybrid courses French/Italian 200 (Intermediate French and Italian for Spanish Speakers). It was our explicit goal from the beginning to provide students in the entire course sequence not only with a language learning experience that better accommodated their existing language competence, but also with a tangible benefit with regard to the time that they had to spend in the language courses before moving on to the upper-division level. Advances in technology, the lack of classrooms, and our universities' timely graduation policy further contributed to our desire to offer another teaching format. The development of hybrid courses had just started on our campus at that time, and we seized the opportunity to develop these 6-unit hybrid format courses that combine two semesters' worth of French/Italian into one semester.

The creation of these hybrid courses presented a number of curricular and administrative challenges. First of all, there were pedagogical concerns about merging a year's worth of teaching materials into a single semester with a significant hybrid (online) component. Second, we needed to find instructors with the necessary energy and enthusiasm to teach an intensive class and were willing to do the required training for the online component. Furthermore, we could not clearly gauge whether the students would be willing to enroll in this course given its particular make-up and the above-described administrative challenges. As we assess the outcome of our curricular innovation, in particular the creation of these hybrid courses, from today's perspective, we find that our early experiment with hybrid courses in the French/Italian for Spanish Speakers project had an unintended benefit for the department overall during the recent economic crisis. Because our students in the French and Italian for Spanish Speakers courses reacted well to the 6-unit hybrid courses (and the obvious saving of time and credit hours), we created duplicate 6-unit hybrid courses for all our regular first- and second-year language courses and moved them through the curricular process. At the height of the economic crisis in California (Fall 2012), the department came under intense pressure to drastically reduce its number of course offerings. The fact that we are now able to offer 6-unit hybrid courses allows us to accommodate both the administration's and the students' demand for an accelerated progress through the basic language course sequence. In Spanish, for example, we started to offer one section of Spanish 100 (combined first- and second-semester Fundamentals of Spanish in a single 6-unit hybrid course) in Fall 2012 and added the equivalent for the second year (Span 200) in Spring 2013. Today, we offer three well-enrolled sections of Span 100.

Developing these hybrid courses caused us to work more closely with new technologies and the online student management tools that accompany our textbooks and ultimately improved our entire curriculum. This work could not have been accomplished without the energy and tenacity of many tenured and part-time faculty as well as numerous Teaching Associates (TAs) who have taken leadership roles in the development of these courses by experimenting with online quizzes and alternative synchronous and asynchronous online teaching tools. Especially beneficial is this work for our graduating MA students/TAs who can enrich their CVs with the acquired knowledge in this field and the experience gained from teaching a variety of different courses.

4. Instructors and Instruction (Teaching Materials):

Since 2001, the department's entire lower-division language program has been directed by the Language Coordinator (LC) who also trains and mentors the Teaching Associates and part-time instructors. TAs from all languages take the Teaching Methodology course together, normally during their first semester in the MA program. They establish relationships with their peers in other languages from the beginning and frequently work together even though they do not teach the same language. Since I, as Language Coordinator, was involved in the French/Italian for Spanish Speakers project very early and taught a course in 2009, I also made this project a topic of our Methodology course discussion and workshops. Many TAs, notably the ones with language competences in French and Spanish (or other languages), showed interest and, through the NEH workshops, started to participate in the project. They visited courses taught by their colleagues and small-group training workshops and gradually started teaching first- or second-semester

French/Italian for Spanish Speakers courses. In Italian, for example, we recruited a native speaker of Spanish, Violet Pasquarelli-Gascon, who is also fluent in Italian, to teach our first courses in Italian for Spanish Speakers courses. Today, all French/Italian for Spanish Speakers courses are taught by TAs or part-time instructors whose roles often go beyond teaching the courses and now include the development of teaching materials, training of new TAs, and collaboration with our high-school partners.

One of the most frequent questions we receive pertains to the qualification of the instructors and their language knowledge of Spanish. It is important to point out that we continue to teach French and Italian with a primarily task- and proficiency-oriented Communicative Approach to which we add specifically and carefully designed intercomprehension modules that direct students toward significant commonalities in syntax and morphology among Romance languages. As a general rule, Spanish functions always as the primary support language when we teach French while Italian, and occasionally also Portuguese, are used to provide further evidence of the systemic similarities among these Romance languages (accordingly, French and Portuguese function as support languages in Italian classes). It would be impossible to require any of our instructors to be fluent in all these languages. As it happens, all instructors in our French/Italian for Spanish Speakers project have significant competencies in Spanish. However, while it is certainly helpful if teachers of Italian/French for Spanish Speakers courses can converse with their students in Spanish, should this be necessary for clarity's sake, advanced- or superior-level oral proficiency is certainly not a requirement. On the other hand, a solid working knowledge of Italian or French and Spanish grammar is necessary for the instructor to adequately understand and present the points of connection, be they morphological or syntactic, between the target language (French or Italian) and the primary (Spanish) or occasional secondary (Portuguese) support languages.

The following describes how our intercomprehension modules are integrated into the otherwise Communicative Approach. First of all, both traditional and French/Italian for Spanish Speakers courses use the same textbook and cover the same amount of work (chapters). This is a fundamental prerequisite for the point I made earlier about students switching from the traditional to the intercomprehension sequence (or vice versa) during the first year. For reasons of consistency and coherence at all levels and in all sections, all instructors need to cover the same amount of material to reach the same benchmarks with regard to the course goals and student learning outcomes so that students are adequately prepared for the upper-division curriculum.

The principal goal of the intercomprehension modules is to facilitate the students' understanding of already present yet dormant knowledge in the area of morphology, grammar, or culture. A short discussion of the concept of verb conjugation will serve to illustrate the difference between a standard approach in any of the current French or Italian textbooks whose default assumption is that all learners in the classroom have little to no knowledge of verb conjugation as it exists in French or Italian. Such an assumption was more accurate some 30 or 40 years ago when the demographic and linguistic background of our students was less varied than today. As a result, most of these textbooks continue to lead students through a carefully prepared yet very lengthy path that begins normally with a treatment of subject pronouns (often with the additional restriction to the first to third person singular) and a chapter-by-chapter presentation of regular ar- er- or ir patterns followed by irregular patterns down to such subtleties as verbs with changing accent marks or spelling changes. Irregular verbs such as "avoir," "être," "faire," or "aller" are introduced along the way and where appropriate to the other topics covered. This *tabula rasa* approach to students whose native or acquired languages (Spanish, Portuguese, or German for that matter) treat verb conjugation more like French and Italian has led to a fundamentally flawed and inefficient teaching approach for a growing number of students. In contrast to this, our intercomprehension modules purposely awaken dormant knowledge through systemic and sustained comparisons using multiple Romance languages (Spanish, Italian, or Portuguese) to make obvious what Spanish-speaking students already know. The attached sample lesson on verb conjugation demonstrates how students are asked to work with various languages to develop their understanding of verb conjugation and also meta-linguistic competence. (Footnote 4: For an example of how this is presented in *Juntos: Italian for Speakers of English and Spanish*, see Appendix.)

4.1 Classroom conduct and language use

One of the most significant outcomes of our project is the collective realization that certain classroom behaviors of the past have been detrimental to the actual patterns of communication among students and between student and instructor. While immersion and communication in the target language still has high priority for us, we also realized that it could easily have a stifling impact on students' willingness to participate in class. Countless classroom observations provide evidence that an instructor's push to have students speak exclusively in the target language can also lead to silence rather than communication. One of the fundamental pillars of intercomprehension is the idea that a group of people can communicate with one another because they understand the other's native language but do not speak it. The same principle is, in essence, applied in our French/Italian for Spanish Speakers courses (and to a lesser degree also in our traditional language courses). For example, students in an Italian for Spanish Speakers class speak by default English and Spanish and in some cases also other languages. The instructor uses the target language (Italian) close to 100 percent of the time. Students are also asked to make every effort to use Italian but are allowed to use Spanish (or English) when they want to contribute but cannot find the necessary word or construction in Italian to say what they think is important to add. This is neither a waste of effort from an intellectual point of view—
since the student makes a contribution to a class discussion, for instance—nor is it a waste in terms of language acquisition. If the student understood the instructor's question in Italian and provides a perfectly logical reply in Spanish he or she demonstrates at least comprehension of Italian. This seemingly small change in our approach to classroom interaction had a significant impact on our students' overall behavior. They feel empowered and rather than remaining silent because they feel embarrassed to make a mistake in the TL, they contribute using the language with which they are most comfortable. This code switching or *interlanguaging* contributes positively to the student's learning experience and to a more vibrant classroom atmosphere.

After some experimentation with the format in which we introduced our intercomprehension modules into our communicative approach, we found it most efficient and effective to divide our 4-hour weekly schedule into three hours of communicative and one hour of intercomprehension lessons. Syntactic or morphological connections, or "bridges" as we call them, between the target and support languages are carefully developed by our instructors and introduced whenever a given grammar point is covered in the textbook. For example, there is significant overlap in the way reflexives are used in Spanish, French, and Italian. Whenever reflexives are covered in the French textbook, the instructor introduces his intercomprehension module. The same applies to the Italian for Spanish Speakers class, where reflexives are treated at a different point in the textbook. Because the Italian and French teachers work closely together, they can use each other's intercomprehension modules simply by switching one language from target to support language and vice versa. This procedure maximizes the use of the textbook.

What greatly facilitates the learning of French/Italian to speakers of Spanish is the fact that the need for traditional "teaching" is greatly reduced. If students are properly exposed to the syntactic or morphological connections through qualitatively and quantitatively adequate input, or bridges, they simply "get" the point.

This type of teaching has had and continues to have an astounding impact not only on our students but also on our instructors as it has significantly stretched and expanded the boundaries of our Communicative Language Teaching paradigm.

5. NEH Grant and its Impact

It is fair to say that the French/Italian for Spanish Speakers project made a significant leap forward after we received a $100,000 grant from the National Endowment for the Humanities (NEH). The impact that this recognition by the NEH had on our work in the department, the college, and with respect to our collaboration with the French and Italian Consulates in Los Angeles and the Embassy of France in Washington cannot be overstated. The announcement of the grant in various CSULB campus publications was followed by a series of reports on radio (NPR), television (Univision), and in print (the Spanish International News Agency EFE) that further cemented the value of this project. For the first time, students who were enrolled in one of the courses or who had graduated from the program had an opportunity to express their personal views and impressions of this project and the impact it had on their academic career and personal life. One of the most striking values of the project, expressed by numerous Spanish heritage speakers, was the psychological boost they received from having their Spanish language recognized as an academic asset and not as a linguistic liability.

At the department and college level, the NEH grant provided us with some sort of "protection" from course cuts. At a time when the campus and the department still experienced budgetary pressures and calls for more cuts, the possibility of losing single courses or even the entire sequence was a constantly recurring problem. Given that we experienced occasionally low enrollments (around 15 students) in some of the courses, offering the entire course sequence was never guaranteed. The situation became significantly better with the NEH grant because the research and outreach/training aspect of the grant were directly linked to the French/Italian for Spanish Speakers courses themselves because they represented the only locus where we could conduct research and provide hands-on training for our instructors. These classes were also the only place where we could test the teaching modules that we started to produce.

Aside from the financial, administrative, and scheduling benefits that we have gained from this 3-year NEH grant (Fall 2011 to Fall 2014), it has enabled us to make significant advances in our understanding of the intercomprehension method in conjunction with a critical assessment of our approach to communicative language teaching and learning. It has furthermore provided much-needed visibility on campus for our department. Finally, as the article by Ida Lanza and Daine Hartunian illustrates, the NEH grant has cemented our collaborative work with community colleges and high schools in our area.

On November 1, 2014, we concluded our 3-year NEH grant with a final meeting at the campus of CSULB with approximately 20 instructors who have contributed a tremendous amount of thought, time, and energy to this project. Their contributions and feedback from the classroom where they tried out this new method have been extremely helpful. For the first time, we will also welcome administrators from CSULB, Long Beach City College, Los Angeles Unified School District, the French and Italian Consulate in Los Angeles, and various high schools in Long Beach and San Pedro to celebrate the success of this project and discuss its expansion beyond Southern California.

BIBLIOGRAPHY

Donato, C., Oliva, C.J., Romero, M., and Zappador-Guerra, D. (2014). *Juntos: Italian for Speakers of English and Spanish.* https://csu.redshelf.com/book/53536/juntos-italian-for-speakers-of-english-and-spanish-9780990728801-clorinda-donato-cedric-joseph-oliva-manuel-romero-daniela-zappador-guerra

Kramsch, C. and Huffmaster, M. (2014). Multilingual practices in the foreign language classroom. In J. Cenoz and D. Gorter (Eds.), *Language and Intercultural Communication in the New Era* (pp 23-38). London: Routledge.

Kramsch, C. (2014). Teaching Foreign Languages in an Era of Globalization: Introduction. *The Modern Language Journal,* 98 (1): 296-311.

Kramsch, C. (2009). *The Multilingual Subject.* Oxford: Oxford University Press.

APPENDIX

Lesson 18
Il presente

In Italian and Spanish, the present tense of regular verbs is formed by dropping the infinitive ending and adding regular personal endings.

habla**r** → habl	am**are** → am
habl**o**	am**o**
habl**as**	am**i**
habl**a**	am**a**
habl**amos**	am**iamo**
habl**áis**	am**ate**
habl**an**	am**ano**

come**r** → com	prend**ere** → prend
com**o**	prend**o**
com**es**	prend**i**
com**e**	prend**e**
com**emos**	prend**iamo**
com**éis**	prend**ete**
com**en**	prend**ono**

vivi**r** → viv	dorm**ire** → dorm
viv**o**	dorm**o**
viv**es**	dorm**i**
viv**e**	dorm**e**
viv**imos**	dorm**iamo**
viv**ís**	dorm**ite**
viv**en**	dorm**ono**

Stem changes

The stems of regular verbs sometimes change in the present tense. The tables below introduce some common stem changes in Italian and Spanish.

| e → ie | o → ue | e → i | u → ue | stem + y | stem → isc |
empezar	poder	pedir	jugar	construir	capire
empiezo	puedo	pido	juego	construyo	capisco
empiezas	puedes	pides	juegas	construyes	capisci
empieza	puede	pide	juega	construye	capisce
empezamos	podemos	pedimos	jugamos	construimos	capiamo
empezáis	podéis	pedís	jugáis	construís	capite
empiezan	pueden	piden	juegan	construyen	capiscono

Sometimes a letter is added or omitted to maintain certain sound.

| stem − i || stem + h ||
cominciare / mangiare		cercare / spiegare	
comincio	mangio	cerco	spiego
cominci*	mangi*	cerchi	spieghi
comincia	mangia	cerca	spiega
cominciamo*	mangiamo*	cerchiamo	spieghiamo
cominciate	mangiate	cercate	spiegate
cominciano	mangiano	cercano	spiegano

Mona Lisa in the Classroom:
An Educational Proposal for Integrated
Training in Intercomprehension

Diego Cortés Velásquez

1. Introduction

Intercomprehension studies is a relatively recent field with a highly interdisciplinary connotation: It is linked to all those disciplines that deal with the study of the closeness between languages (mutual intelligibility, semicommunication, receptive multilingualism, and so on), to those that deal with comparisons between languages such as Comparative Linguistics and Contrastive Analysis (Blanche-Benveniste, 2001), and at the same time related to those subjects whose aim is the acquisition/learning of languages (Second Language Acquisition Studies, bilingualism, plurilingualism/multilingualism, heritage language learning).

Language acquisition/learning may also include research that has IC as its main objective. Over the last two decades several application proposals have been developed in order to achieve this objective, some of which have been quite successful (see Bonvino in this volume). The implementation of these educational proposals, inspired by the IC approach, has led to the emergence of some important factors:

a) IC constitutes an answer to plurilingual education and has been encouraged on various occasions by EU member states (i.e., White Paper on Education and Training, 1995);
b) it has highlighted some aspects of communicative competence such as partiality and the existence of the phenomenon of approximation (Blanche-Benveniste, 2008);
c) it has provided significant knowledge regarding input in acquisition (what is learned in a language course and in an IC-based course and how input is processed during comprehension);

d) it has provided important observations on the assessment used by traditional methods: e.g., the lack of listening practice, which is extremely important in language learning;
e) it has contributed to the implementation of plural approaches in which more than one language is studied in a single course, which is in contrast to the idea of singular approaches with just one language;
f) it has emphasized the positive transfer that learners of closely related languages may make based on the transparencies that they have in common, as opposed to the approaches of a contrastive analysis in which similarities between languages may even be seen as an obstacle to a "perfect" L2 acquisition.

The aim of this work is first to describe EuRom5, one of the most widespread tools for teaching IC, and then to describe a typical training session with EuRom5; afterward, some experiences characterized by special contexts will be described and some concrete examples of teaching activities will be proposed that have been developed as a result of EuRom5 trainers' various classroom experiences. A program will be proposed for a more in-depth and extended development of oral comprehension and for collaborative work online of target audiences with specialized languages.

2. EuRom5: Synthesis and Strengths

EuRom is the name of a method for the simultaneous learning of Romance languages using an IC approach (see Bonvino in this volume), and it originated from the seminal work of Claire Blanche-Benveniste (1997) in the early nineties. The long experience gained by Blanche-Benveniste and her research team during the realization of the EuRom4 project was transferred to the publication of the handbook *EuRom4: simultaneous Romance languages teaching method*, released in 1997 by La Nuova Italia press.

EuRom5 is the enlarged and revised edition of EuRom4. This new edition, coordinated by Elisabetta Bonvino, includes Catalan and takes into account the experience gained through years of using the method in many courses.

EuRom5 is addressed to speakers of one of five languages (Portuguese, Spanish, Catalan, Italian, and French), adults with a good educational background and who are good readers in L1. The objective of EuRom5 is to train the learner to understand texts dealing with general topics in a short time (approximately 35/40 hours). At the end of the course, the students can reach B1 or partial B2 level; that is, they are able to read newspaper articles by themselves or different texts related to their interest areas, using a dictionary to look for those few words they cannot understand. The aim of EuRom5 (as for EuRom4) is not a complete mastery of the four languages. In such a limited time, only "an incomplete" knowledge included in the partial competences is possible.

This incomplete competence is however perfectly adequate and will help beginners to be more relaxed, as it shows learners how to follow an autonomous comprehension program (Blanche-Benveniste, 1995).

The EuRom5 method is essentially based on five factors, implicit in the initial hypothesis, which largely mirror the guidelines of most modern language education:

- Similarity between Romance languages
- Transfer and exploitation of a learner's personal knowledge as an important contribution in the classroom
- Approach to simultaneous learning of languages
- Attention to the reading process
- Introduction of "authentic" texts (Gilmore, 2007; Mishan, 2005) into the learning situation

EuRom is therefore a method—founded on the principles of intercomprehension (cf. Bonvino and Escudé in this volume)—for development aimed at reading ability. For this reason, paying attention to the process, strategies, and techniques of reading has always played a central role. Reading in L2 is seen as a complex combination of linguistic-cognitive processes, since it involves the reader using various strategies, in order to reconstruct the meaning of a text in a flexible and interactive way. In this connection, the objective of the EuRom5 method is firstly to try and help learners to understand and interpret a text using a global approach to the meaning and by learning how to reutilize those reading mechanisms that they already know in their mother tongue, as well as using their knowledge of the world and making use of inference too. Learners also need to learn to decode texts by splitting up some words or by identifying important similarities between their L1 and other languages, exploiting interlinguistic transparency without losing sight of the entirety of comprehension, and integrating textual and extra textual information.

Table 1 summarizes the main features of EuRom5 from the point of view of learners and trainers.

Learner	is immediately exposed to a text in a language never studied before
	deals with several languages in the same session
	listens to the reading of the text by a native speaker
	can read the translation of the title in five languages
	deals with understanding the meaning by him/herself
	can use several hints and tips
Trainer	makes it easy
	encourages the learner
	promotes independent use of strategies and cooperation
	may not have a high level of competence in all languages
	leads the learner to autonomy

Table 1. EuRom5 methodological aspects for learners and trainers

Furthermore, it should be emphasized that one of the pivotal points of EuRom is what has been defined as "the right to approximation" in comprehension, as argued by Blanche-Benveniste (2008, p. 58). She states that those who are good readers in their L1 are able to understand a text without being interrupted in their reading by words they do not know. They do not proceed "word by word," but rather by sets of words. They base their reading on inferences on various levels before guessing some of the unknown words. Good readers therefore accept, for short or long periods, that they have areas of approximate comprehension. They use different types of comprehension for the same text, some of which are very approximate, while others are more precise.

Thus readers do not necessarily always need to understand all the words and details of a text. They may accept and be happy with understanding the overall meaning, something that also happens when they read texts in their own L1.

3. Description of a EuRom5 Session

From the very first session the learners have to deal with a text in a language they have never studied before, and the goal is trying to understand it. In order to facilitate comprehension, the translation of the title and the reading out loud of the entire text are provided. After reading and listening to the text, the learner tries hard to understand the meaning in a completely independent way. This kind of activity concerns languages never studied before by the learners, and since it is based on the *problem solving* method, it is experienced as a stimulating challenge, which increases motivation, thus relieving the learner's anxiety.

Since the learners have never experienced any explicit teaching of these languages, they generally join in the challenge with enthusiasm.

In order to verify if learners have understood and mainly to share the path taken toward the correct or wrong meaning with the entire class, the so-called "transposition of the text in L1" (Bonvino et al., 2011) is required. The transposition is not a real translation; it is rather similar to the *thinking aloud technique* (Bowles, 2010). This transposition using the learner's mother tongue is very interesting to observe: The reader proceeds step by step through gradual adjustments.

During this phase, the learners have the chance to ask questions about the main differences between the target languages and their native tongue. Their second choice would be relying on the strategies suggested by the tutor or on other contextual aids supplied by the handbook.

During the experimentations we have noticed that the starting point of the intercomprehension process is the proximity between languages, which is evident in the lexical transparency. The vocabulary is the main factor on which the understanding of a text depends. If it is transparent, from one language to another, it enables comprehension also in the case of complex syntactic structures. This phenomenon is widespread in Romance languages, in which there are many potentially identifiable lexical elements.

In Table 2 stages of a EuRom5 session are described.

	Stage 1
Listening to the recording of the text performed by a native speaker	• Encourage a comprehensive approach to the text and capture relevant information • Identify the construction of the sentence and any symmetries between groups of words • Clarify any opaque spellings
	Stage 2
Reading the text from the title translated into five languages	• To grasp the main idea • To create hypotheses and inferences about the content of the article and the meaning of linguistic items
	Stage 3
"Transposition" of text into L1	• To make explicit the cognitive processes (hypothesis and strategies) by readers • Co-construction of text meaning (*problem solving*, individual and collective)
	Stage 4
Consultation of aids for comprehension	• To confirm or refute the hypotheses formulated about the content of the text and the meaning of lexical items • To overcome an obstacle to understanding

Table 2. Description of EuRom5's methodological stages (adapted from Fiorenza and Bonvino, 2011)

In order to provide a better description of a session, a dialogue is shown here in which a Spanish-speaking student, whom we refer to here as Juan,[1] takes part in a EuRom session. We follow Juan as he reads a complex text that has not been simplified in a language that he has never studied. In order to analyse Juan's reading and comprehension processes we used a visual representation (*Tables 3, 4, and 5*) that is not flattened on the linear dimension and accounts for the successive approximations that lead to comprehension. This visualization of the interaction in class between trainer and learner aligns the Italian text on the paradigmatic axis with the transposition of meaning carried out by Juan and with all the attempts and observations that accompany this reading:[2] On the horizontal axis there is the sequence of positions—syntagmatic—which defines the construction; on the vertical axis there is the possible paradigmatic realization of each position.

---

[1] By using Juan's experience we can summarize the experience of using the EuRom manual in Spain and Latin America.
[2] The tool that makes it possible to simultaneously show the syntagmatic and paradigmatic dimensions is showing sequences in a grid, a system defined by Claire Blanche-Benveniste and her collaborators (for further details see Blanche-Benveniste et al. 1979, and Bonvino & Cortés (in prep.).

Figure 1 shows the Italian text on which the session was based. The grid only shows the first 5 lines.

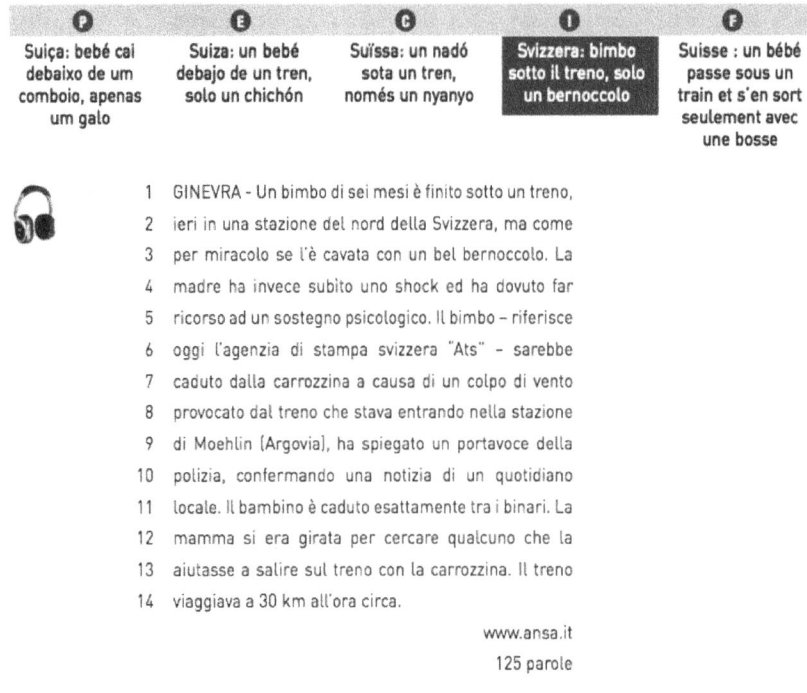

Figure 1. Screenshot of text I1A.

Table 3. Analysis grids for the interaction between Juan and his EuRom5 trainer

Juan managed to understand the text by himself. By observing the visualization adopted for the comprehension process, it can be noted that comprehension sometimes seems to start from a few key words and then spreads out until it covers or "constructs" the entire text, thanks to inferential processes. "Yesterday" was deduced from the linguistic context, thus filling an informative gap. It should be noted that not understanding the word "yesterday" would not impair the comprehension of the general meaning of the text. From these short exchanges it can be inferred that the trainer is a facilitator who tends not to supply translations, but rather encourages learners and suggests strategies.

	ma	come	per	miracolo	se l'è cavata	con un	bel	bernoccolo
J:	mas	como	por	milagro				
T: *Mira el título*								
J:						un	¿bello?	chichón
J:	pero	como	por	milagro	se hizo solo	un		chichón

Table 1. Analysis grids for the interactions between Juan and his EuRom5 trainer

As can be seen from the table above, some points were not translated so correctly, for example "se l'è cavata." In the case of "ha invece subìto uno shock" (table 5) too, the Spanish-speaking reader faces a twofold difficulty linked to the interruption of the verbal syntagm by the word "invece," apart from its lexical opacity, and by the verb "subìto" initially mistaken for a false friend "sùbito." The tutor's strategic advice is to skip over the obstacle and go on, which immediately makes it possible to understand the meaning of the text.

	la madre	ha	invece	subito	uno	shock	ed	ha dovuto	far ricorso	ad un	sostegno psicologico
J	la madre					shock					
J						shock es trauma					
J	subito será 'enseguida', ¿no?										
J	la madre			tuvo enseguida	un	trauma					
T	"subito" no es 'enseguida', sáltalo										
J	la madre	sufrió			un	trauma	y	tuvo que pedir			sostegno
J									es parecido a entonces debe ser	sostener apoyo psicológico	
T									sí, perfecto es		apoyo psicológico
J	la madre	sufrió			un	trauma	y	tuvo que pedir			apoyo psicológico

Table 5. Analysis grids for the interactions between Juan and his EuRom5 trainer

The teacher, whom we prefer to call "trainer," is in this case a facilitator who intervenes only when necessary. A trainer's main task is understanding the real difficulties in comprehension as well as encouraging, inciting, and stimulating group participation. Above all he must allow students to set their own pace and guide them along their individual paths for the acquisition of comprehension abilities. His main goal is not "to teach" something but to guide the comprehension process. Basically the student already knows everything he/she needs in order to understand. In the brief passage shown in the grid, the trainer gives the input necessary for exploiting the information given ("look at the title"), for skipping information that is not particularly important (" 'subito' isn't 'enseguida'; skip it"), or for continuing. He did not need to give any grammatical explanations.

The method adopted is in fact of an inductive kind. The teacher provides neither grammar rules nor the translation of texts. This fact is extremely important given that some less careful critics of this method have perceived a revival of the grammatical-translational method, which is still far more widely used in language teaching than people think (Larsen-Freeman, 2000), while the process of constructing meaning by means of EuRom still uses translation but puts much more emphasis on the processes underlying comprehension.

In table 6 a comparison is presented between the Grammar-Translation method and the EuRom5 method.

Grammar Translation method (As described by Jack C. Richards and Theodore S. Rodgers, 2001)	EuRom5 method
Deductive	Inductive
The goal of foreign language study is to learn a language in order to read its literature or in order to benefit mental discipline and intellectual development.	The goal of Romance languages study is to develop high competence of student's reading comprehension of closely related language in order to consult information from original sources.
Reading and writing are the major focus; little or no systematic attention is paid to speaking or listening.	Reading comprehension is the main goal. Writing in the target language is never requested. A certain amount of attention is paid to listening because it can help with reading comprehension. Furthermore, reading comprehension can be considered the starting point for developing listening skills.
Vocabulary selection is based solely on the reading texts used, and words are taught through bilingual word lists, dictionary study, and memorization. In a typical Grammar-Translation text, the grammar rules are presented and illustrated, a list of vocabulary items is presented with translated equivalents, and translation exercises are prescribed.	Every text has a glossary with the less transparent words that the student can consult, if necessary. The glossary is presented in the five languages to show lexical links in Romance languages. Grammar (actually called "Reading Grammar") is presented as an aid at the end of the handbook to explain the most interesting phenomena that can hinder reading comprehension. It was built from real difficulties found by learners during experimentation. No exercises prescribed.
The sentence is the basic unit of teaching and language practice. Much of the lesson is devoted to translating sentences into and out of the target language, and it is this fo-	The whole text is the basic unit of work. Comprehending the meaning is the problem-solving based focus of EuRom5.

cus on the sentence that is a distinctive feature of the method.	
Accuracy is emphasized. Students are expected to attain high standards in translation, because of the high priority attached to meticulous standards of accuracy.	The right of approximation is claimed. Students are asked to say what they understand and are not requested to be accurate, especially in the first sessions.
Grammar is taught deductively—that is, by the presentation and study of grammar rules, which are then practiced through translation exercises.	Grammar is faced inductively and is not the objective. The starting point is the text and the goal is to understand it. Some grammatical facts are shown as an aid to understanding better. No practice through translation exercises is provided. Reading texts aloud and transposition and continuous comparison between languages produce in-depth metalinguistic observations.
The student's native language is the medium of instruction. It is used to explain new items and to enable comparisons to be made between the foreign language and the student's native language.	The student's native language is the medium of instruction because it allows the transfer of knowledge in order to understand the text.
Just one language is studied at a time.	Four languages are studied in every session on the principle that knowing one language allows learners to understand several closely related languages.

Table 6. Comparison between the Grammar-Translation method and the EuRom5 method

Finally, it can be concluded that the role of the trainers is basically that of being a guide rather than a teacher.[3] What tutors really need to teach are a few formulas or linguistic facts, which in any case the best students will be able to discover by themselves. Trainers should keep this basic thought in

---

[3] In Italian the word 'docente' is good to use because it derives from the Latin 'DUCERE' which means 'to lead.'

mind every time they lead a session; as Blanche-Benveniste and Valli (1997) stated, "students learn what they find out by themselves."

3. Classroom Experiences

Since Blanche-Benveniste's idea became the EuRom method in the early 1990s, many IC courses have been taught in Europe and America. In the initial stage, several of these were conducted as part of research in order to test a corpus of texts identified by the team. Later, some European universities started using the EuRom4 handbook as an introductory course for linguistic learning, and in this way, the method became one of the most widespread tools for teaching IC.

In 2007, 10 years after publishing EuRom4 and having considered the introduction of some new features, Blanche-Benveniste decided to entrust a new edition to her pupil and collaborator Elisabetta Bonvino. The new edition of EuRom5 appeared in 2011 completely renewed and including Catalan as the fifth language. Subsequently, several courses have been organized in many universities.

Even if IC is not considered in a prototypical view a language teaching approach, it seems that the paradigm has slowly started to change. According to the REDINTER website (cf. Bonvino in this volume), which collects data from IC studies, the EuRom method has been used in more than 50 courses in the past 10 years, which is likely an underestimate if we consider that any educational institution includes IC as part of its program.

As part of the goal of this paper, two classroom experiences are described below that have been taught with EuRom5 in the past few years, one characterized by a blended program at Roma Tre University in 2012, and the other by a multilingual information management program at the Externado University of Bogotá.

The IC course carried out at the Università degli Studi Roma Tre in May 2012 (Educational College for Languages and Languages, Faculty of Arts and Philosophy) was a chance to carry out a didactic program in a *blended* form, in which the manual and the site related to EuRom5 were used and the method described above (cf. § 2) was followed. The course made it possible to evaluate the online use of EuRom5 for the first time, thanks to the site's having recently been set up. The course consisted of 16 classroom hours together with a guided self-learning program on reading and listening skills.

There were 18 students in the group, most of whom were Italian-speaking,[4] enrolled in the three-year degree course in Modern Languages for International Communication at Roma Tre. All the participants knew, to varying degrees, at least one of the following languages: English (B1/C1), French (A1/B2), German (A1/B2), Spanish (B1/C1), Russian (A2/B1), Arabic (B1), or Portuguese (A2). The objective of the course was to give the participants the tools for developing receptive skills in four unknown Romance languages simultaneously (Portuguese, Spanish, Catalan, and French).

Students took part in the course enthusiastically, and all the activities offered were carried out as planned. The high level of motivation was stimulated not only by the fact that all the students concerned were doing language courses, but also by their curiosity about an experimental and innovative course that could also be inserted into their study plan.

The program for each classroom lesson included an approach to the texts in unknown languages that followed the EuRom5 procedure and used the manual. Apart from these lessons, students were able to do a guided self-learning activity that focused on reading and listening skills. With a view to this, certain activities were proposed and organized in various modules (A, B, C, and D), which students could use by accessing a section dedicated to the EuRom5 course set up on the Moodle platform and made available by the Centro Linguistico d'Ateneo (CLA) at the Università Roma Tre.

The main objectives of the section dealing with reading were to monitor the self-learning reading programs for linguistic and didactic research and to make learners more aware of their own reading and comprehension processes. The reading activities consisted of a series of texts from the EuRom5.com site, preceded and followed by questionnaires to be filled out in order to gather data on the metacognitive behavior of the students (Fiorenza, 2012, pp. 56–57).

The listening activities consisted of two phases: preparing for the listening by means of a perceptive training with intensive listening work (identifying items in the sound flow, distinguishing items, and so on) and listening to texts that last for about one minute and are recordings of radio news programs in a podcast format that are available from iTunesStore Italia or Radio

---

[4] Most of the students were mother tongue Italian. Two were bilingual with a Romance L1 (Spanish and Rumanian). One had an L1 that was not a Romance language (Albanian).

France International for Portuguese, Spanish, and French and podcasts from iCat.cat, a Catalan broadcaster, for Catalan. These podcasts provide authentic material that has not been created for didactic purposes, and roughly the first minute of such broadcasts is used. Blanche-Benveniste made some suggestions about the initial oral IC training, which were widely followed. An initial point is the need to favor a more "standard" spoken language compared to more spontaneous spoken language to start with in the field of IC, since "il est plus facile de passer du plus formel au moins formel que de faire le trajet inverse" (Blanche-Benveniste, 2009, p. 20). The oral comprehension section also included the compilation of metacognitive questionnaires before and after the listening activities.

As far as the results of the reading activities are concerned, participants generally displayed an improved capacity for the perception of language systems, in the sense that they were able to integrate general things with details, or rather to reconstruct (even though only partially) the systems of more than one Romance language in a relatively short space of time. In many cases, at the end of the program students confirmed that they no longer perceived the Romance languages as being separate and often wanted to continue with this type of study, especially to develop other abilities too (oral comprehension and production).

From the point of view of the reading and listening metacognitive strategies, it can be noted that learners

a. acquire a greater capacity to regulate their learning processes;
b. seem to progressively increase the planning of their reading activities in terms of times, methods, and purposes;
c. seem to increase their attention to the text and their capacity to regulate their reading speed and to monitor their comprehension levels;
d. the data gathered seems to indicate those who are better at listening activities tend to plan better and focus their attention on decoding texts. Specifically, these students plan their listening activities by thinking about similar texts that they may have listened to in the past;
e. from the point of view of the bottom-up process, it was possible to ascertain the importance of the ability to recognize words

(which also includes the segmentation and recognition of the lexical units boundaries);
f. from the point of view of the top-down process, it has been possible to ascertain how good listeners consciously make greater use of inferences than less-good listeners. In particular they tend to reconstruct the meaning of a text by starting from the words they understand and in doing so activating *expectancy grammar*. Good listeners have shown that they are able to connect what they understand with what they know about a topic, and they can also use their own experiences to help with their comprehension;
g. transfer is one of the most important mechanisms in IC. The data gathered suggest that good listeners have been able to help themselves by using their mother tongue, because they were also more aware of this mechanism.

Following an assessment that was organized based on the certificates that students had for various languages, almost all of which were above a B1 level (Fiorenza and Bonvino, 2011). These results, achieved in a short space of time, are at the same time quite modest but also of great importance. They are modest in the sense that they cover only reading and listening (not production) of very specific types of texts. Yet they are very important since this high level of competence has been reached not in one but in four different languages and above all because this type of competence is one of the most important currently, given that most information is written down, either on paper or using multimedia.

In summer 2013 a series of three EuRom5 courses was organized by the Departamento de Derecho de los Negocios de la Facultad de Derecho de la Universidad Externado de Colombia. The purpose of the program was to enable students to develop their competence in reading newspaper articles in four Romance languages, with the aim that developing this competence would subsequently allow the participants to consult texts in their original language that relate to their professional fields and that the information consulted could then be used for reworking the tests in Spanish.

For this reason the courses were designed from the point of view of multilingual information management, which means that, via task-based activities, participants had to deal with various sources of information in different languages and then to manage the data collected from reading articles in the four languages studied (Portuguese, Catalan, Italian, and French) in order to rewrite a text in Spanish. Therefore the emphasis was not so much on the languages as on the content of the texts.

The program was divided into four phases:

- an introductory phase with EuRom5 to enable students to acquire the skills necessary for decoding the various degrees of transparency in the Romance languages (spelling similarities, morphosyntactic and lexical elements, and so on)
- a phase to enable students to start reworking and rewriting the information taken from new newspaper articles dealing with current affairs and news. For this part it was useful to prepare a dossier with up-to-date international news material, published in the languages studied in class, and to present the following type of activities to the class:
    o identify the information contained in the articles;
    o identify the specific information in each article;
    o rewrite the identified information into a piece of writing in their L1.
- a phase including the identification of a topic in which all the class are interested. It was necessary to prepare a dossier with excerpts and articles.
- an assessment of the level of understanding and ability to process information.

The courses, in which 28 people took part altogether, lasted 21 hours each and were organized in 3-hour sessions. The participants were mostly researchers, teachers, and students in the fields of public and international law. They all had Spanish as their native language apart from one English speaker who used Spanish as a bridge language.

The course concentrated on the EuRom5 method (cf. § 2), and the manual was therefore used in all the sessions. All the sessions made use of the manual and the site (for oral support). Starting from the fourth session new materials were introduced consisting of articles dealing with current affairs, and the introduction of these articles was the most novel and interesting part of this experience. Students were asked to carry out a task in which they had to produce a brief article in Spanish using the information included in each article. The task was composed of the following phases:

  i. individual reading: each student had a limited amount of time available (about 10 minutes) in order to skim read the articles.
  ii. comparisons with the other students with the aim of identifying the ideas contained in each article. This phase was very important as it led to a "co-construction" of the meaning of the text.
  iii. writing up the article.
  iv. sharing and commenting on the results with the rest of the class.

The riddle surrounding the enigma of Leonardo Da Vinci's famous painting the Mona Lisa, taken from the French text 20C from EuRom5, which was the basis for constructing a rewriting task and was used as an example for expository clarity. The work session was constructed around the French text, with the addition of some articles dealing with this topic that had recently been published in Portuguese (tab.3), Catalan (tab.2), Italian (tab. 3), and French (tab.4). The main theme of the texts is the identity of Mona Lisa, and the facts and theories reported in each article diverge slightly so that by reading each article different and important facts can be extracted.

Cientistas analisam ADN da alegada "Mona Lisa"

09/08 17:38 CET

Continua a saga para descobrir quem foi Lisa Gherardini, a alegada jovem que serviu de modelo para a famosa "Mona Lisa", de Leonardo da Vinci.

Esta sexta-feira, na Basílica da Anunciação, em Florença, cientistas italianos abriram a cripta onde estão os restos mortais de Francesco del Giocondo, marido de Gherardini, e dos dois filhos do casal. É nas ossadas dos dois filhos que está centrada, agora, a atenção dos estudiosos.

Os cientistas estão entusiasmados com mais esta etapa.

Table 7. An extract from the article in Portuguese[5]

---

[5]From the www.Euronews.com site

Els arqueòlegs creuen que un esquelet trobat a Florència pot ser el de la suposada Monna Lisa

Apareixen les restes de dues dones al convent de Santa Ursula, on va ser enterrada Lisa Gherardini

Dijous, 4 d'octubre del 2012 - 12:11h.   EUROPA PRESS / Barcelona

Dos esquelets, probablement de dues dones, són la nova troballa realitzada aquest dimarts pels arqueòlegs que fa temps que busquen les restes de Lisa Gherardini (1479–1542), la dona que podria haver estat la model de Leonardo da Vinci per a la 'Monna Lisa', al convent de Santa Ursula, a Florència, on va ser enterrada la suposada musa de l'artista italià.

Table 8. An extract from the article in Catalan

Monna Lisa, l'ultimo esame per il mistero delle spoglie

Aperta la cripta dei martiri, dove sono contenute le ossa di una parte della famiglia della prima modella di Leonardo. Si farà l'esame del Dna per confrontarle con le presunte spoglie della donna. L'appello alla Francia: "La Gioconda in Italia"

L'esame del Dna per tentare di svelare il mistero delle spoglie della Gioconda di Leonardo. Dopo 300 anni, a Firenze, questa mattina è stata aperta la Cripta dei Martiri dietro l'altare maggiore della Chiesa della SS.Annunziata. All'interno della tomba sono custoditi i resti del marito di Monna Lisa, Francesco di Bartolomeo del Giocondo e dei suoi due figli. Il primo, Bartolomeo, avuto dalla prima moglie e l'altro, Piero, di Lisa Gherardini, che l'uomo ebbe per seconda moglie.

Table 9. An extract from the article in Italian

> ### Mona Lisa, es-tu là ?
>
> 09/08/2013 17:38 CET
>
> Depuis plus de 500 ans, scientifiques et amateurs d'art tentent de percer les secrets de Mona Lisa. Des chercheurs de Florence continuent ainsi de suivre la piste de Lisa Gherardini, la femme qui aurait inspiré Leonard de Vinci.
>
> Après avoir découvert des ossements qui pourraient lui avoir appartenu, ces chercheurs ont décidé d'ouvrir le caveau où sont enterrés son mari et ses fils, le caveau de la famille des Giocondo.
>
> Ils pourront ensuite comparer l'ADN de ces squelettes aux ossements déjà retrouvés.

Table 10. An extract from the article in French

The classroom activity included a work session lasting three hours and was organized as follows: First of all, the French text 20C was read, according to the EuRom method (cf. § 2). Then photocopies of the other four articles were handed out, and the students were asked to skim read them: They were given about four minutes for each one in order to discourage a bottom-up type of reading (word for word). Students were then asked to work in groups of four, and the end product of the task was an article written in Spanish that included all the possible information contained in the four articles in their original languages. Working in groups led to observations about the text and a stimulating debate centred on the co-construction of the meaning. Students had to focus on the following main aspects:

- sharing their understanding of the texts: have we understood the same thing?
- identifying the important informative nuclei; which is the most interesting information?
- checking coherence in the news contained in the five sources of information. Do the articles contradict one another? Do they report the same events? the same hypotheses?
- deciding the layout of the final text: What slant should they give to the article?

- selecting the information in order to prepare the final text; which information should they use to enrich the article?

From a constructivist point of view, the work done in class was stimulating because it allowed students to:

- concentrate on the co-construction of the meaning (not of the linguistic facts) by using the skills developed during the course;
- prepare a test in Spanish, produced by consulting texts in languages that had not been studied before the course;
- compare their opinions with those of the other students;
- exploit the knowledge of the more expert students (for example those who already knew some French) with the idea of creating a proximal development area.

4. Conclusions

It is obvious that the training proposed by EuRom5, but also by other tools used for IC teaching, follows a different paradigm from that of the well-known communicative approach in its notional-functional realization (Finocchiaro and Brumfit, 1983). That is to say there is no presentation of teaching units dealing with various functions such as "greeting people," "making introductions," or "offering something," nor is there any teaching of specific notions of space, time, number, gender, and so on. There are also no activities for practising languages such as pattern drills or role-plays. The objectives of EuRom5 are ambitious and modest at the same time. They are ambitious inasmuch as the aim is to enable the reader to read complex texts that represent a linguistic input that has not been adapted for students and that, in the most widespread paradigm for language learning, would only by approached after at least 300 hours of lessons. Yet they are modest, since the aim is to understand only one type of text, not a novel or a poem and not even a speech or conversation between native speakers.

From the point of view of the learners' perception of the EuRom5 method, many aspects made a positive impression, especially the following:

- the centrality and autonomy of the learner;
- the simultaneity of the languages and the speed of the program;

- the "*focus on meaning*," or rather the attention paid to understanding the content of the articles together with the freedom of learners to choose which linguistic aspects to study in more detail, thus respecting the subjectivity of each individual learning path;
- exposure to complex input from the very first learning phases;
- the development of reading and comprehension strategies;
- thinking about languages and language.

In conclusion it may be asked whether it is possible to go beyond the comprehension of the texts included in the EuRom5 training course, how more skills could be integrated, and, if necessary, how the other abilities could be integrated and with what tools and learning programs.

Starting with the experiences described in this article, we have tried to consider these questions and attempted to develop some proposals, since we are convinced that the competences achieved by means of a EuRom5 training program can be capitalized on in a program that takes into account the immediate linguistic needs of learners.

Beginning with the experience drawn from the course held at Roma Tre University, it has been ascertained that a blended learning course is extremely fruitful, not only in developing reading comprehension, which is the main aim of the EuRom5 method, but also in integrating oral comprehension. Allowing students to manage the audio is one of the characteristics of the work online that provides the most advantages to learners. Furthermore, the web platform makes it easy to carry out the metacognitive questionnaires that make it possible to monitor students' comprehension and at the same time to give them a kind of training that is often neglected in language courses.

By taking inspiration from the course held in Bogotá, during which much attention was paid to the professional fields of the participants, a program may be hypothesized that we will call a "Multilingual Information Management (MIM)" profile. As can be seen from table 7, the program can be divided into four phases that take learners from a so-called "zero" phase of knowledge of the languages (in which zero is equivalent to the spontaneous level) to a phase in which they can capitalize on their own knowledge and are able to carry out a process of reworking of the information they consult in more than one language. The basic idea is that making use of information in the original language makes it possible to multiply the sources and thus expand the available information. This profile corresponds to the requirements of university students and researchers who need to use publications in their original language that are not necessarily in English.

Profile 1: Proposal for Multilingual Information Management

- Profile: Multilingual Information Management
- Target public: university students/researchers and speakers of one Romance language (i.e., Spanish)
- Main objective: to read texts in Portuguese, Catalan, Italian, and French.
- Total hours: 34

		Input	Description
Stage 1			
Starting point	16 hrs.	EuRom5	Training cycle with the EuRom5 handbook
Stage 2			
Doing the reading	8 hrs.	Newspaper articles on current news	Training cycle with newspaper articles and a task-based approach.
Stage 3			
Let's go to the core	8 hrs.	Papers related to the subject chosen by the group	At the beginning of the course the teacher and the students choose a subject depending on their academic interests

	Stage 4		
Assessment	4 hrs.	Final examination	Final examination should consist in writing a paper with information extracted from several articles on the same subject (i.e., Spanish colonial campaigns, International law)

The last phase, regarding the assessment of the program by means of different pieces of work (Jamet, 2010), raises the awkward question of how to assess IC-based training. In the practical case of this profile, the trainer will be able to ask students to prepare a test in the working language by using a series of texts dealing with the chosen topic and written in the languages studied. In order to assess the written work the trainer will need to create a suitable grid that takes various aspects into consideration:

a) the completeness of the information.
- It can be answered the question: can students exploit the information contained in the texts?;
b) the coherence of the reported information.
- It can be answered the question: can students organize the information in the text?;
c) the veracity of the reported information.
- It can be answered the question: can students interpret the information reported in the texts?

The hypotheses presented here are meant as a starting point for teachers to use in their didactic planning both for introducing EuRom into their language lessons and for proposing programs based entirely on IC.

BIBLIOGRAPHY

Blanche-Benveniste C., Borel B., Deulofeu J., Durand J., Giacomi A., Loufrani C., Meziane B., Pazery N. (1979). Des grilles pour le français parlé, *Recherches sur le français parlé*, 2, 163-204.

Blanche-Benveniste, C. (1995). *Le projet Eurom4: comprendre les langues aujourd'hui*. Paris: La Tilv.

Blanche-Benveniste, C., Valli, A., Mota, A., Simone, R., Bonvino, E., & Uzcanga Vivar, I. (1997). *Eurom4: méthode d'enseignement de quatre langues romanes*. Firenze: Nuova Italia Editrice.

Blanche-Benveniste, C. & Valli, A., (1997). L'expérience d' Eurom4: comment négocier les difficultés. *Le français dans le monde*, [special issue], 110-115.

Blanche-Benveniste, C. (2001). Nouveaux apports de la grammaire contrastive des langues romanes. In I. Vivar Uzcanga, E. Pombo Llamas, & J. M. Pérez Velasco (Eds.), *Presencia y renovación de la lingüística francesa* (pp. 41–54). Salamanca: Ediciones Universidad de Salamanca.

Blanche-Benveniste, C. (2008). Aspetti lessicali del confronto tra lingue romanze. Esiste un lessico europeo? In M. Barni, C. Bagna, & D. Troncarelli (Eds.), *Lessico e apprendimenti* (pp. 47–66). Milano: Franco Angeli.

Blanche-Benveniste, C. (2009). Suggestions de recherches à mener pour entraîner la perception orale d'une langue romane à d'autres. In M. C. Jamet (Ed.) *Orale e intercomprensione tra lingue romanze. Ricerche e implicazioni didattiche* (pp. 19–32). Venezia: Le Bricole, Editrice Cafoscarina srl.

Bonvino, E., Caddéo, S., Pippa, S. & Vilaginés Serra, E. (2011) *Leggere e capire 5 lingue romanze: português, español, català, italiano, français*. Milan: Hoepli.

Bowles M.A. (2010). *The Think-Aloud Controversy in Second Language Research*. New York/London: Routledge Taylor & Francis Group.

Commission of the European Communities (1995). White Paper on Education and Training—Teaching and Learning—Towards the Learning Society. Available at: http://europa.eu/documentation/official-docs/white-papers/ index_en.htm.

Finocchiaro, M. & Brumfit, C. (1983). *The Functional-Notional Approach*. New York, NY: Oxford University Press.

Fiorenza, E. (2012). *Intercomprensione tra lingue romanze e lettura in L2. Tesi di Laurea Magistrale*. Università degli Studi Roma Tre, Unpublished

Fiorenza, E. & Bonvino, E. (2011). L'intercomprensione dall'italiano o verso l'italiano: un percorso fra le lingue romanze. *Revista de Italianística*, XXI–XXII, 161-179.

Gilmore, A. (2007). Authentic materials and authenticity in foreign language learning. *Language Teaching*, 40, 97–118.

Jamet, M.C. (2010). Intercomprensione, Quadro comune europeo di riferimento per le lingue, Quadro di riferimento per gli approcci plurilingui e valutazione. *Synergies Europe*, 5, 75–98.

Larsen-Freeman, D. (2000). *Techniques and Principles in Language Teaching*. Oxford: Oxford University Press.

Mishan, F. (2005). *Designing Authenticity into Language Learning Materials*. Bristol: Intellect.

Richards, J. C., & Rodgers, Theodore S. (2001). *Approaches and Methods in Language Teaching* (2nd Edition). Cambridge: Cambridge Language Teaching Library.

Italian and French for Spanish Speakers:
San Pedro High School - LAUSD
A Practical Study of the Logistics of Teaching Another
Romance language to Spanish Speakers

Ida Lanza and Diane Hartunian

1. Introduction

This article examines the practical application of intercomprehension strategies in high-school Italian 1 and French 1 for Spanish speakers courses. The objectives for offering these courses are to give students who already speak one Romance language (Spanish) an opportunity to learn a second using their knowledge of Spanish as a spring-board. The synergies among the Romance languages enable these students to learn French and Italian at an accelerated pace. It is our goal to cover two years of content in one, so that these students may skip the traditional Italian 2 or French 2 and go to the third level in year 2, eventually moving to the AP level in year 3. The article will examine the materials being used, the techniques employed on a day-to-day basis, and the data generated by various assessments to determine if intercomprehension techniques and these types of classes do indeed give students the basics necessary to move to a more advanced level of language acquisition more quickly.

In mid-August of 2013, San Pedro High School, in the Los Angeles Unified School District South Division, for the first time offered Italian 1 and French 1 for students who are Spanish speakers. The school counselors promoted the courses in the Spring of 2013 during their visits to the local middle schools that feed San Pedro High School. The response and enthusiasm were overwhelming; both Italian 1 and French 1 for Spanish Speakers had 50+ students registered in each class at the beginning of the Fall semester. After the first three weeks of schedule changes and adjustments, each class ended up with 40+ students.

San Pedro High School is located in San Pedro California, which is the port of L.A. The student population is as follows:

Year	A	%	B	%	C	%	D	%	E	%	F	%	G	%	Tot.
2011-12	22	0.9	36	1.4	26	1.0	25	1.0	229	9.2	1717	69.1	430	17.3	2485
2010-11	20	0.7	40	1.5	25	0.9	21	0.8	244	9.1	1925	71.7	409	15.2	2684
2009-10	31	1.1	74	2.6	0	0.0	22	0.8	259	9.0	2001	69.7	485	16.9	2872
2008-09	21	0.7	38	1.3	39	1.3	16	0.5	233	7.8	2074	69.7	555	18.6	2976
2007-08	27	0.9	43	1.4	42	1.4	17	0.6	259	8.4	2085	67.7	607	19.7	3080

A: AI/Alaskan; **B**: Asian; **C**: Filipino; **D**: Pacific Island; **E**: Black; **F**: Hispanic; **G**: White;

http://search.lausd.k12.ca.us/cgi-bin/fccgi.exe?w3exec=schoolprofile&which=8850

Our students come from highly varied backgrounds, and their knowledge of Spanish is just as heterogeneous. Some can speak and understand spoken Spanish but cannot read or write it; others have attended some schooling in a Spanish-speaking country from one to eight years. In the Italian 1 class, 100 percent come from homes where Spanish is the primary language; 17 percent are listed as Limited English Proficient (LEPs) and are taking separate English as a second language classes to support their English classes; 11 percent are classified as Gifted and Talented (GATE); 2 percent have Individual Education Plans (IEPs) and 2 percent have specific discipline issues. In the French class, 100 percent are from Spanish-speaking homes, 0 percent are LEPs, 7 percent are GATE, 9 percent have IEPs, and 12 percent have discipline issues. So, even though our students are all Spanish speakers, their competency varies greatly, and this fact poses many challenges for our large classes with little technology.

As high-school teachers in the LAUSD school district we are mandated by our district to help LEPs improve their English language skills. Therefore, we not only must teach them a new language, but we must also tend to their English competence. In addition to teaching our credentialed subjects, all teachers are now expected to help students with their English writing proficiency, as described in the new Common Core Standards that California has adopted. Language teachers are considered part of the teachers of "Technical subjects," group and we may be partially evaluated on the basis of our students' scores on the English CCS standardized tests that began in the Spring of 2015. (This last point has not yet been implemented in California, but it is already the case in Florida and New Jersey.)

It is in this context, therefore, that intercomprehension theories and strategies can help all of our students across all the languages they need to master, manipulate, and produce throughout their high-school careers and beyond. In general, the students are excited about learning another Romance language, and they appreciate that their knowledge of Spanish gives them an advantage in the acquisition of either French or Italian. They can readily use Spanish cognates to figure out the meaning of many words, and those who know some Spanish grammar can transfer the patterns from the Romance language they speak to the one they are learning.

2. ITALIAN 1 FOR SPANISH SPEAKERS

In class, I (Ida Lanza) use Italian as much as possible, switching to Spanish and English as necessary to get a point across or to help students see patterns and similarities. The students can comprehend approximately 70–80 percent of what I am saying in Italian, so I try to keep speaking in Spanish or English to a minimum. On the other hand, I encourage my students to use whatever language they are most comfortable with—Spanish, English, or Italian—to ask questions, clarify ideas, or justify a position. Intercomprehension is the reality of my classroom. I find it liberating and empowering both for me and for my students. I am sure there are proponents of the purely communicative approach (TPR etc.) who will be shaking their heads in disapproval, but code switching happens in real life, and whatever methodology keeps students engaged, thinking, talking, and exploring, helps them learn more about the connections among Spanish, Italian, and English.

Although the students in Italian for Spanish Speakers are given the standard LAUSD-approved textbook—*Oggi in Italia* (8th edition)—in class we use a wide variety of materials including an Italian text—*Progetto Italiano Jr.*

1 and 2 along with the CDs and videos that accompany that text. In class we also use the video site YABLA.com for additional listening practice. One strategy I use in all my Italian classes and that I have found to be extremely effective is the use of songs to engage the students. Songs are the only way to encourage students to read a text more than once; they learn vocabulary, grammar, and idiomatic expressions in context; the combination of text and music stimulates both sides of the brain and helps put the information into long-term memory. We listen to the songs for an entire month, reading the text, singing along, and doing exercises that focus on the vocabulary, grammar, and idioms. At the end of the month, there is an assessment based on students' work with that song. Even though I only have anecdotal evidence for the effectiveness of this activity, the students enjoy the songs, sing along, and often memorize the songs, telling me that the songs get "stuck in their heads" and they find themselves singing them at home. Italian 3 students can still sing the songs from Italian 1. For my Italian for Spanish Speakers class, I am changing some of the songs I used in traditional Italian 1 to songs that the Latino students already know in Spanish. Many Italian singers, Laura Pausini, Tiziano Ferro, Nek, Eros Ramazzotti, etc., have Spanish versions of their Italian songs. Often the students are surprised to learn that these singers are Italian. Since the songs have both Italian and Spanish versions, they can be compared for meaning, to see if they translate exactly, and if not, to determine the differences in each text. I encourage them to listen to Italian radio and Internet stations to find songs that they like, and some of the song choices that we use come from their selections. Another criterion I use to choose a song, besides its availability in both Spanish and Italian, is presence of the grammar structures on which we are focused for that month.

 The first song I use in all Italian 1 classes is "L'Italiano," by Toto Cutugno. After a class discussion about how many words they already know in Italian from both Spanish and English, we listen to the song and look for cognates in all three languages, followed by the identification of those words that are only cognates in Italian and Spanish. I have provided the text and exercises that I used this past semester (Fall 2013) in the Italian for Spanish Speakers class. Every class of Italian 1 loves this song, without exception, for it resonates greatly for the Spanish-speaking students who are often already familiar with the song in Spanish. With its statements about identity and the questioning of stereotypes, the lyrics offer numerous opportunities for approaching Italian culture as a means through which to reflect on culture in general. Additionally, the song has acquired international cultural currency as the Italian theme song when the Italians defeat other teams in soccer. In addition to singing the song in Italian and Spanish, Cutugno also recorded French, Romanian, and Russian versions of the song. A perusal of Cutugno on the web reveals an inordinate number of sites and fan clubs, including http://lyricstranslate.com/it/Toto-Cutugno-L%E2%80%99italiano-lyrics.html, a site that offers translations of the song from Arabic to Slovenian, with multiple translations made available in a number of languages. These websites and their content offer more possibilities for the development of culturally and linguistically rich reflections, especially in the area of intercomprehension. For example the website for Cutugno's Romanian fan club is legible to speakers of other Romance languages, thanks to the many cognates and similar structures. Brief forays into other Romance languages can indeed provide reinforcement to the task of learning French and Italian, and, as many of the contributions to the volume have shown, they contribute to the further development of the metacognitive language skills that promote accelerated learning among multilinguals. This lesson that appears below has been applied successfully in college classrooms as an intercomprehension exercise that works well in courses of French for Spanish speakers as well.[1]

---

[1] The version of the lesson presented here has been developed by Ida Lanza, San Pedro High School, in collaboration with Clorinda Donato, California State University, Long Beach.

"Un Italiano": an exercise in Intercomprehension and Intercommunication created by Ida Lanza, San Pedro High School in collaboration with Clorinda Donato, CSU Long Beach	
	Un vero e proprio inno all'italianità, che consacra la fama di **Toto Cutugno**, agli inizi degli anni '80, per la precisione al **festival di San Remo** nel 1983. Una certa elite culturale lo catalogò, come a volerlo disprezzare, al genere nazional-popolare. In effetti è la canzone che cantano i nostri emigrati all'estero, le nostre mamme indaffarate in cucina, e i bambini che giocano. Almeno così è stato per molto tempo. Del resto il canto, per un Italiano, è vita, e se non canta *"muore"*. Clichès? Stereotipi? Luoghi comuni? Forse. Utili, comunque, per analizzare, comprendere, riflettere sulla condizione identitaria di un popolo che si accinge a festeggiare tra colori e musica la sua nascita. [2] http://guide.supereva.it/bibliofilia/interventi/2011/01/chi-e-litaliano-vero

---

[2] All rights to the song music and lyrics remain with the authors; song and lyrics are used only for educational purposes according to the copyright exception for educators. Notwithstanding the provisions of sections 17 U.S.C. § 106 and 17 U.S.C. § 106A, the fair use of a copyrighted work, including such use by reproduction in copies or phono-records or by any other means specified by that section, for purposes such as criticism, comment, news reporting, teaching (including multiple copies for classroom use), scholarship, or research, is not an infringement of copyright.

Italian	Spanish 1	Spanish 2	French	English
Lasciatemi cantare	Déjenme cantar	Quiero cantar muy alto	Laissez-moi chanter	Let me sing
Con la chitarra in mano	Con la guitarra en mano,	Con la guitarra en mano,	Avec la guitare à la main	with my guitar in hand;
Lasciatemi cantare ... Sono un italiano!	Déjenme cantar, Soy un italiano	Quiero cantar muy alto, Soy un italiano.	Laissez-moi chanter Je suis un italien	Let me sing, I am an Italian
Buongiorno Italia gli spaghetti al dente	Buen día Italia los fideos al dente	Aunque esté lejos y aunque pase el tiempo	Bonjour Italie, les spaghetti "al dente"	Good morning, Italy, with spaghetti "al dente,"
Un partigiano come presidente,	Un partisano como presidente	Yo no me olvido ni un sólo momento,	Et un partisan comme président	A partisan as president
Con l'autoradio sempre nella mano destra	Con el stereo en la mano derecha	De ese bellísimo país donde nací	Avec l'auto-radio toujours dans la main droite	a radio (IPod) always in my right hand
Un canarino sopra la finestra	Y un canario sobre la ventana.	Y que siempre está en mi pensamiento.	Et un canari sur la fenêtre	a canary on the window (sill).
Buongiorno Italia con i tuoi artisti	Buen día Italia con tus artistas	Soy de esa Italia que ama los artistas	Bonjour Italie, avec tes artistes	Good morning Italy with your artists
Con troppa America sui manifesti,	Con demasiado America en los anuncios.	Tan pintoresca y tan colorista	Avec trop d'Amérique sur tes affiches (pub)	With too much America on your posters
Con le canzoni fatte con amore e cuore,	Con las canciones, hechas con amor, y corazón	Con su poesía, con su amor, con sus canciones,	Avec les chansons avec amour Avec le coeur	With songs, with love, with heart,
Con più donne sempre meno suore.	Con mas mujeres y menos monjas.	Y esas chicas que despiertan ilusiones	Avec de plus en plus de femmes moins bonnes soeurs (relig.)	With more women and less nuns.
Buongiorno Italia, buongiorno Maria, Con gli occhi pieni di malinconia,	Buen día Italia, buen día María, Con los ojos llenos de melancolía	Cuando despierto y digo "buenos días" Echo de menos a esa Italia mía,	Bonjour Italie Bonjour Marie Avec les yeux plein de mélancholie	Good morning Italy, good morning Maria With eyes full of melancholy (sadness).
Buongiorno Dio ... sai che ci sono anch'io.	Buen día dios, sabes que estoy aquí tambien.	Buongiorno sí, soy así gracias a ti.	Bonjour Dieu Tu sais aussi qu'il y a moi	Good morning God, you know that I am here too.
Lasciatemi cantare Con la chitarra	Déjenme cantar Con la guitarra en mano,	Quiero cantar muy alto con la guitarra en	Laissez-moi chanter Avec une guitare à	Let me sing with my guitar in hand

in mano,	mano		la main	
Lasciatemi cantare Una canzone piano piano	Déjenme cantar, Una canción lento lento	Quiero cantar muy alto que yo soy un italiano,	Laissez-moi chanter Une chanson doucement doucement	Let me sing with a very slow song
Lasciatemi cantare, Perché ne sono fiero	Déjenme cantar Porque estoy orgulloso	Quiero cantar muy alto, que lo oiga el mundo entero	Laissez-moi chanter Car j'en suis fier	Let me sing, because I am proud of it.
Sono un italiano, Un italiano vero	Soy un italiano. Soy un italiano, verdadero.	Soy un italiano, un italiano sincero.	Je suis un italien Un italien vrai	I am Italian, a real Italian.
Buongiorno Italia che non si spaventa Con la crema da barba alla menta, Con un vestito gessato sul blu	Buen día Italia, que no se espanta, Con la crema para barba a la menta Con traje grisáceo sobre azul	Cuando la noche me deja en silencio, Dentro de mí oigo como un lamento Amores que en Italia conocí,	Bonjour Italie, qui ne s'épouvante pas Et avec la mousse à raser à la menthe Avec un habit tendant vers le bleu	Good morning Italy that is never scared With mint-scented shaving cream With a blue pinstriped suit
E la moviola la domenica in TV.	Y la movida los domingos en la tv	Y que pasaron como ráfagas de viento.	Et le ralenti le dimanche à la TV	And an old time movie on the TV every Sunday
Buongiorno Italia col caffè ristretto,	Buen día Italia con el café estrecho	Y aunque al final me vuelva la alegría	Bonjour Italie, avec le (café) "ristretto"	Good morning Italy with extra-strong espresso
Le calze nuove nel primo cassetto	Los calcetines nuevos en el primer cajón,	A veces siento la melancolía,	Les chaussettes neuves dans le premier tiroir	With new socks in the first drawer
Con la bandiera in tintoria E una Seicento giù di carrozzeria	Con la bandera en la tintorería Y un seiscientos con la carrocería estropeada.	Al recordar a la italiana tan hermosa Que yo tanto, tanto, mucho quería.	Avec le drapeau en teinturerie Et une Fiat 600 cabossée	With an Italian flag at the dry-cleaners And a dilapidated (FIAT) 600
Buongiorno Italia, buongiorno Maria,	Buen día Italia, buen día María,	Cuando despierto y digo "buenos días	Bonjour Italie Bonjour Marie	Good morning Italy, good morning Maria
Con gli occhi dolci di malinconia,	Con los ojos llenos de melancolía	Pensando siempre en esa Italia mía,	Avec les yeux plein de mélancholie	With eyes full of melancholy (sadness).

Buongiorno Dio ... lo sai che ci sono anch'io.	Buen día dios, sabes que soy inclusive yo.	Buongiorno sí, soy así gracias a ti.	Bonjour Dieu Tu sais aussi qu'il y a moi	Good morning God, you know that I am here too
Lasciatemi cantare Con la chitarra in mano,	Déjenme cantar Con la guitarra en mano	Quiero cantar muy alto con la guitarra en mano	Laissez-moi chanter Avec une guitare à la main	Let me sing with my guitar in hand
Lasciatemi cantare Una canzone piano piano.	Déjenme cantar, Una canción lento lento	Quiero cantar muy alto que yo soy un italiano	Laissez-moi chanter. Une chanson doucement doucement	Let me sing with a very slow song
Lasciatemi cantare, Perché ne sono fiero:	Déjenme cantar Porque estoy orgulloso	Quiero cantar muy alto, que lo oiga el mundo entero	Laissez-moi chanter Car j'en suis fier	Let me sing, because I am proud of it.
Sono un italiano, Un italiano vero.	Yo soy un italiano, Un italiano, verdadero.	Soy un italiano, un italiano sincero.	Je suis un italien Un italien vrai	I am Italian, a real Italian.
			La la la la la la la..... Laissez-moi chanter Avec une guitare à la main	Let me sing with my guitar in hand
			Laissez-moi chanter Une chanson doucement doucement	Let me sing with a very slow song
.			Laissez-moi chanter Car j'en suis fier	Let me sing, because I am proud of it.
			Je suis un italien Un italien vrai	I am Italian, a real Italian.

Esercizio #1: Data _____ (Analysis of the text)

Sing along or read the words in Italian to your partner.
1) What is a noun? (sostantivo – nome)

2) How do you know a word is a noun in English? (en español, in italiano)

3) Using the translations, underline all the nouns in Italian in the song. (en español, in English)

4) Discuss similarities and differences with your partner (Discutan las similitudes y las diferencias con su compañero).

Esercizio #2: Data

Sing along or read the words in Italian to your partner.
1) Translate the following: (in italiano e in spagnolo)

   A. Let me sing

   B. With my guitar in my hand

   C. Good Morning

   D. I am Italian

   E. A real Italian

Observation: how many cognates (le parole analoghe, las palabras similares) are there in the Italian and Spanish translations

2) Circle all the nouns in English and Spanish that are plural.
3) How do you know they are plural?

4) Highlight the nouns in Italian that correspond to the plural nouns in English.
5) What do you notice about the plurals in Italian?

6) Discuss with your partner the differences and similarities in forming plurals among the three languages.
7) Write down your conclusions

Esercizio # 3: Data

Sing along or read the words in Italian to your partner.
Cultural comprehension: (Pueden contestar en inglés, español o italiano; Potete rispondere in inglese, spagnolo, o italiano) Discuss with your group.

1) What does "spaghetti al dente" mean to you?

2) What is a nun?

3) What is a partisan?

4) What does it mean to be "melancholy"?

5) Have you ever had an "espresso"?

6) Have you ever had a "cappuccino"?

7) What do you think the singer means by "too much America on the posters"?

Esercizio #4: Data _____

Sing along or read the words in Italian to your partner.
1) Try to translate the following into English or Spanish without looking at the song:
   a) Lasciatemi cantare, con la chitarra in mano.

   b) Sono un italiano, un italiano vero.

   c) Lasciatemi cantare una canzone piano piano.

   d) Lasciatemi cantare perché ne sono fiero.

   e) Buongiorno Italia, buongiorno Maria.

2) Come si dice?

a) with my guitar	d) I am proud
b) Let me sing	e) Good morning
c) very slowly	f) in hand

Esercizio # 5: Data _____

1) Sing along or read the words in Italian to your partner
2) What is the subject of a sentence?

   _____

3) What is a pronoun?

   _____

4) In the following sentences, underline the subject pronoun in Italian, Spanish and English (el pronombre sujeto - il pronome soggetto)

Io sono italiano	Yo soy italiano	I am Italian
Tu sei americano.	Tu eres americano	You are American
Lui è messicano.	Él es mexicano	He is Mexican
Lei è guatemalteca	Ella es guatemalteca	She is Guatemalan
Noi siamo salvadoregni	Nosotros somos salvadoreños	We are Salvadorian
Voi siete peruviani	Vosotros sois peruanos. (Ustedes son peruanos)	You(all) are Peruvian
Loro sono costaricani	Ellos son costarricenses	They are Costa Rican

5) Come si dice in italiano?
   a) I_____(yo)
   b) you_____(tú)
   c) he_____(él)
   d) she_____(ella – usted)
   e) we_____(nosotros)
   f) you (all)_____(vosotros – ustedes)
   g) they_____(ellos/ellas)

Esercizio # 6 Data: _____

1) Sing along or read the words in **Italian** to your partner.
2) Using the examples from exercise 5, conjugate (coniugate – change the verb according to the subject) the verb

"to be"	"essere"
I am	
You are	
He is	
She is	
We are	
You all are	
They are	

3) Come si dice? (Try translating without looking at the song)
   a. Let me sing with my guitar in hand.
   _____

   b. Let me sing with a very slow song.
   _____

   c. Let me sing, because I am proud of it.
   _____

   d. I am Italian, a real Italian.
   _____

Esercizio # 7 Data
_____

1) Sing along or read the words in **Italian** to your partner.
2) What is a preposition? ¿Qué es una preposición? (discuss with a partner)
   _____
3) Can you find 10 examples of prepositions in English? in Spanish?
   _____

4) Look at the song and using the English and Spanish translations, find and box in the prepositions in Italian.
5) List the Italian prepositions you have found:
   _____

6) Which preposition is the most common in this song?
   _____

Esercizio # 8: Data _____

1) Sing along or read the words in **Italian** to your partner.
2) With your partner, say the word, spell the word in Italian and then say the word again, ask your partner what it means.

a. buongiorno	f. espresso
b. cantare	g. bandiera
c. chitarra	h. donna
d. manifesto	i. cuore
e. spaghetti	j. canzone

Esercizio # 9: Data _____

1) Sing along or read the words in **Italian** to your partner without looking at the paper.
2) Tell you partner what the song is about without looking at the translations
3) Write down 3 concepts you learned about the Italian language and/or culture in listening to this song and doing the exercises:

   I. _____

   II. _____

   III. _____

4) ¿Te gusta esta canción? ¿Por qué? Indiquen 3 ejemplos de la cancíon que apoyan su opinión. (Do you like this song? Why? Use 3 examples from the song to support your opinion.) (Ti piace questa canzone? Perché? Dai tre esempi dal testo.

   _____
   _____
   _____

5) Why do you think that this song continues to be so popular throughout the world and in so many different cultures? Is this song appealing to your culture? Why or why not? Why do you think that Toto Cutugno added the new verse— "lasciateci cantare perché siamo fieri, siamo italiani, italiani veri"—to the song when he sang it again at San Remo in 2013, thirty years after its debut in 1983?

   _____
   _____
   _____
   _____
   _____

6) Find other websites that feature this song in other languages. What did you discover?

   _____
   _____
   _____
   _____

2.1 *Rationale for the various types of exercises:*

In many of the exercises, the students work with partners or groups of three and four to analyze the text and deduce the grammatical patterns we are discussing. I use this particular song at the very beginning of the semester, as the students are learning the similarities and differences in pronunciation in spelling and in word meaning. Several of the exercises are a vehicle for them to practice all of these aspects of the new language. While learning basic concepts in Italian, I do encourage them to write and explain in whichever language they feel most comfortable at this point in time. Intercomprehension is about communicating ideas in the most effective and efficient way for both speaker and listener. If they write in Spanish or English, it also gives me insight into their academic knowledge of those languages. In addition, our school is focusing on writing across the curriculum, using evidence from the text, and the final exercise for this song asks them for an evaluation, which must be supported by three specific examples from the text to support their opinion. We are trying to encourage all students, in every grade level, and in every subject, to use the text as the basis of their work. By using the same academic language over and over in all content classes, the students can be slowly acclimated to the new demands of the Common Core Standards.

While the songs are a good way to begin the class every day, obviously they are not the only activities in which the students participate. The text *Progetto Italiano Jr. 1* has many visuals, pictures and videos, extensive listening exercises, conversations, descriptions, ads for various products, and so on. Students are exposed to a variety of registers and thematic lexicons, which encourage them to use the vocabulary in simple, created conversations.

I have found that I can speak Italian almost 90 percent of the time and the students are able to understand almost everything; they can also read moderately difficult texts and listen to conversations with relative ease. When speaking they often confuse the Spanish and English words and the pronunciation of the combinations, *ce, ci, che, chi, ge, gi, ghe, ghi, sce sci, sche, schi,* as well as the double consonants, which are a challenge for Spanish speakers. In addition, because they perceive Italian as being relatively "easy" for them, they often do not complete homework assignments and do not practice enough to do well on assessments. At the end of the first semester, Italian 1a, I had an equal number of As and Bs (17), five Cs, and one D. No one failed the class, but I was surprised that I had any Cs or Ds at all. General observations of the results imply that students who were literate in Spanish did much better than students who were not. Students who are identified as gifted and talented also did very well, because they could apply their knowledge of English language and grammar to Italian even if they did not know Spanish grammar. Students with special needs (IEP students) are having a difficult time with the written language but do fairly well when the tasks are oral. Students who have a limited knowledge of written Spanish have the most difficult time switching from the Spanish sounds to the Italian sounds. We realize that these findings are fully corroborated by heritage language researchers, who also find that literate heritage students in Spanish can handle the written language and grammar rules better then the heritage students whose knowledge of Spanish is largely conversational. Nonetheless, all students do well with spoken French and Italian, too. We look forward to incorporating more of the work from the heritage language research community into our work as teachers of French and Italian for Spanish Speakers.

The material in *Progetto Italiano Junior 1 and 2* is very user friendly, and many of the topics interest and motivate the students. The program comes with audio CD's of conversations, videos with Italian subtitles, and many suggestions for other websites to visit to improve and increase their language acquisition. However, the books are the property of the school, and we do not have enough for the students to take home a copy and have them in school too. They also cannot write in them since they are not consumable books that are replaced every year. If we allow students to take them home, many of them forget them when they come to class; moreover, at least 15 percent will not be returned at the end of the semester. (This happens every year with our standard text, *Oggi in Italia*.) Since our department has limited funds and the funds from the Italian government are not guaranteed year-to-year, we use the text only in class. We know that student progress would be improved if students could take the books home to practice their language skills. Without the book and accompanying technology, many of the students study neither the notes nor the official text, *Oggi in Italia*. The two texts are organized in completely different ways, and *Oggi in Italia*'s audience consists primarily of college students.

Most high-school students are extrinsically motivated, and our students in the Italian and French for Spanish Speakers courses are no different; they want to pass the course and get their credits for graduation. (LAUSD now has A–G requirements for all students to graduate from high school, and that means that the students must take a World Language other than English for at least two years.) Up until this year languages were considered electives for those who did not want to attend college. However, the push now is to prepare all students for college while at the same time giving them the skills necessary to get a job right out of high school. In addition, students can no longer pass a class with a D; they must get a C or better or they will have to repeat the class. After level 2 there is usually a big drop off of students who continue to level 3 (about 50 percent) and an even further drop off at the AP level (approximately 80 percent drop).

3. Observations for French for Spanish Speakers 1

The French 1 class for Spanish speakers is comprised of students who have varying levels of proficiency in Spanish, from native speakers to students who have limited proficiency. All students are proficient in English. The class is taught at the 90 percent ACTFL target language level, and the students' input level is very advanced. Although the program is still in the beginning stages, a shift in the language acquisition paradigm can be noted, almost from the onset. Some observations include:

Vocabulary

- From a lexical perspective, students are quick to comprehend French vocabulary on a variety of themes well beyond the beginning level. Because of the high level of cognates in French and Spanish, and English, thematic vocabulary can be taught at a much faster pace. While the pronunciation in French is more challenging, once students can comprehend the distinctive sounds in French, word recognition is not a difficult task. Furthermore, many expressions are very similar to Spanish. Fr.: "faire la queue; Sp.: hacer cola," Fr.: "tout le monde; Sp.: "todo el mundo," Fr.: "il vaut mieux tard que jamais," Sp.: "más vale tarde que nunca," not to mention expressions with avoir, i.e., Fr.: "avoir faim, soif, froid; Sp.: tener hambre, sed, frio," to name a few.

Verb Conjugations

- Due to the similarities of French and Spanish verbal paradigms, verb conjugations that are usually covered over a period of four semesters in high school can be mastered during the first year.

Culture

- Another salient aspect is the cultural component. The students in French 1 for Spanish Speakers display a genuine connection to French culture. French cinema is one way to expose students to both language and culture. What has been remarkable is the way in which students have connected to the linguistic and cultural aspects of French cinema both in class and beyond the school setting. Their level of engagement and interaction with the content is comparable to students who have attained an advanced level of high school French, equivalent to at least French 3.

- To cite an example, "La môme" ("La Vie en rose"), the renowned 2007 film about the life of legendary singer Edith Piaf, is normally programmed for second semester level 2, or level 3, at the secondary level. Students usually connect with the music and themes at a more advanced level. Because of the similarity in cultural themes in the Hispanic and francophone worlds, students in the Spanish speakers class display a keen interest in the songs and cultural aspects of the music and life of Edith Piaf. On their own initiative, students continued viewing the film outside class and shared with their families. Interestingly, parents of students commented on the fact that Spanish versions of Piaf's songs are well known in Latin America, and the songs all sound familiar to them. In other words, the Hispanic cultural schema of Spanish-speaker learners of French facilitate and accelerate the learning process.

4. Moving Forward: Challenges and Rewards

Our hope is that at least half of the students in Italian 1 and French 1 for Spanish Speakers will move on to level 3, thus increasing the numbers of students at that level by a third (from 40 to 60); subsequently, we would like to have at least 20 students go on from level 3 to the AP level in both languages.

This would double the number of students we usually have in AP each year, which now stands at five.

Our biggest challenges have been the following: first, the lack of individual technologies in the classroom that would help students work at their own pace. At the college level, students are required to do homework online with online workbooks, participate in chat-room discussions with fellow-students from the class and/or the instructor, create and comment on blogs etc. Even though most students have a computer and Internet access at home, given the lower socio-economic standing of many students, not all of them have Internet access all the time, and we cannot create a situation of inequity with regard to the modality in which course material is accessed. Our classrooms have only one computer, a projector, and visualizer. The French teacher has spent her own money for the iPad she uses, and she also pays for her own wireless connection since the school's wifi is very slow and often crashes when there are too many people online at any given time. We use as much technology as the situation permits; I have subscribed to the YABLA website, which has video clips accompanied by written dialogue in Italian and English that can be turned off. We use these clips as Exit Tickets, to practice new vocabulary, and to become more familiar with different registers and regional accents. For the songs, I rely on YouTube, which has many versions of the songs we are learning in class. Many students download the songs to their phones or music players and listen to them during the day. Our second challenge is the lack of specific material for this new course; some sort of basic reader/textbook created for Latino-American speakers of Spanish who wish to learn another Romance language at the high-school level is sorely needed. I know that several colleges including CSULB (California State University, Long Beach) are in the process of putting together the material and lessons that they use in their French and Italian for Spanish Speaker courses. There are certainly texts of this sort in Europe and Latin America, specifically for French learning Spanish in France, Italians learning Spanish in Italy, and vice versa. However, here in the United States, available texts always assume English as the primary language, and no intercomprehension strategies or activities are included in these standard texts.

Since we have had only one semester of both classes, it is difficult to draw long-term conclusions from the results so far. We are progressing a little more quickly than we would in a standard Italian 1 or French 1 class. I would usually cover six or seven chapters of *Oggi in Italia* in Italian 1 over the course of a year, while in this class of Spanish speakers I hope to get to chapter 12, which would include the present, past perfect, imperfect, and the future tenses. For the students who demonstrate proficiency in the use of these concepts, I will recommend that they move on next year to Italian 3, while those who still seem to be struggling with the basic tenets of the structure will go to Italian 2. We do not anticipate having enough students to create an Italian 2 or French 2 for Spanish Speakers at this time. Our objective is to prepare more students for the level 3 and AP classes. We obviously will have more data at the end of this semester, and we will be able to see if our hypotheses are correct and if we are at least heading in the direction we have envisioned for the students in these classes.

Schools with large Latino populations need to find ways to use their students' knowledge of their rich cultures and native idioms to acquire new knowledge. Students become proud of their heritage when they see that it is validated as a learning tool that can open new doors of opportunity in the acquisition of other Romance languages at school. The intercomprehensive approach has given us tools for teaching that closely mirror our reality. Students want to learn about new languages and cultures, but their awkward self-consciousness and the lack of authentic situations in which to practice their new language can create obstacles in the learning process. Instead, intercomprehension, with its multilingual, language arts approach, encourages students to express their observations, ideas, and opinions in the language in which they feel most comfortable as they transition to the new language(s) they are learning and using. Languages as practice in the here and now is the focus of intercomprehension, rather than sets of abstract, disembodied rules that often never make it from the textbook into the contact zone.

Afterword

Since this article was written, we were able to add a few statistics about the Italian for Spanish Speakers class. Out of a class of 40, 11 (27.5 percent) went on to Italian 3 and 2 (5 percent) went directly to Italian AP. Thus 28 percent of my Italian 3 class comes from the Italian 1 for Spanish Speakers (11/39). The others are continuing in Italian 2. Having 11 additional students in Italian 3 has had a great impact on the Italian program at San Pedro

High School. For the first time in three years, the administration has given me a separate Italian AP class, which I am confident will lead to better AP outcomes. In the past I have had a combination Italian 3/AP, which is logistically very challenging to teach and leaves both levels deficient due to lack of time and attention to their needs. I am particularly proud of two students, Bani Sandoval from El Salvador, and Andrea Orozco from Mexico. Both young ladies have been in the United States only a few years; they are straight-A students, having transitioned out of ESL in just a couple of years. They took Italian 1 for Spanish Speakers last year, and this year they are both in Italian AP. Both entered a writing contest sponsored by the Italian Government and NIAF called "Scrivo in italiano," and Bani Sandoval won first prize for level 1 students in Southern California. I knew the minute I read her essay, "Gelato," that she would win because not even college students write as well as she does. We look forward to more outcomes of this kind, especially now that we are using the textbook *Juntos: Italian for Speakers of English and Spanish*, written by Clorinda Donato, Cedric Oliva, Manuel Romero, and Daniela Zappador-Guerra, all from CSU Long Beach.

CONTRIBUTORS

ELISABETTA BONVINO is professor of Second language Learning and Teaching in the Departement of Languages and Literature at the Università Roma Tre where she has been working since December 31, 2004. She is the Director of the Language Centre of Roma Tre; Coordinator of the Ufficio della Certificazione dell'italiano per stranieri. Her primary areas of interest are Intercomprehension among Romance languages. She has been the coordinator of the research project and author of the manual "EuRom5: read and understand five Romance languages" one of the most important manual on the Intercomprehension.

DIEGO CORTÉS VELÁSQUEZ is currently professor of foreign language education at Rome Università degli Studi Internazionali (UNINT) and a Postdoctoral Fellow at Linguistic Center (CLA) of Università degli Studi Roma Tre. He obtained his PhD in Linguistics and teaching Italian as a second language in Siena Università per Stranieri in 2013. He has worked in several Italian and European projects which main objective was the education to plurilingualism. His main research field is intercomprehension among Romance languages.

ROBERTO DOLCI is Associate Professor of Educational Linguistics and Language Pedagogy at the University for Foreigners of Perugia. His research interests are language education policies and teacher training. He is member of the Scientific Committee of the Italian Language Resource Laboratory at the John D. Calandra Italian American Institute, Queens College, CUNY. He is co-editor of TILCA, (*Teaching Italian Language and Culture in America*), and is member of the Observatory for Italian Language and Culture in the USA of the Italian Embassy in Washington.

CLORINDA DONATO is the George L. Graziadio Chair of Italian Studies at California State University, Long Beach and Professor of French and Italian. She was the principal investigator for the National Endowment for the Humanities grant to Hispanic Serving Institutions, "Teaching French and Italian to Spanish Speakers," 2011-2014. She is a specialist in eighteenth century French and Italian literature, but also works in the field of Romance language acquisition.

PIERRE ESCUDÉ is a Professor at the University of Bordeaux (France). His research focuses on the didactics of languages as they coexist within individuals (bilingualism, multilingualism) or inside specific social circles, especially at school. An Expert with the Council of Europe on minority languages, he has edited Jules Ronjat's pioneering work on bilingualism (Peter Lang, 2013) and a textbook on intercomprehension (Clé International, 2010). He has also piloted two programs on didactics engineering: euromania (www.euromania.com)—the first European textbook integrating curriculum subjects and Romance languages, and euroforma, an intensive university-level training course focusing on the methodology of intercomprehension. From 2009 to 2013, he worked with the team of the California South University in Long Beach on a groundbreaking method directed towards teaching Romance languages (French, Spanish, Italian, Portuguese) and English.

FABRIZIO FORNARA is a PhD candidate in Instructional Systems and Learning Technologies and an Italian and Spanish language Teaching Assistant at Florida State University. He is also a PhD candidate in Spanish Linguistics at the University of Barcelona, Spain. His research focuses on instructional design principles and educational technologies applied to second language learning; intercomprehension among languages; and computer assisted language-learning (CALL) trends.

DIANE HARTUNIAN teaches French and Spanish at San Pedro High School in the Los Angeles Unified School District. She has a doctoral degree in Spanish Renaissance literature from the Catholic University of America. Diane completed her undergraduate work in Mexico where she learned French, and graduate studies in Aix-en-Provence, France, Ms. Hartunian has extensive experience teaching at both the high school and college levels. Along with NEH training in intercomprehension from California State University, Long Beach, Ms. Hartunian teaches the French for Spanish Speakers program at San Pedro High School. Currently, Ms. Hartunian is completing a certification program in in online teaching through the California Community College Consortium.

MARKUS MULLER received his PhD from UCLA in French Literature in 1998 and is currently Chair of the Department of Romance, German, Russian Languages and Literatures and Associate Professor of French at California State University, Long Beach. From 2001 to 2013, he served as the department's coordinator of the lower-division language and Teaching Associate training program. His research interests span from 19th-century French and German fantastic literature to second language acquisition, teaching methodology and most recently the topic of Intercomprehension.

IDA L. NOLEMI-LANZA is the Chair of the World Language Department of San Pedro High School in San Pedro. She participated in the National Endowment for the Humanities grant to Hispanic Serving Institutions, "Teaching French and Italian to Spanish Speakers," 2011-2014, and as a result of that study she has initiated Italian for Spanish Speakers at San Pedro High School. She has received several grants from the Italian Government to increase the number of students taking AP Italian, and she received the 2013 Coccia-Inserra Award for excellence and innovation in teaching Italian language and culture from the Coccia Institute for the Italian Experience in America of Montclair State University.

CEDRIC JOSEPH OLIVA is the Language Program and Teaching Associate Program Coordinator for the Department of Romance, German, Russian Languages and Literatures at California State University, Long Beach. Dr. Oliva teaches Intercomprehension, Romance Linguistics, and Teaching Methodology, as well as French and Italian for Speakers of English and Spanish. He received his PhD in Anglophone and Romance Languages and Literatures and was awarded theAllocation de Recherche. His current research focus is on intercomprehensive and multilingual teaching strategies applied to the teaching of French and Italian to Speakers of English and Spanish.

BARBARA SPINELLI is Senior Lecturer at Columbia University and Assistant Professor of Second Language Acquisition at the University for Foreigners in Perugia, Italy. She collaborates with the Centre for Language Assessment and Certifications as a teacher trainer and involves in language testing and European research projects. Her main research areas are: Network-based Language Learning, Curriculum Design, Plurilingual and Intercultural Education. She has published articles in ISL journals. She is the co-author of the Profilo della lingua italiana Livelli A1, A2, B1, B2 del QCER.

ANTHONY JULIAN TAMBURRI is Distinguished Professor of European Languages & Literatures and Dean of the John D. Calandra Italian American Institute. He is past president of the Italian American Studies Association (IASA) and of the American Association of Teachers of Italian (AATI). His authored books include: *Una semiotica della ri-lettura: Guido Gozzano,*

Aldo Palazzeschi, Italo Calvino (Cesati, 2003); *Una semiotica dell'etnicità: nuove segnalature per la letteratura italiano/americana* (Cesati, 2010); *Reviewing Italian Americana: Generalities and Specificities on Cinema* (Bordighera, 2011); and *Re-reading Italian Americana: Specificities and Generalities on Literature and Criticism* (Fairleigh Dickinson, 2014). His is co-editor for translations, with Robert Viscusi and James Periconi, of *Italoamericana: The Literature of the Great Migration, 1880-1943* (Fordham, 2014); with Giordano and Gardaphé, *From The Margin: Writings in Italian Americana* (Purdue, 2000 2nd ed.); and he has edited two dozen other collections. He is executive producer and host of the TV program, *Italics*, and one of the co-founders of the Italian American Digital Project. He directs the Italian Series for Fairleigh Dickinson University Press.

IRENE ZANINI-CORDI (PhD, University of California, Berkeley) is Associate Professor of Italian at Florida State University. Her interests span the Italian Renaissance, 18th- and 19th-century literature and culture, women writings, contemporary Italian literature and Second Language Acquisition. She has published extensively on Italian women writers and 18th- and 19th- century Italian literature. Her first book, *Donne sciolte* (Longo Editore, 2008) deals with the theme of abandonment, while her current book project focuses on Social Network Theory and explores the dynamics of female empowerment within the 18th- and 19th- century literary salons.

INDEX OF NAMES

Aalto, Eija, 102, 132
Allières, Jacques, 99–100
Altschuler, Glenn, 8, 26
Amselle, Jean-Loup, 22
Anquetin, Mathilde, 152, 164
Appel, Gabriela, 134
Aracil, L.V., 82, 100
Atanasoska, Tatjana, 102, 132

Bach, Svend, 34, 57
Bachelard, Gaston, 95, 100
Baetens Beardsmore, Hugo, 11, 22
Baker, Colin, 11, 22, 66, 77
Baucom, Linda, 22
Bec, Pierre, 90, 100
Beerkens, Roos, 67, 77
Benucci, Antonella, 43, 57
Berruto, Gaetano, 36, 57
Bettoni, Camilla, 41, 57
Bialystok, Ellen, xxi, 22
Blackledge, Adrian, 67, 77
Blanc M.H.A., 11, 24
Blanche-Benveniste, Claire, 30, 34, 57–58, 122, 127, 132, 146, 164, 191–194, 203, 205, 216
Blommaert, Jan, 102, 132
Bloomfield, Leonard, xxi, 11, 22
Boekman, Klaus, 102, 132
Bolen, C.M., 22
Bonvino, Elisabetta, 29–59, 152, 164, 191–194, 195, 196, 203, 206, 216
Boorstin, Daniel, 2, 22
Borel, Bernard, 216
Bourciez, E., 100

Bouvet, Éric, 38, 58
Bowles, Melissa A., 39, 58, 195, 216
Brecht, Richard, 25
Bréelle, Dany, 38, 58
Brumfit, Christopher, 212, 216
Brunet, Jacqueline, 34, 57
Bush, George W., 2, 4, 6, 22
Bybee, Joan, 108, 132

Caddéo, Sandrine, 33–35, 43, 57–58, 64, 77, 86, 100, 121, 125, 132, 152, 164
Canagarajah, A. Suresh, 66, 77, 108, 132
Candelier, Michel, xxi, 20–22, 58, 110, 112, 132
Capucho, Filomena, 34–35, 49, 56–58
Carvalho, Ana Maria, 68, 75–77
Castagne, Eric, 72, 77, 125, 132
Castellotti, Véronique, 115, 134
Cenoz, Jasone, xxi, 11, 14–15, 19–20, 22, 103, 104, 107, 132, 133
Chapelle, Carol, 162, 164
Charlet-Mesdjian, Béatrice, 86, 100
Clinton, William, 2, 4, 23
Coleon, M., 25, 78
Conti, Virginie, 121, 132
Cook, Vivian, 14, 23
Cope, Bill, 101, 102, 132, 133
Cortés Velásquez, Diego, 43, 57–58
Coste, Daniel, 37, 58
Creese, Angela, 67, 69, 77–78

Dabène, Louise, 33–34, 59

da Silva, Antonio J.B., 68, 77
Debyser, Francis, 33, 59
De Carlo, Maddalena, 44, 57–59, 152, 164
Degache, Ch., 40, 57–59
de Pietro, Jean-Francois, 132
de Saussure, Ferdinand, 88, 100
Deulofeu, José, 216
Diez, Friedrich Christian, 90, 100
Dolci, Roberto, 1–27, 77
Donato, Clorinda, 61–78, 173, 174, 188
Doyé, Peter, 49, 59, 152, 164
Doyle, Dennis, 23
Duperron, Lucile, 23
Durand, Jacky, 215

Easley Pearson, Denise, 25
Escudé, Pierre, 34–35, 37, 57, 59, 64, 78–100, 107, 121, 122, 127, 128, 133

Fabbro, F., 11, 23
Facciol, Raymond, 132
Farrell, Martin Peter, xxi, 23
Finocchiaro, Mary Bonomo, 212, 216
Fiorenza, Elisa, 41, 58, 196, 204, 206, 215, 217
Flattau, P.E., 2, 23
Flores, Nelson, 18, 24, 102, 133
Freire, Juliana Luna, 68, 77
Furman, Nelly, xxi, 9, 24

Garbarino, Sandra, 57–59
Garcia, Ofelia, 18, 24, 67, 78, 102, 108, 116, 133
Garrett, Nina, 162, 164
Gass, Susan, 38, 59
Giacomi, Alain, 216

Gillespie, Joan, 25
Gilmore, Alex, 193, 217
Goldberg, David, xxi, 9, 24
Gorter, Durk, xxi, 11, 14–15, 20, 22, 104, 107, 133
Grin, Francois, 121, 132
Grosjean, François, 24

Halliday, Michael K., 101, 133
Hamers, J.F., 11, 24
Hayward, F.M., 24
Heiberger, Greg, 152, 164
Hernández-González, Carmen, 90, 100
Hornberger, Nancy, 66–67, 77–78
Huffmaster, Michael, 188

Jaffe, Alexandra, 69, 78
Jamet, Marie-Christine, 33–34, 43, 57–58, 64, 77, 121, 125, 132, 214, 215, 217
Janin, Pierre, 34, 37, 59, 63, 78, 107, 121, 122, 127, 128, 133
Jessner, Ulrike, 107, 116, 133
Jimenez-Jimenez, Antonio, 24
Junco, Reynol, 152, 164

Kalantzis, Mary, 101, 102, 132-134
Kano, Naomi, 108, 133
Kasper, Gabriele, 15, 24
Klein, Horst, 34, 59
Klein, Wolfgang, 40, 59
Konoeda, Keiko, 134
Kramsch, Claire, xxi, 14–15, 19, 24, 66, 78, 102, 103, 104, 107, 108, 109, 117, 130, 131, 133, 172, 174, 188
Krashen, Stephen, 38, 59, 147, 164
Kress, Gunther, 102, 133
Kruze, Larisa, 25

Kumagai, Yuri, 130, 133

Lantolf, James, 114, 134
Lave, Jean, 114, 126, 134
Larsen-Freeman, Diane, 200, 217
Le Pichon Vorstman, Emmanuelle, 115, 134
Leung, Constant, 107, 108, 134
Link, Holly, 66–67, 78
Loken, Eric, 152, 164
Long, M., 14, 24
Lőrincz, Ildikó, 132
Loufrani, Claude, 216
Lusin, Natalia, xxi, 9, 24

Macnamara, John, xxi, 25
Martin, K.E., 59
Martin, P., 69, 77–78
Mastrelli, Carlo Alberto, 34, 57
Maurais, Jacques, 25
May, Stephen, 14, 24–25, 61, 78, 102, 108, 134
McBride, Kara, 152, 164
Meissner, Franz Joseph, 34, 40, 47, 58
Meziane, Boudjema, 216
Mishan, Freda, 193, 217
Mohajeri Norris, Emily, 25
Morris, Michael A., 1, 25
Mota, Antónia, 216

Naharro, M., 11, 25
Nichols, P.C., 25, 67, 78
Nishimata, Miyuki, 133
Norton, Bonny, 104, 134
Nunan, David, 109, 134

Ochs, Elinor, 19, 25
Oliva, Cedric Joseph, 61–78, 188
Oliviero, Carmela, 75, 78

Ollivier, Christian, 33, 49, 60
O'Malley, J. Michael, 60
Orahood, Tammy, 25
Ortega, Lourdes, 14, 25, 108, 134
Overstreet, Mark, 23

Paradis, Michael, 11, 25
Parizzi, Francesca, 112, 135
Pascual, Xavier, 132
Pavlenko, Aneta, 104, 116, 134
Pazery, Nelly, 216
Pennycook, Alastair, 25, 110, 135
Piccardo, Enrica, 102–103, 115, 135
Pippa, Salvador, 41, 58, 152, 164, 216
Potowski, Kim, xxi, 25, 75, 78

Reboullet, André, 33, 60
Reinheimer-Rîpeanu, Sanda, 90, 100
Richards, Jack C., 201, 217
Rivers, William, 25
Robinson, John, 25
Rodgers, Theodore S., 201, 217
Romero, Manuel, 78, 188
Ronjat, Jules, 87–88, 95, 100
Rubin, Donald, 26
Rundstrom Williams, Tracy, 26

San Felice, Laura, 75, 78
Santosuosso, John, 2, 26
Saravanan, Vanithamani, 102, 135
Sato, Shinji, 133
Seidlhofer, Barbara, 107, 135
Shih, Ru-Chu, 164
Shohamy, Elana, 1, 26
Siaya L.M., 24
Simões, Antônio Roberto Monteiro, 78
Simone, Raffaele, 36, 60, 216
Skorton, David, 8, 26

Spinelli, Barbara, 101–143
Spolsky, Bernard, 1, 26
Stavans, Ilan, 117, 135
Stegmann, Tilbert, 34, 59
Steinberg, Michael, 25
Sutton, R.C., 26
Sylvan, Claire, 102, 108, 116, 133

Tamburri, Anthony J., 23, 77
Tasmowski, Liliane, 90, 100
Teyssier, Paul, 90, 100
Tillman, Martin, 26
Titone, Renzo, xxii, 11, 26
Thompson, J.W., 26
Trooboff, Stevan, 26

Uzcanga Vivar, Isabel, 216

Valdes, Guadalupe, xxii, 11–12, 27, 60
Valli, André, 146, 164, 203, 216
Vandergrift, Larry, 38, 60
van Geert, Paul, 107, 135
Vilaginés Serra, Eulalia, 152, 164, 216
Vygotsky, Lev, 114, 134

Wagner, Johannes, 14–15, 23–24
Wei, Li, 109, 116, 135
Wenger, Etiénne, 114, 126, 134–135
Whiteside, Anne, 108, 133
Wiedemann, Lyris, 77–78
Wright, S., 1, 27

Zappador-Guerra, Daniela, 78, 188

www.ingramcontent.com/pod-product-compliance
Lightning Source LLC
Chambersburg PA
BHW080322170426
3193CB00017B/2874